"Top stuff. Super clev[...] [...]t is really top notch. Basically, I'm jealous. [...]

— BEN TEMPLESMITH
(ARTIST OF *30 DAYS OF NIGHT* AND *FELL*)

"This is the insanity cooked up in the minds of writer Brandon Seifert and artist Lukas Ketner, and it's only gotten better with every new issue of WITCH DOCTOR."

— IGN

"A superbly smart and riveting medical thriller filled with off-the-wall characters"

— FANGORIA

"Holy cow, [...]ll. I have seen the future, and its name is WITCH DOCTOR... Seifert's script is nic[...]d lean, with loads of cleverness, and Ketner's art reminds me a bit of Rick Veitch in pl[...], of my pal Bill Willingham in others, all without being derivative in the slightest."

— CHRIS ROBERSON
(WRITER OF *iZOMBIE*)

"If you're go[...] to trust anyone's judgment in horror comic books, it should be the creator of *The Wal[...] Dead*. Robert Kirkman knows a good horror and the first comic book series to be [...]ially released by his Skybound imprint, WITCH DOCTOR, has emerged as an imme[...]e hit."

— L.A. WEEKLY

"With a wi[...]g premise and some fantastic ideas at play, WITCH DOCTOR has by far been one o[...] favorite miniseries of the year."

— AIN'T IT COOL NEWS

"Four out o[...] e stars!"

— COMIC BOOK RESOURCES

"An intelli[...] haracter study nestled shamelessly and lovingly in the arms of a creature feature. W[...] DOCTOR reminds readers how well comics can do horror."

— TIM SEELEY
(WRITER OF *HACK/SLASH*)

"Seifert and[...] ner are on the verge of something potentially huge with their medical-horror pr[...] Huge in the way *Hellboy* and *The Goon* are huge. If they play their cards right, Dr. [...] will be making house calls for a very long time to come."

— BROKEN FRONTIER

"The comic[...] at horror fans have been waiting for. Not only is it creepy as all hell, not only does it bring disturbing imagery, but it offers a take on the genre never seen before."

— BLOODY DISGUSTING

"Drips with retro-gore fun"

— PASTE MAGAZINE

"Eminently entertaining"

— 109

WITCH DOCTOR™

VOLUME 1: UNDER THE KNIFE

THE WRITING
(including the letters)
BRANDON SEIFERT

THE ART
LUKAS KETNER

THE COLORS
SUNNY GHO *(chapters 0-2 & chapter 3 pages 2-7)*
ANDY TROY *(chapter 4 & chapter 3 pages 1, 8-22)*
JAMIE GRANT *(cover of chapter 0)*

THE EDITOR
SINA GRACE

SPECIAL MEDICAL CONSULTING
KAREN ANDERSEN

FOR SKYBOUND ENTERTAINMENT
Robert Kirkman- CEO
J.J. Didde- President
Sina Grace- Editorial Director
Shawn Kirkham- Director of Business Development
Tim Daniel- Digital Content Manager
Chad Manion- Assistant to Mr. Grace
Sydney Pennington- Assistant to Mr. Kirkham
Feldman Public Relations LA- Public Relations

FOR INTERNATIONAL RIGHTS INQUIRIES, PLEASE CONTACT SK@SKYBOUND.COM

www.skybound.com
www.witchdoctorcomic.com

FOR IMAGE COMICS

Robert Kirkman
Chief Operating Officer

Erik Larsen
Chief Financial Officer

Todd McFarlane
President

Marc Silvestri
Chief Executive Officer

Jim Valentino
Vice-President

Eric Stephenson
Publisher

Todd Martinez
Sales and Licensing Coordinator

Sarah deLaine
PR & Marketing Coordinator

Branwyn Bigglestone
Accounts Manager

Emily Miller
Administrative Assistant

Jamie Parreno
Marketing Assistant

Kevin Yuen
Digital Rights Coordinator

Tyler Shainline
Production Manager

Drew Gill
Art Director

Jonathan Chan
Senior Production Artist

Monica Garcia
Production Artist

Vincent Kukua
Production Artist

Jana Cook
Production Artist

www.imagecomics.com

WITCH DOCTOR, VOL. I: UNDER THE KNIFE. First Printing: December 2011. Published by Image Comics, Inc. Office of publication: 2134 Allston Way, 2nd Floor, Berkeley, California 94704.

ISBN: 978-1-60706-441-1.

PRINTED IN THE USA

For information regarding the CPSIA on this printed material call: 203-595-3636 and provide reference # EAST – 416340

To Karen. For appreciating this intensely weird thing I've found myself doing — and for helping me get the details right.

— Brandon

For Mom, Dad, Tara, and Dane.

— Lukas

And for Shannon T. Stewart, from both of us. Couldn't have done it without you, buddy.

The creators would like to thank Jimmie Robinson, Mike Dringenberg, Joshua Williamson, Joe Keatinge, Steve Lieber, Chris Roberson, Darick Robertson, and Tony Lee (for their assistance and encouragement); Brian Bendis; Tony Morgan, Ken and Mike Carriglitto; Bob Schreck; Allison Baker; Katie Moody (for general awesomeness and for submitting Lukas to the Russ Manning Awards without telling us); Susan Auġér and everyone else we've met through Whitechapel, Panel & Pixel and Sequential Workshop; Floating World Comics, Sequential Art Gallery, Bridge City Comics, Larry's Comics, and Hollywood Things From Another World; Karen Andersen, Lauriel Earley and Allison Stickles (for consulting with Brandon on the medicine and biology); and to Mike Mignola, Joss Whedon, Warren Ellis, Bernie Wrightson, Eric Powell and Steven Moffat (for the inspiration).

Special thanks to Scott Allie and Kohel Haver. And to Robert Kirkman, JJ Didde, Sina Grace, Shawn Kirkham, and everyone at Skybound and Image Comics for giving them the opportunity to make this.

Who is your favorite writer in comics? Or your favorite artist?

Just think about that for a minute.

Now... do they actually WRITE stories? Do they actually DRAW pictures?

Think about those questions. Are they writing stories, introducing new environments, creating characters? Do they shape new worlds for you to experience, visually invent new things to look at, introduce you to a new way of seeing something?

Or are they interpreting your favorite characters from your childhood for a modern generation?

There's something to be said about taking an idea that's as old, tired and played out as something like, say... Spider-Man and making it seem unique and compelling again. It takes a certain level of skill to be sure. But is it writing? Is it drawing?

Sometimes I feel like it's comparing a painting to a jigsaw puzzle.

The pieces are there. It's just a matter of plugging in a plot, grabbing some well-defined toys and having them go through the motions in hopefully, a new way. Or, a matter of taking a design that's stood the test of time and making the eyes bigger, slapping on a new belt, or adding random lines to a classic costume. That's corporate comics... there's no innovation, nothing thought-provoking or challenging coming out of that cold, calculated, comics-by-the-numbers system.

I crave something NEW.

WITCH DOCTOR is that something... it's new, original... and exciting.

On every page you're meeting a new character, visiting a new place, being introduced to a new concept... and everything about this book is- in my humble opinion- completely enthralling.

What you're about to read is a fantastic piece of work from two very talented creators, Brandon Seifert and Lukas Ketner.

Brandon is a former medical student, from Alaska, who traveled with the circus for a number of years as a juggler and once sold produce on the side of the road to make ends meet. I don't know if all of that's true, I don't know a lot about him personally, but I do know that he's a great writer with great ideas. You'll see what I mean when you read this book.

Lukas is a commercial artist, also from Alaska. It's a little known fact that he co-created The Dominos Noid and played the youngest kid on *Family Ties*. Again, I don't know him very well so a few of these facts may be incorrect. I can say that his art style is all at once classic and unlike anything you've ever seen. I've rarely seen someone draw otherworldly creatures so... otherworldly. Lukas makes WITCH DOCTOR a joy to look at.

The task of creating something original and truly starting with a blank page is exciting and rewarding but at the time terrifying and extremely risky. These two guys make it seem easy like the most talented seasoned pros in the industry.

When you turn the page in this comic, it's not a matter of HOW the villain will be defeated-- it's IF, and you will know anything can happen along the way.

You're going to love it... now get started!

Robert Kirkman
Backwoods, CA
2011

Robert Kirkman is the creator or co-creator of **The Walking Dead, Invincible, Super Dinosaur, The Infinite** and countless other comics you may not have heard of because they didn't sell so well. He's also the CEO of Skybound, the imprint of Image Comics that produces — among others — this very book. That makes his opinions somewhat biased, but no less accurate.

WITCH DOCTOR #1 Larry's Comics Regional Variant Cover

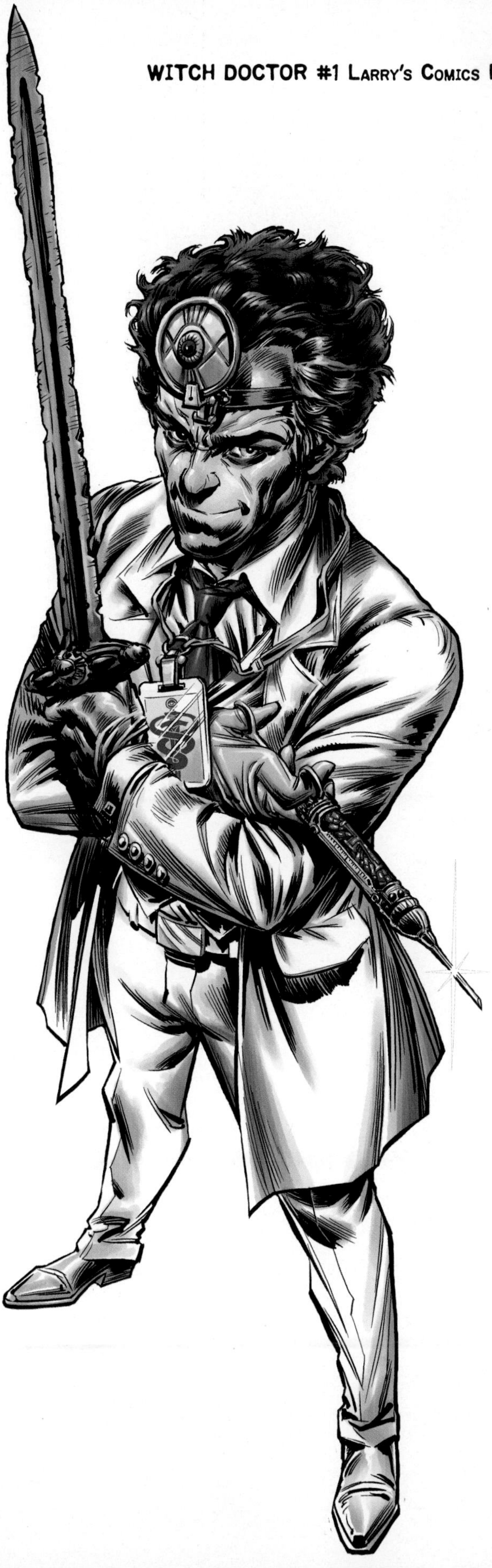

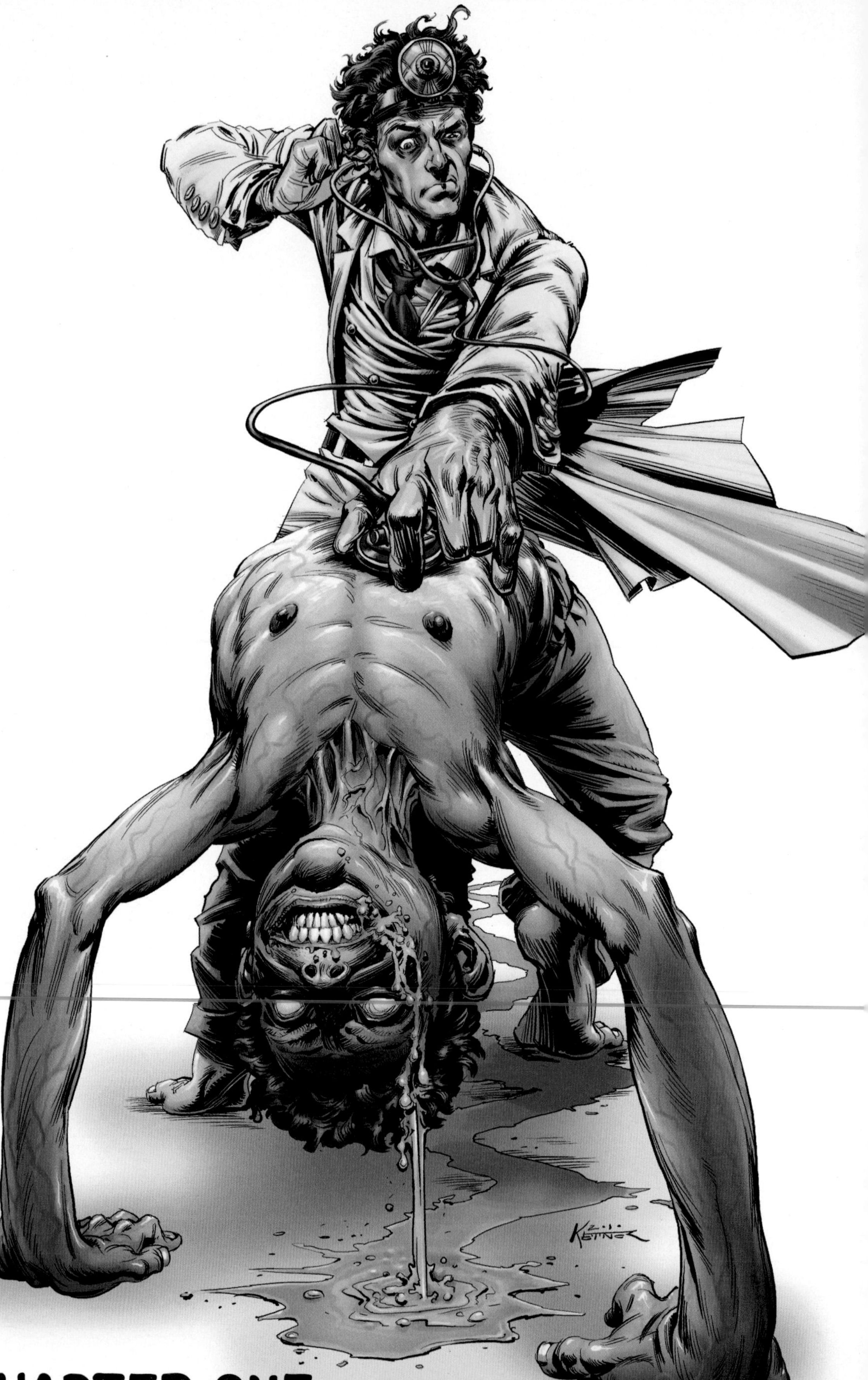

CHAPTER ONE

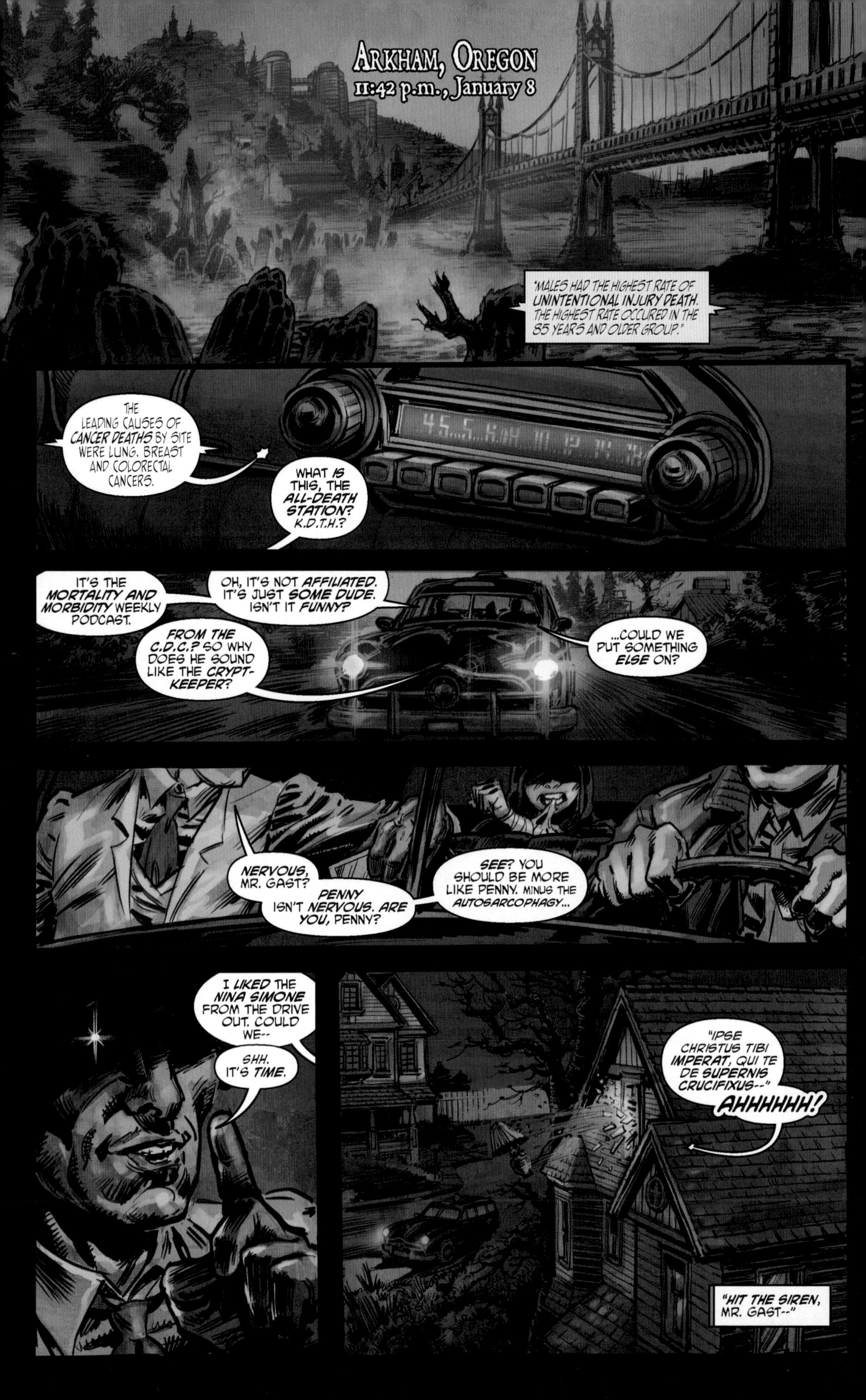
Arkham, Oregon
11:42 p.m., January 8
"MALES HAD THE HIGHEST RATE OF UNINTENTIONAL INJURY DEATH. THE HIGHEST RATE OCCURED IN THE 85 YEARS AND OLDER GROUP."
THE LEADING CAUSES OF CANCER DEATHS BY SITE WERE LUNG, BREAST AND COLORECTAL CANCERS.
WHAT IS THIS, THE ALL-DEATH STATION? K.D.T.H.?
IT'S THE MORTALITY AND MORBIDITY WEEKLY PODCAST.
OH, IT'S NOT AFFILIATED. IT'S JUST SOME DUDE. ISN'T IT FUNNY?
FROM THE C.D.C.? SO WHY DOES HE SOUND LIKE THE CRYPT-KEEPER?
...COULD WE PUT SOMETHING ELSE ON?
NERVOUS, MR. GAST?
PENNY ISN'T NERVOUS. ARE YOU, PENNY?
SEE? YOU SHOULD BE MORE LIKE PENNY. MINUS THE AUTOSARCOPHAGY...
I LIKED THE NINA SIMONE FROM THE DRIVE OUT. COULD WE--
SHH. IT'S TIME.
"IPSE CHRISTUS TIBI IMPERAT, QUI TE DE SUPERNIS CRUCIFIXUS--"
AHHHHHH!
"HIT THE SIREN, MR. GAST--"

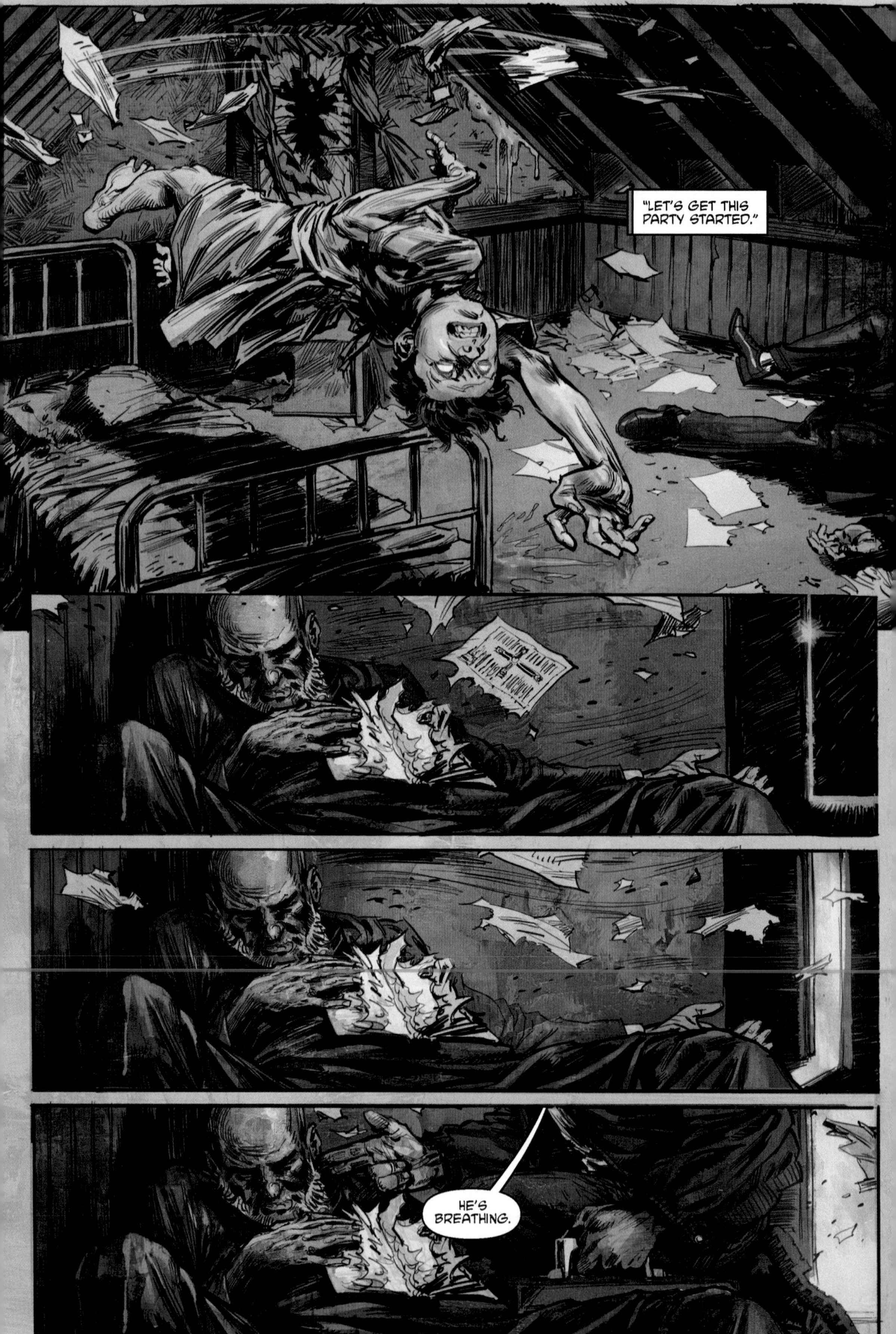
"LET'S GET THIS PARTY STARTED."
HE'S BREATHING.

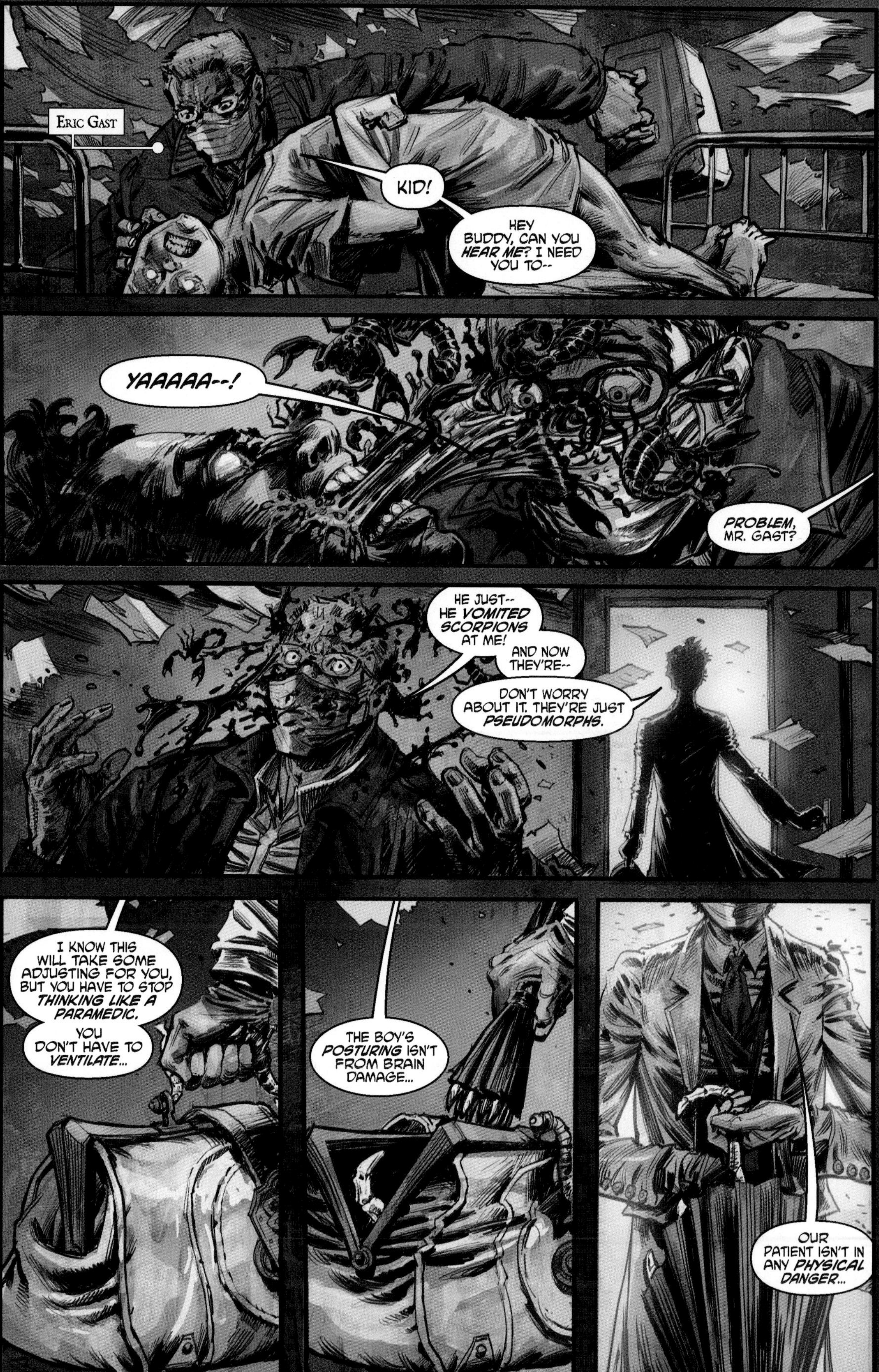
Eric Gast
KID!
HEY BUDDY, CAN YOU HEAR ME? I NEED YOU TO--
YAAAAA--!
PROBLEM, MR. GAST?
HE JUST-- HE VOMITED SCORPIONS AT ME!
AND NOW THEY'RE--
DON'T WORRY ABOUT IT. THEY'RE JUST PSEUDOMORPHS.
I KNOW THIS WILL TAKE SOME ADJUSTING FOR YOU, BUT YOU HAVE TO STOP THINKING LIKE A PARAMEDIC.
YOU DON'T HAVE TO VENTILATE...
THE BOY'S POSTURING ISN'T FROM BRAIN DAMAGE...
OUR PATIENT ISN'T IN ANY PHYSICAL DANGER...

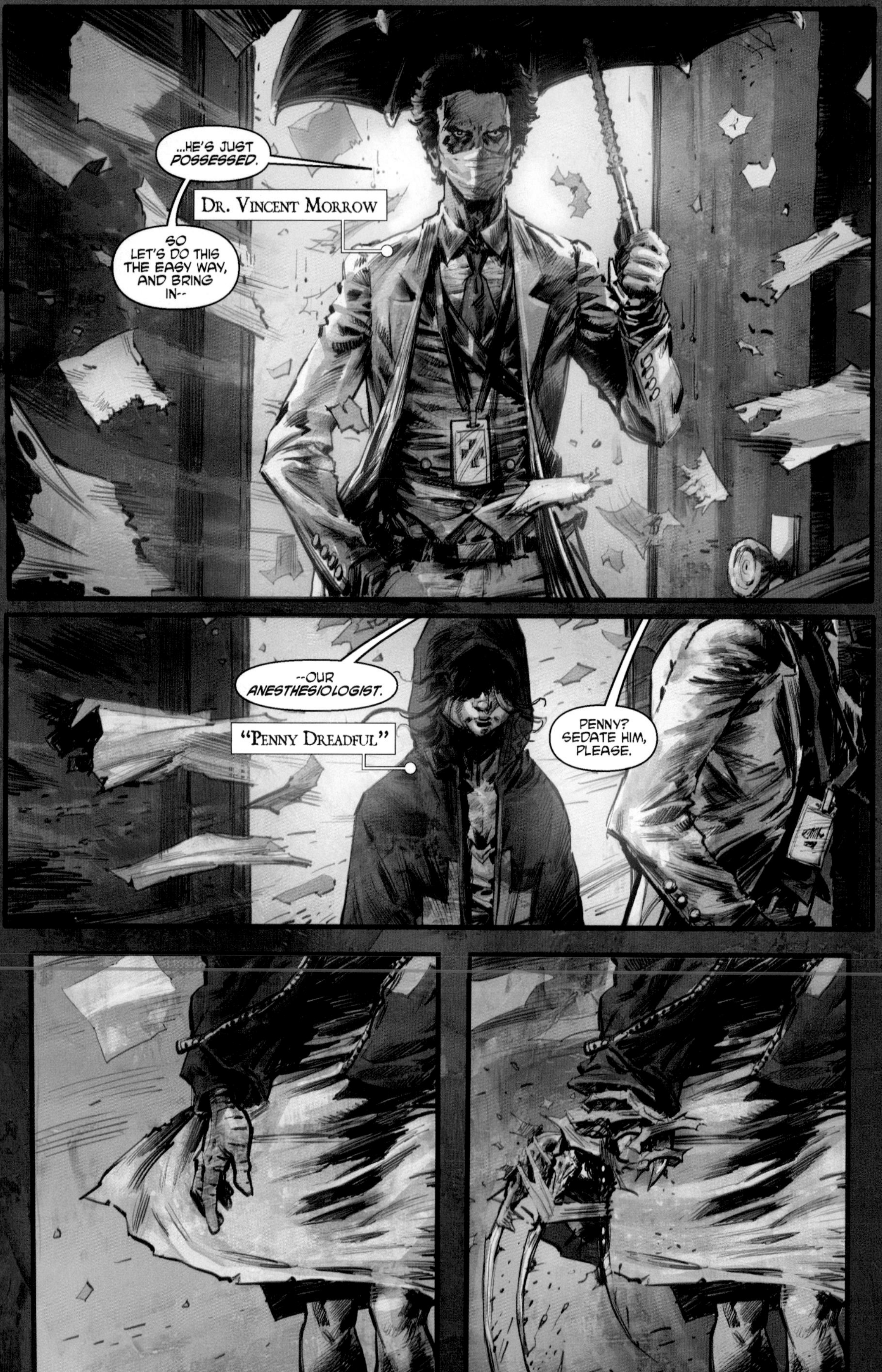
...HE'S JUST POSSESSED.
DR. VINCENT MORROW
SO LET'S DO THIS THE EASY WAY, AND BRING IN--
--OUR ANESTHESIOLOGIST.
"PENNY DREADFUL"
PENNY? SEDATE HIM, PLEASE.

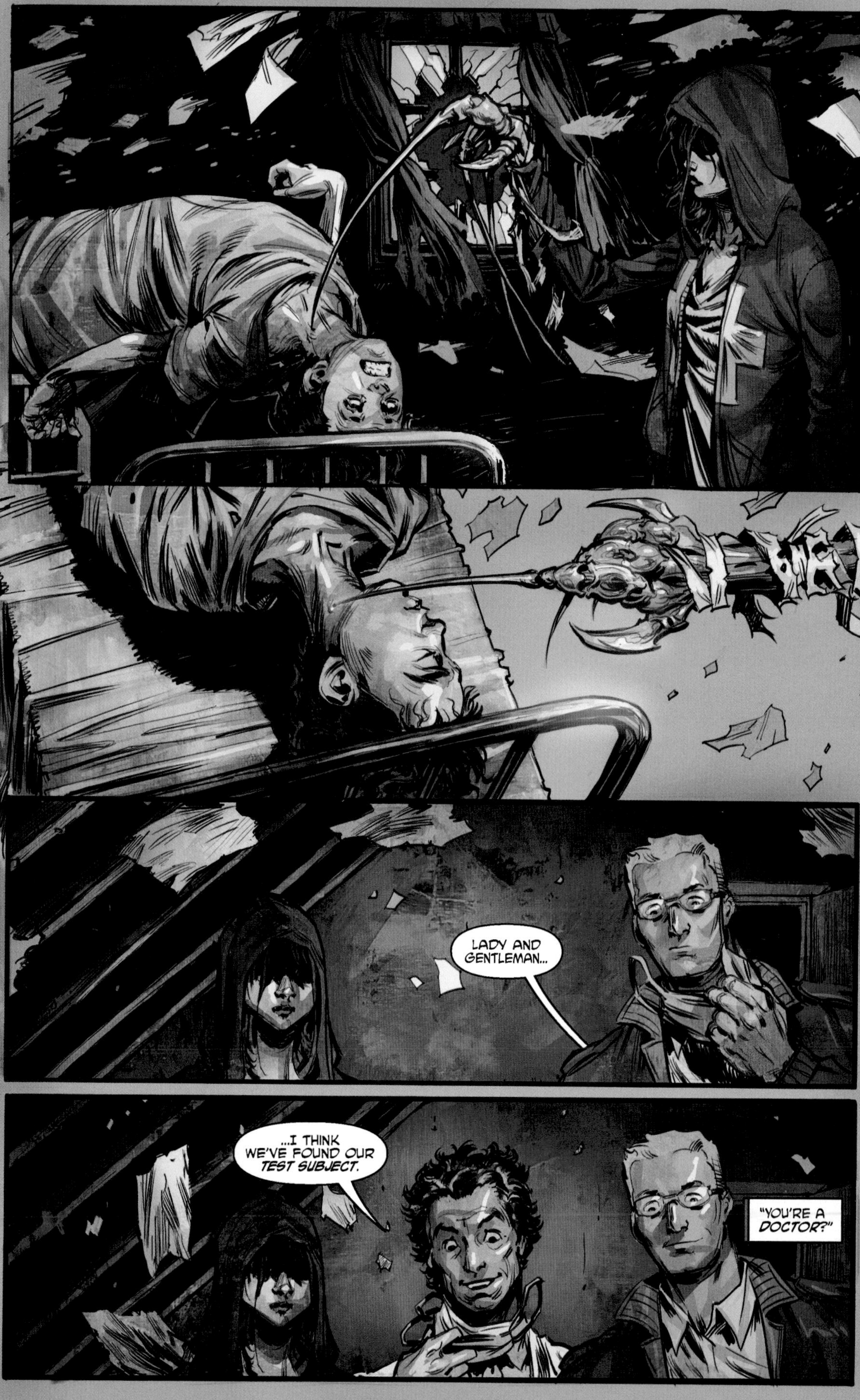
LADY AND GENTLEMAN...
...I THINK WE'VE FOUND OUR *TEST SUBJECT.*
"YOU'RE A *DOCTOR?*"

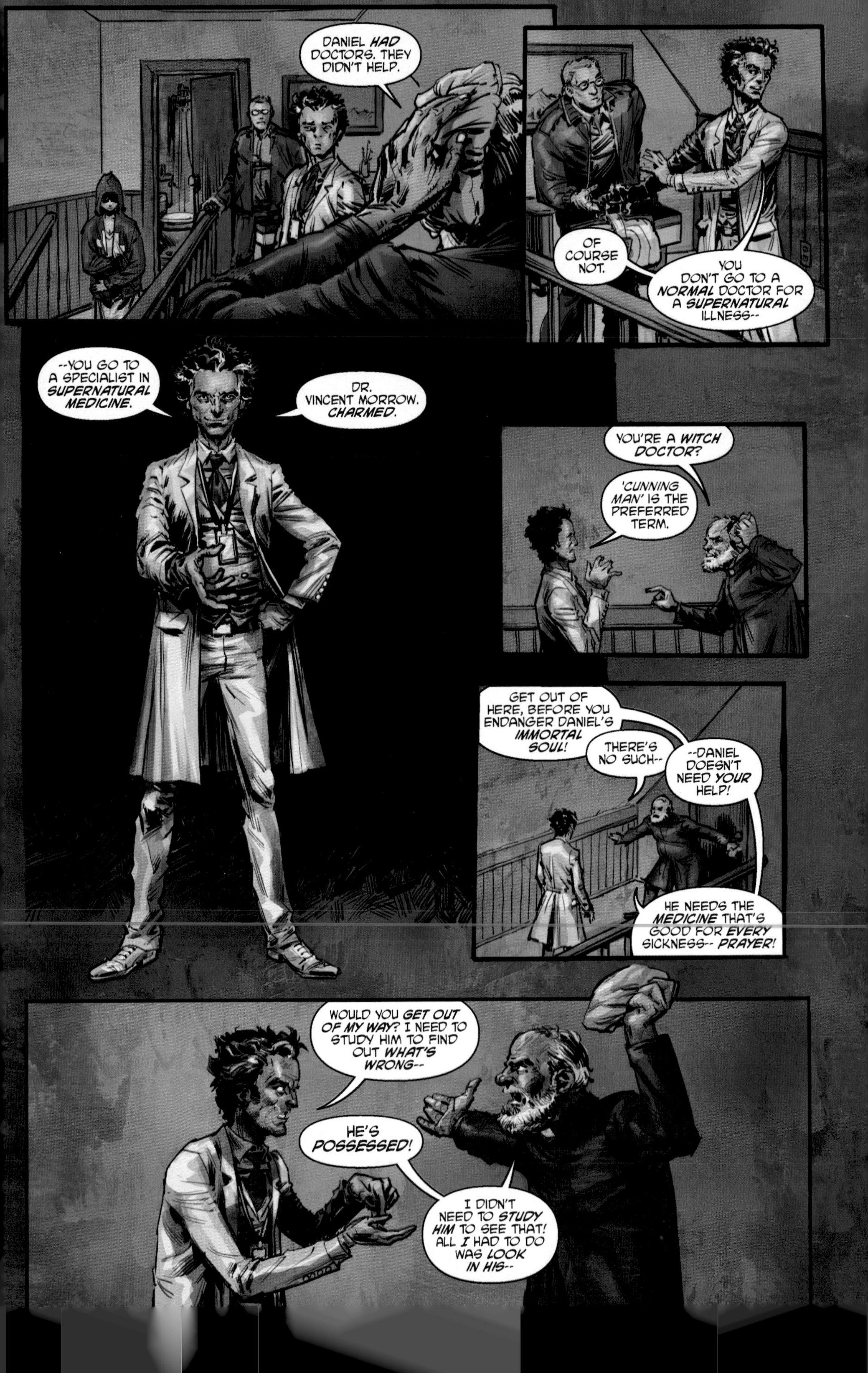
DANIEL HAD DOCTORS. THEY DIDN'T HELP.
OF COURSE NOT.
YOU DON'T GO TO A NORMAL DOCTOR FOR A SUPERNATURAL ILLNESS--
--YOU GO TO A SPECIALIST IN SUPERNATURAL MEDICINE.
DR. VINCENT MORROW. CHARMED.
YOU'RE A WITCH DOCTOR?
'CUNNING MAN' IS THE PREFERRED TERM.
GET OUT OF HERE, BEFORE YOU ENDANGER DANIEL'S IMMORTAL SOUL!
THERE'S NO SUCH--
--DANIEL DOESN'T NEED YOUR HELP!
HE NEEDS THE MEDICINE THAT'S GOOD FOR EVERY SICKNESS-- PRAYER!
WOULD YOU GET OUT OF MY WAY? I NEED TO STUDY HIM TO FIND OUT WHAT'S WRONG--
HE'S POSSESSED!
I DIDN'T NEED TO STUDY HIM TO SEE THAT! ALL I HAD TO DO WAS LOOK IN HIS--

--EYES?

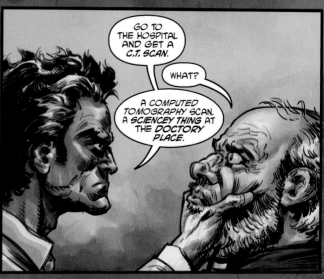

GO TO THE HOSPITAL AND GET A C.T. SCAN.

WHAT?

A COMPUTED TOMOGRAPHY SCAN. A SCIENCEY THING AT THE DOCTORY PLACE.

YOU HAVE A MILD TRAUMATIC BRAIN INJURY -- IN LAYMAN'S TERMS, A CONCUSSION.

WHEN YOU BOUNCED OFF THAT WALL, YOUR BRAIN BOUNCED OFF THE INSIDE OF YOUR SKULL.

...HOW DO YOU--?

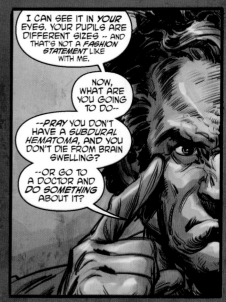

I CAN SEE IT IN YOUR EYES. YOUR PUPILS ARE DIFFERENT SIZES -- AND THAT'S NOT A FASHION STATEMENT LIKE WITH ME.

NOW, WHAT ARE YOU GOING TO DO--

--PRAY YOU DON'T HAVE A SUBDURAL HEMATOMA, AND YOU DON'T DIE FROM BRAIN SWELLING?

--OR GO TO A DOCTOR AND DO SOMETHING ABOUT IT?

YOU MAY EXPERIENCE SOME DISORIENTATION-- DON'T LET THE DOOR HIT YOU ON THE WAY OUT.

NOW, WHERE'D THE PARENTS GET TO? I NEED TO SHOW THEM...

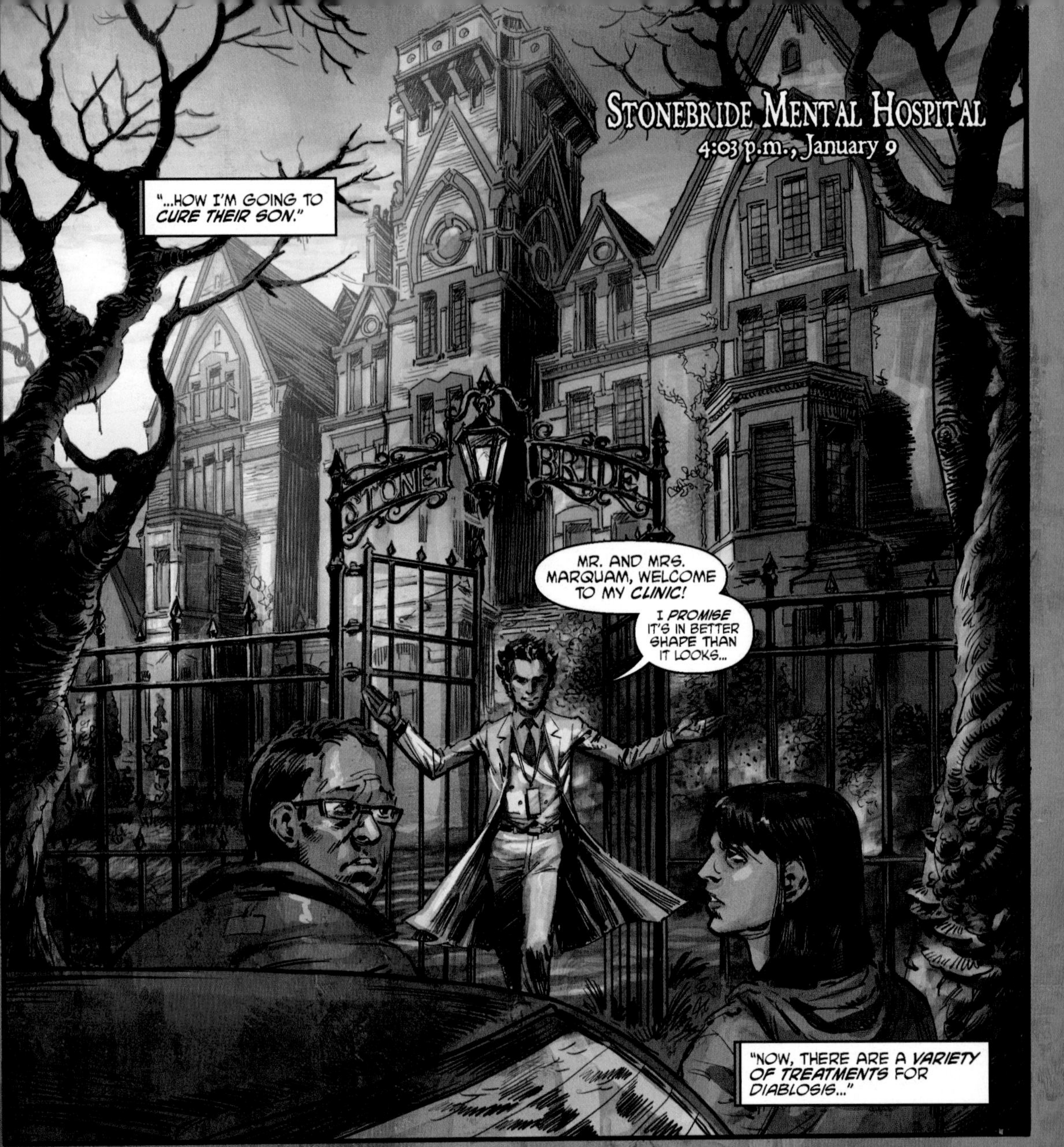
STONEBRIDE MENTAL HOSPITAL
4:03 p.m., January 9
"...HOW I'M GOING TO CURE THEIR SON."
STONE BRIDE
MR. AND MRS. MARQUAM, WELCOME TO MY CLINIC!
I PROMISE IT'S IN BETTER SHAPE THAN IT LOOKS...
"NOW, THERE ARE A VARIETY OF TREATMENTS FOR DIABLOSIS..."

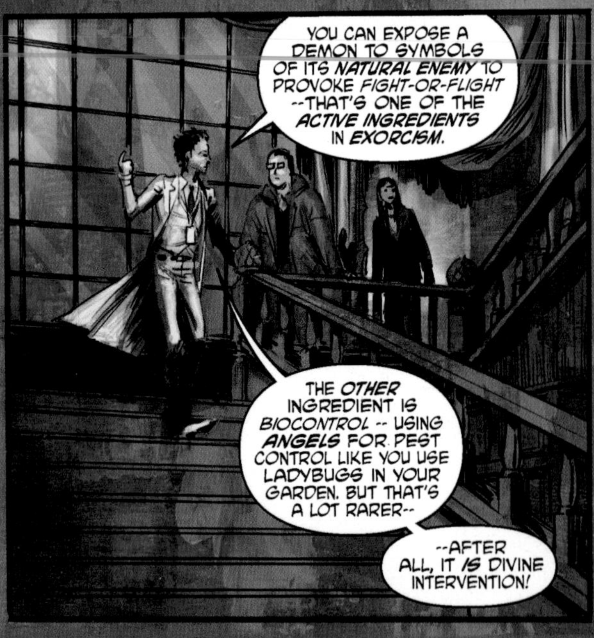
YOU CAN EXPOSE A DEMON TO SYMBOLS OF ITS NATURAL ENEMY TO PROVOKE FIGHT-OR-FLIGHT --THAT'S ONE OF THE ACTIVE INGREDIENTS IN EXORCISM.
THE OTHER INGREDIENT IS BIOCONTROL -- USING ANGELS FOR PEST CONTROL LIKE YOU USE LADYBUGS IN YOUR GARDEN. BUT THAT'S A LOT RARER--
--AFTER ALL, IT IS DIVINE INTERVENTION!

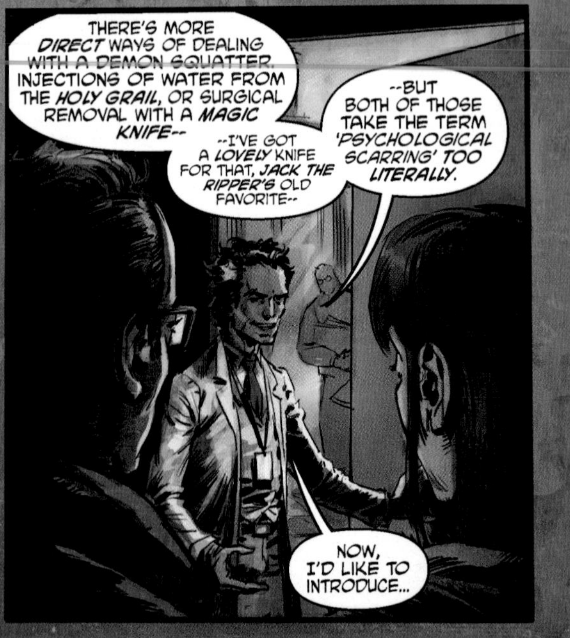
THERE'S MORE DIRECT WAYS OF DEALING WITH A DEMON SQUATTER. INJECTIONS OF WATER FROM THE HOLY GRAIL, OR SURGICAL REMOVAL WITH A MAGIC KNIFE--
--I'VE GOT A LOVELY KNIFE FOR THAT, JACK THE RIPPER'S OLD FAVORITE--
--BUT BOTH OF THOSE TAKE THE TERM 'PSYCHOLOGICAL SCARRING' TOO LITERALLY.
NOW, I'D LIKE TO INTRODUCE...

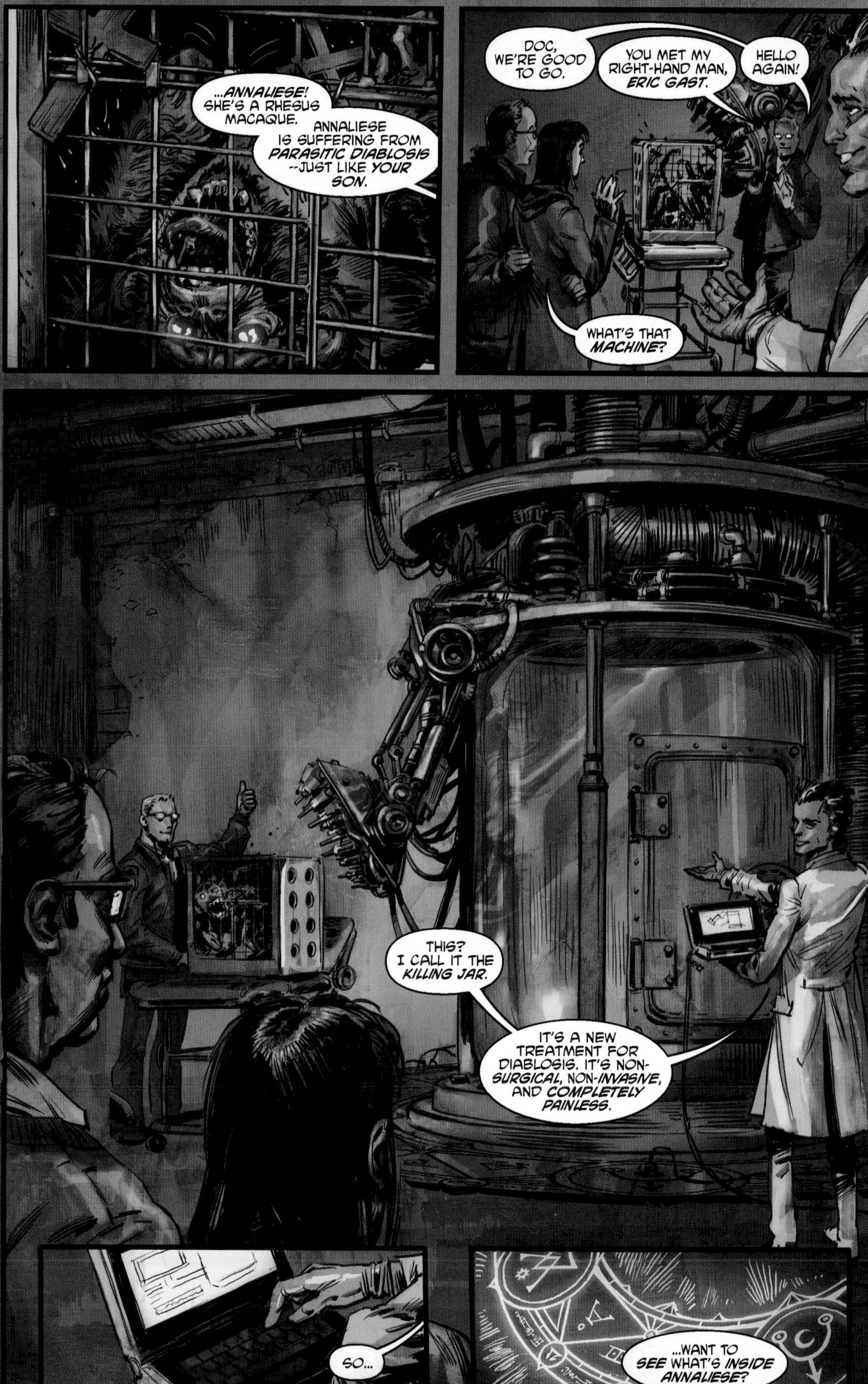
...ANNALIESE! SHE'S A RHESUS MACAQUE.
ANNALIESE IS SUFFERING FROM PARASITIC DIABLOSIS --JUST LIKE YOUR SON.
DOC, WE'RE GOOD TO GO.
YOU MET MY RIGHT-HAND MAN, ERIC GAST.
HELLO AGAIN!
WHAT'S THAT MACHINE?
THIS? I CALL IT THE KILLING JAR.
IT'S A NEW TREATMENT FOR DIABLOSIS. IT'S NON-SURGICAL, NON-INVASIVE, AND COMPLETELY PAINLESS.
SO...
...WANT TO SEE WHAT'S INSIDE ANNALIESE?

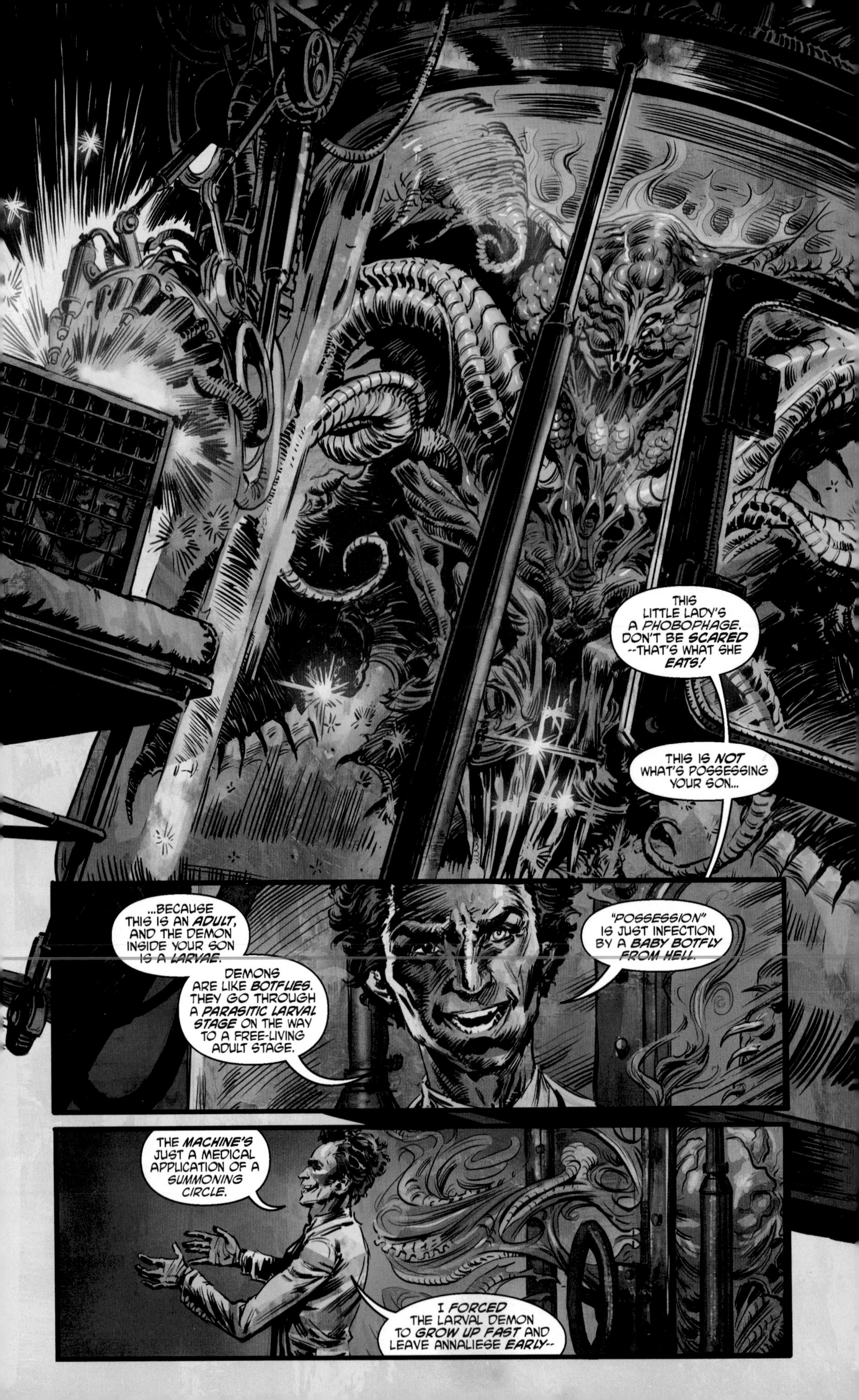
THIS LITTLE LADY'S A PHOBOPHAGE. DON'T BE SCARED --THAT'S WHAT SHE EATS!
THIS IS NOT WHAT'S POSSESSING YOUR SON...
...BECAUSE THIS IS AN ADULT, AND THE DEMON INSIDE YOUR SON IS A LARVAE.
DEMONS ARE LIKE BOTFLIES. THEY GO THROUGH A PARASITIC LARVAL STAGE ON THE WAY TO A FREE-LIVING ADULT STAGE.
"POSSESSION" IS JUST INFECTION BY A BABY BOTFLY FROM HELL.
THE MACHINE'S JUST A MEDICAL APPLICATION OF A SUMMONING CIRCLE.
I FORCED THE LARVAL DEMON TO GROW UP FAST AND LEAVE ANNALIESE EARLY--

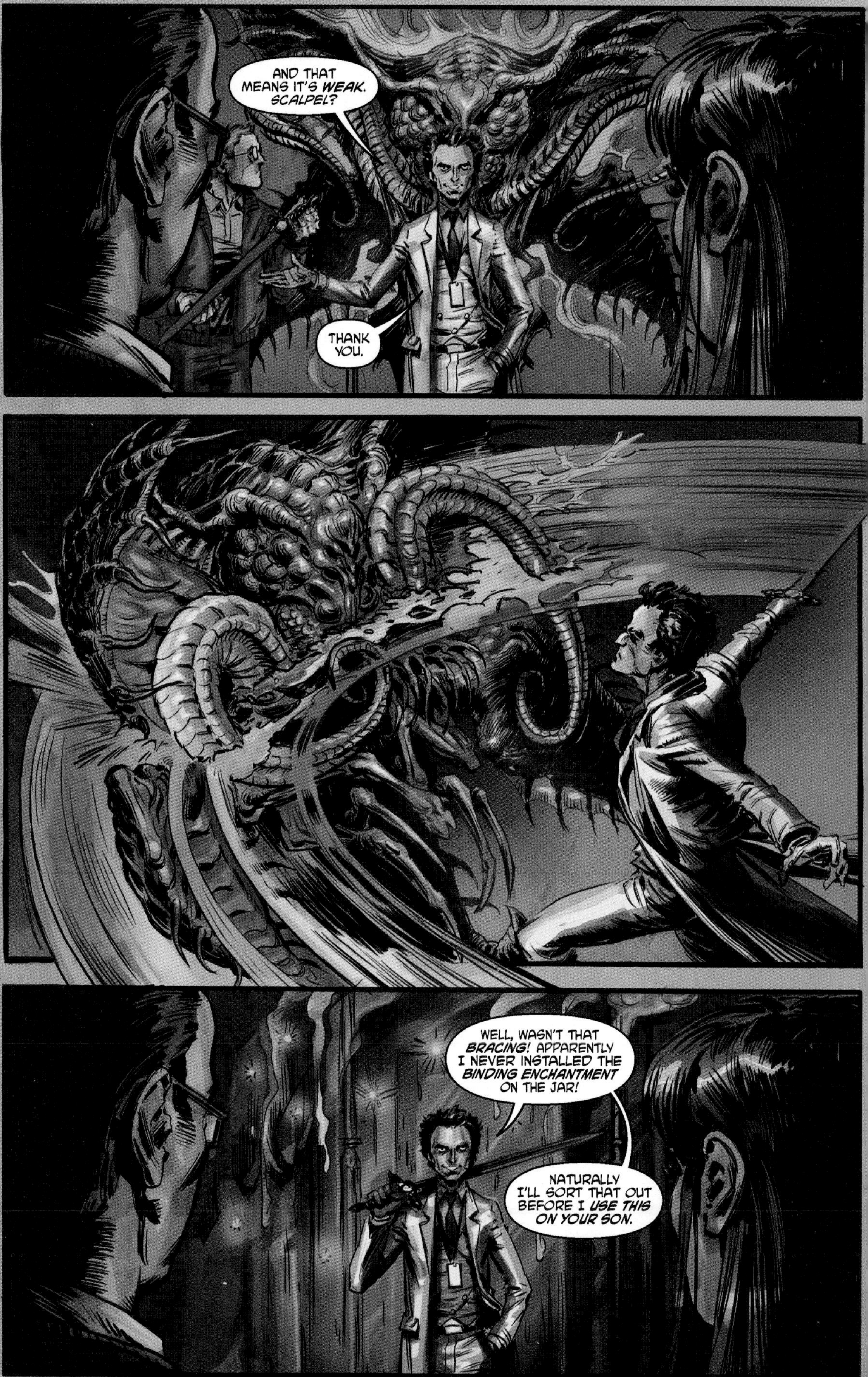
AND THAT MEANS IT'S *WEAK*. SCALPEL?
THANK YOU.
WELL, WASN'T THAT *BRACING!* APPARENTLY I NEVER INSTALLED THE *BINDING ENCHANTMENT* ON THE JAR!
NATURALLY I'LL SORT THAT OUT BEFORE I *USE THIS ON YOUR SON*.

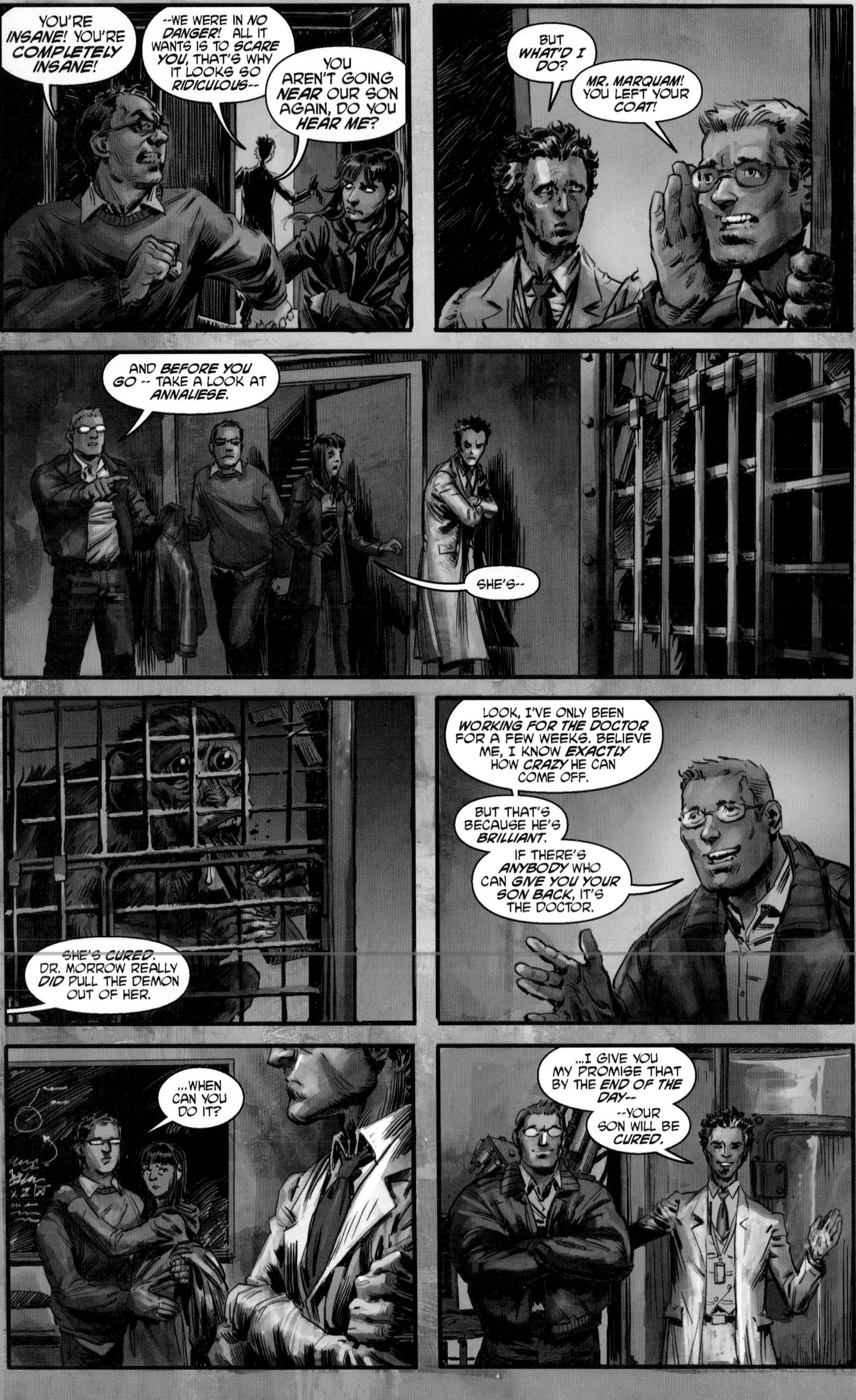
YOU'RE INSANE! YOU'RE COMPLETELY INSANE!
--WE WERE IN NO DANGER! ALL IT WANTS IS TO SCARE YOU, THAT'S WHY IT LOOKS SO RIDICULOUS--
YOU AREN'T GOING NEAR OUR SON AGAIN, DO YOU HEAR ME?
BUT WHAT'D I DO?
MR. MARQUAM! YOU LEFT YOUR COAT!
AND BEFORE YOU GO -- TAKE A LOOK AT ANNALIESE.
SHE'S--
SHE'S CURED. DR. MORROW REALLY DID PULL THE DEMON OUT OF HER.
LOOK, I'VE ONLY BEEN WORKING FOR THE DOCTOR FOR A FEW WEEKS. BELIEVE ME, I KNOW EXACTLY HOW CRAZY HE CAN COME OFF.
BUT THAT'S BECAUSE HE'S BRILLIANT.
IF THERE'S ANYBODY WHO CAN GIVE YOU YOUR SON BACK, IT'S THE DOCTOR.
...WHEN CAN YOU DO IT?
...I GIVE YOU MY PROMISE THAT BY THE END OF THE DAY--
--YOUR SON WILL BE CURED.

WE CAN'T DO IT.

WHAT? WHY NOT?

WELL, JUST *LOOK* AT THE KID'S *TEST* RESULTS!

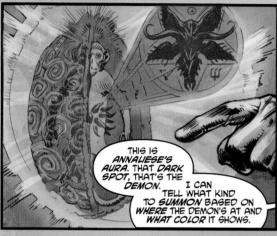

THIS IS *ANNALIESE'S* AURA. THAT *DARK SPOT*, THAT'S THE *DEMON*. I CAN TELL WHAT KIND TO *SUMMON* BASED ON *WHERE* THE DEMON'S AT AND *WHAT COLOR* IT SHOWS.

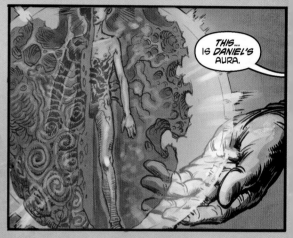

THIS... IS *DANIEL'S* AURA.

THE SCAN'S *WORTHLESS*. I'LL HAVE TO *RECALIBRATE* THE *ETHERIC VOLUME IMAGER.*

SO HOW LONG IS *THAT* GONNA TAKE?

TO PULL OUT EACH OF THE SCANNER'S *CRYSTALS* AND CONSECRATE THEM TO THE *FOUR CARDINAL DIRECTIONS?* A WEEK. A *REEEEALLY TEDIOUS* WEEK.

IS THERE SOME *OTHER* WAY TO FIND OUT WHAT *KIND OF DEMON* DANIEL'S POSSESSED BY? ANOTHER *TEST?*

NO. THERE'S *NOTHING ELSE* I CAN DO!

--YEAH. NOTHING *I* CAN DO...

...BUT IF WE BROUGHT IN A *SPECIALIST...*

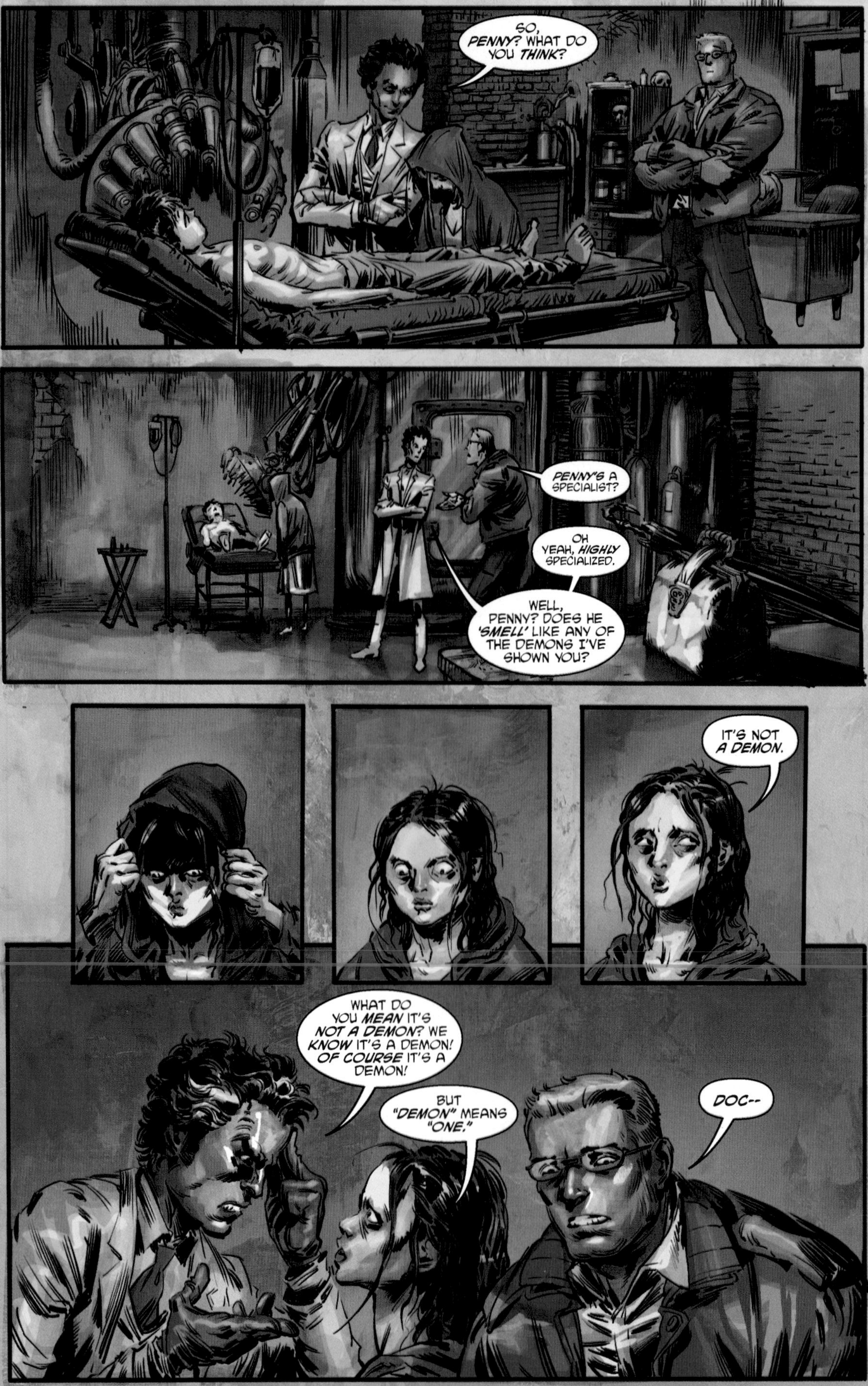
SO, PENNY? WHAT DO YOU THINK?
PENNY'S A SPECIALIST?
OH YEAH, HIGHLY SPECIALIZED.
WELL, PENNY? DOES HE 'SMELL' LIKE ANY OF THE DEMONS I'VE SHOWN YOU?
IT'S NOT A DEMON.
WHAT DO YOU MEAN IT'S NOT A DEMON? WE KNOW IT'S A DEMON! OF COURSE IT'S A DEMON!
BUT "DEMON" MEANS "ONE."
DOC--

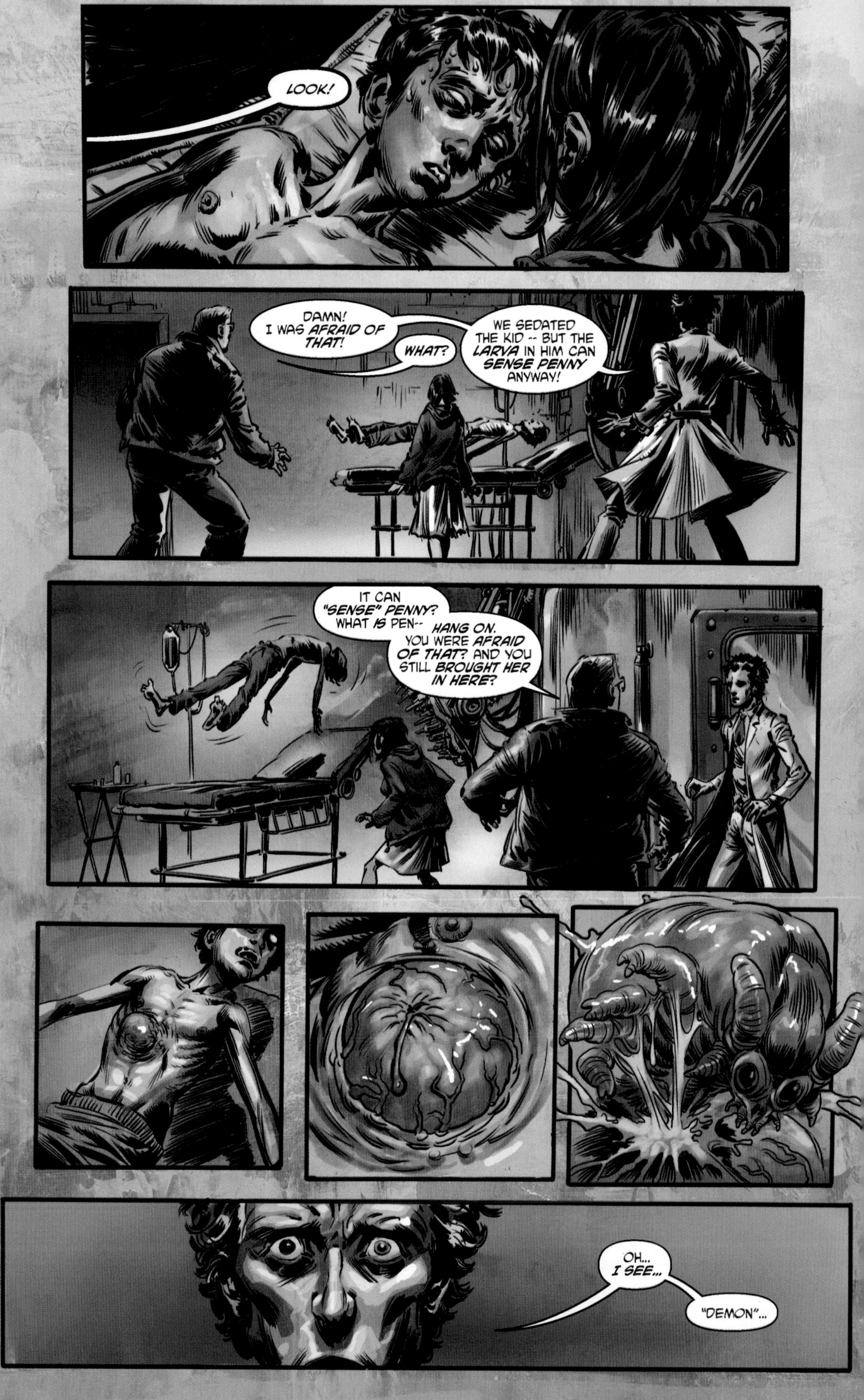
LOOK!
DAMN! I WAS AFRAID OF THAT!
WHAT?
WE SEDATED THE KID -- BUT THE LARVA IN HIM CAN SENSE PENNY ANYWAY!
IT CAN "SENSE" PENNY? WHAT IS PEN--
HANG ON. YOU WERE AFRAID OF THAT? AND YOU STILL BROUGHT HER IN HERE?
OH... I SEE...
"DEMON"...

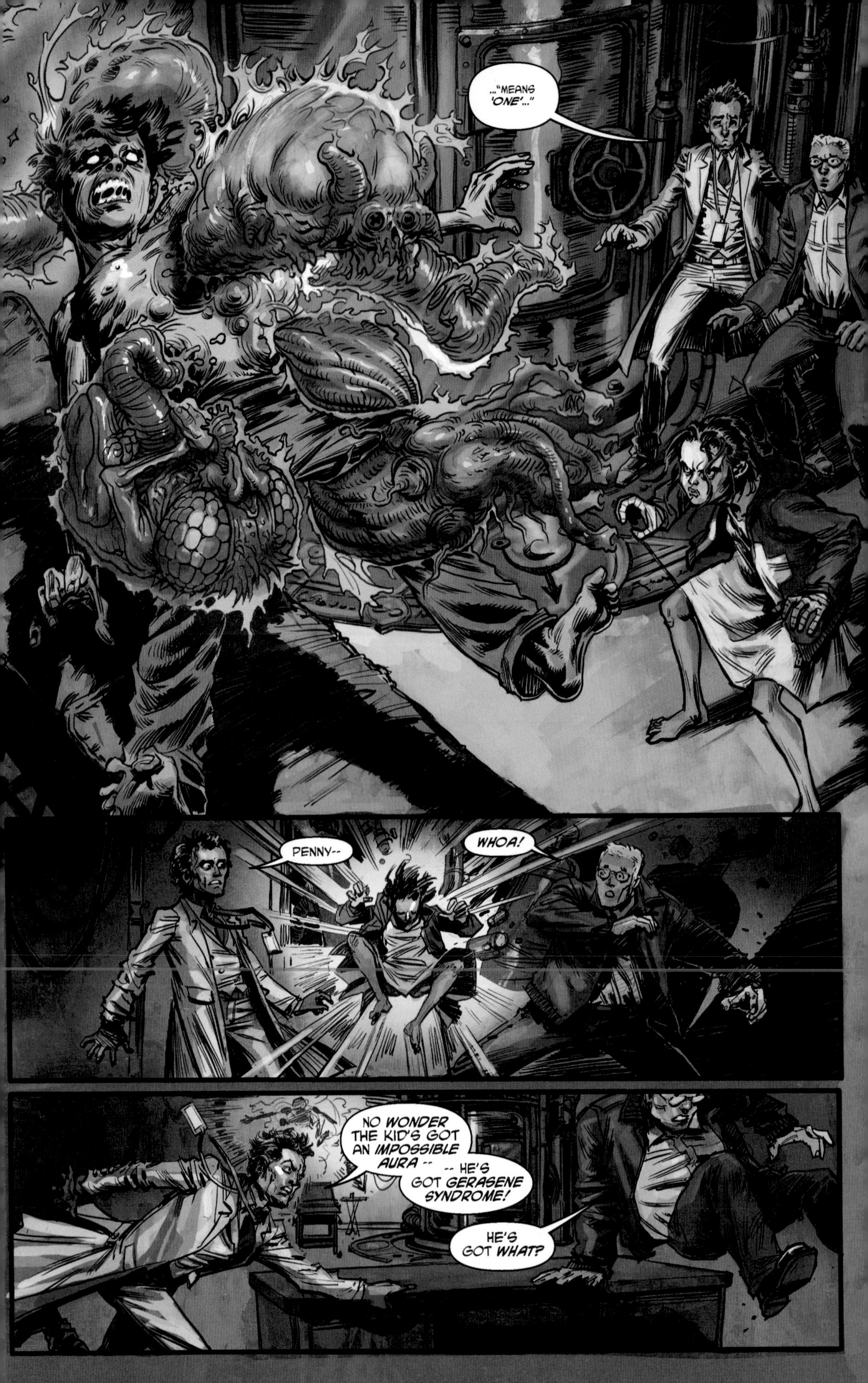
..."MEANS 'ONE'..."
PENNY--
WHOA!
NO WONDER THE KID'S GOT AN IMPOSSIBLE AURA --
-- HE'S GOT GERASENE SYNDROME!
HE'S GOT WHAT?

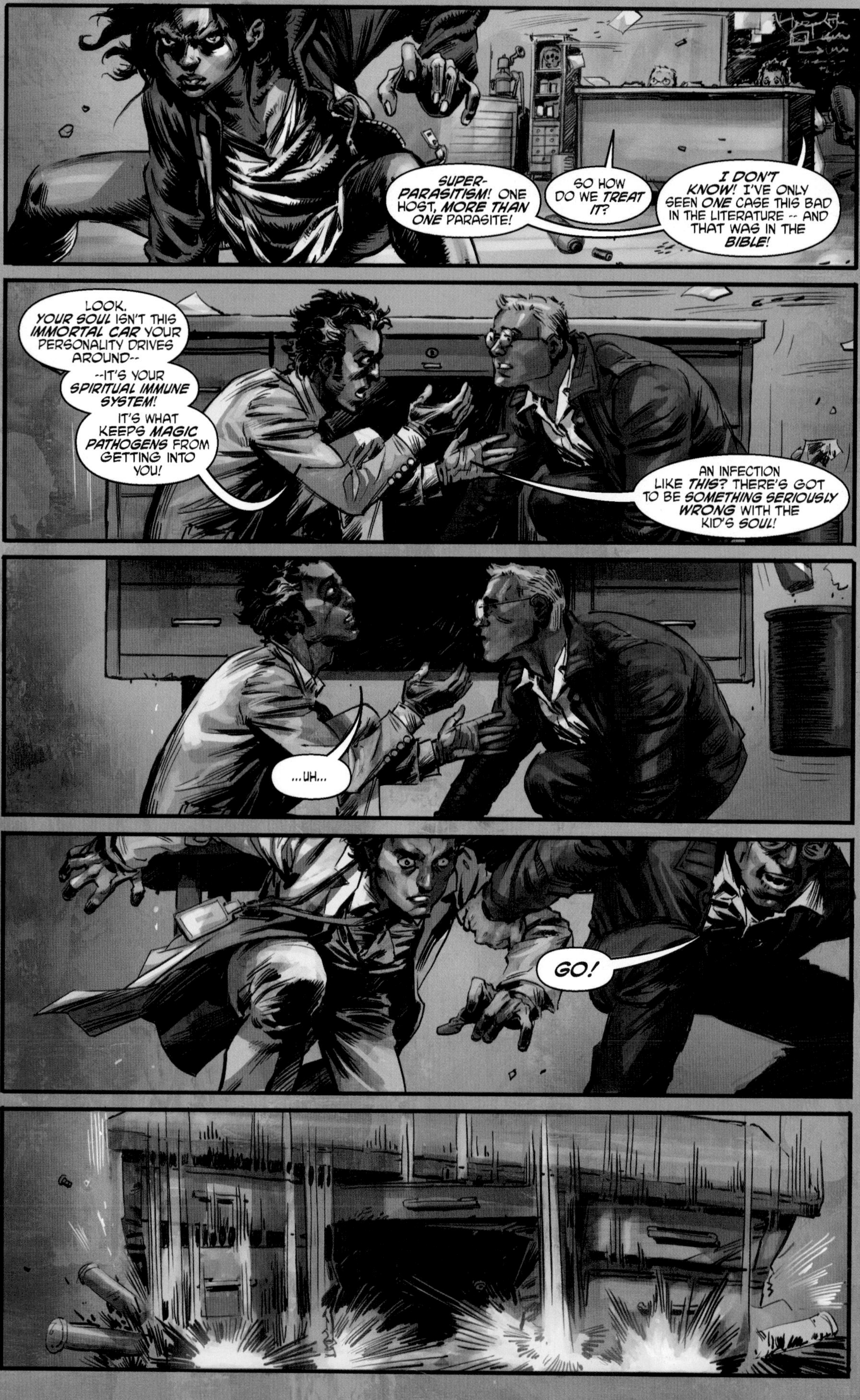
SUPER-PARASITISM! ONE HOST, MORE THAN ONE PARASITE!
SO HOW DO WE TREAT IT?
I DON'T KNOW! I'VE ONLY SEEN ONE CASE THIS BAD IN THE LITERATURE -- AND THAT WAS IN THE BIBLE!
LOOK. YOUR SOUL ISN'T THIS IMMORTAL CAR YOUR PERSONALITY DRIVES AROUND--
--IT'S YOUR SPIRITUAL IMMUNE SYSTEM!
IT'S WHAT KEEPS MAGIC PATHOGENS FROM GETTING INTO YOU!
AN INFECTION LIKE THIS? THERE'S GOT TO BE SOMETHING SERIOUSLY WRONG WITH THE KID'S SOUL!
...UH...
GO!

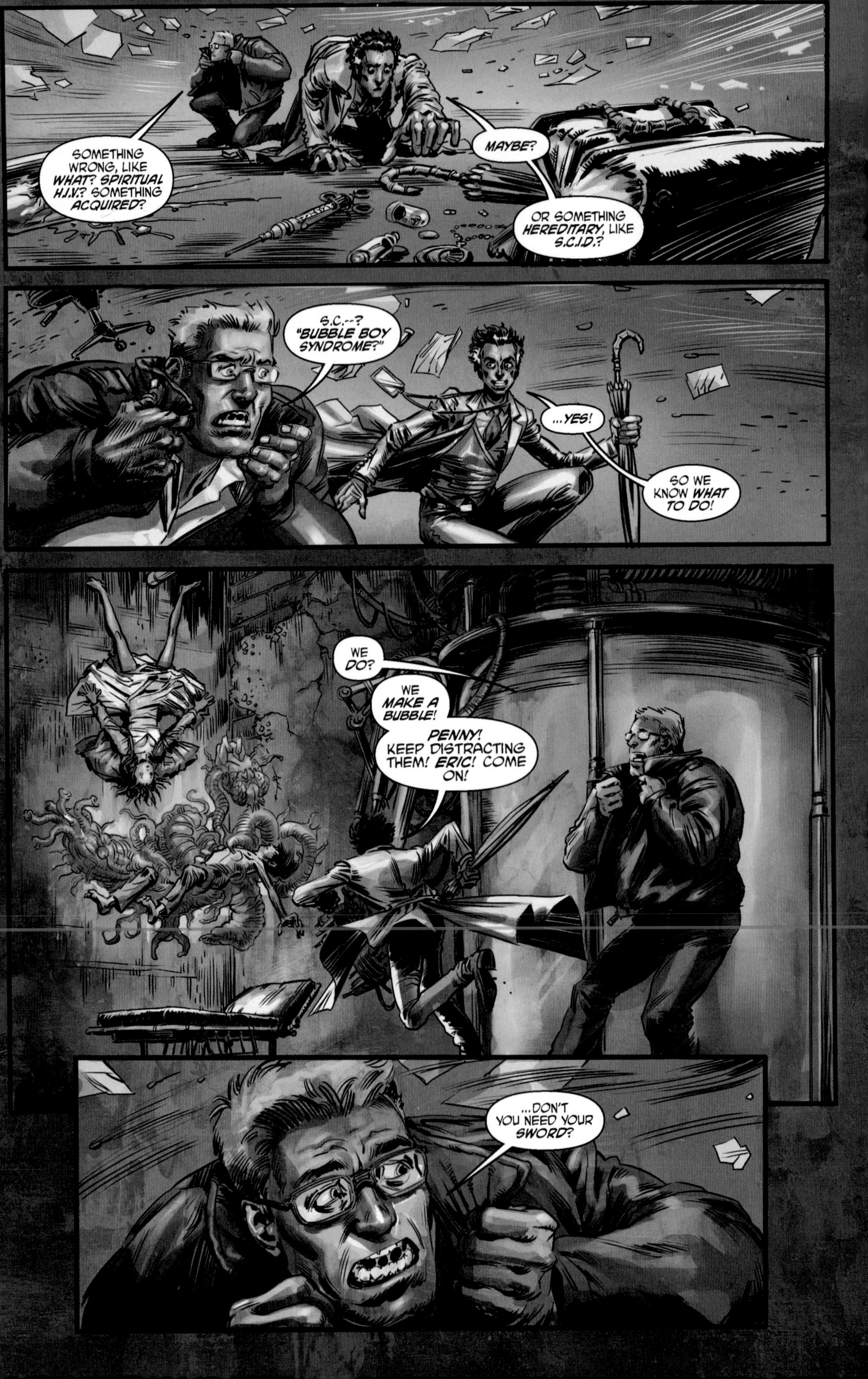
SOMETHING WRONG, LIKE WHAT? SPIRITUAL H.I.V.? SOMETHING ACQUIRED?
MAYBE?
OR SOMETHING HEREDITARY, LIKE S.C.I.D.?
S.C.--? "BUBBLE BOY SYNDROME?"
...YES!
SO WE KNOW WHAT TO DO!
WE DO?
WE MAKE A BUBBLE!
PENNY! KEEP DISTRACTING THEM! ERIC! COME ON!
...DON'T YOU NEED YOUR SWORD?

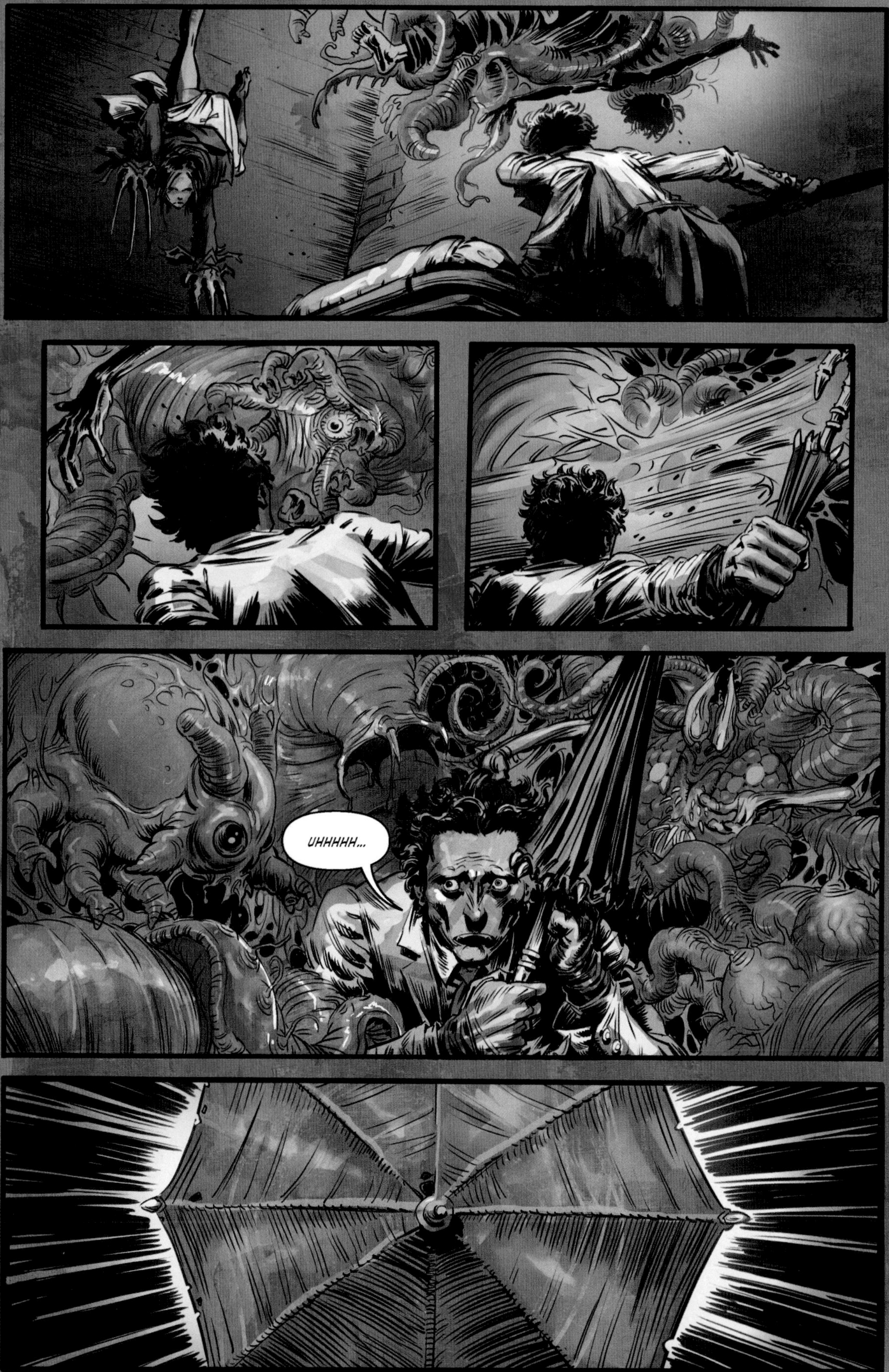
UHHHHH...

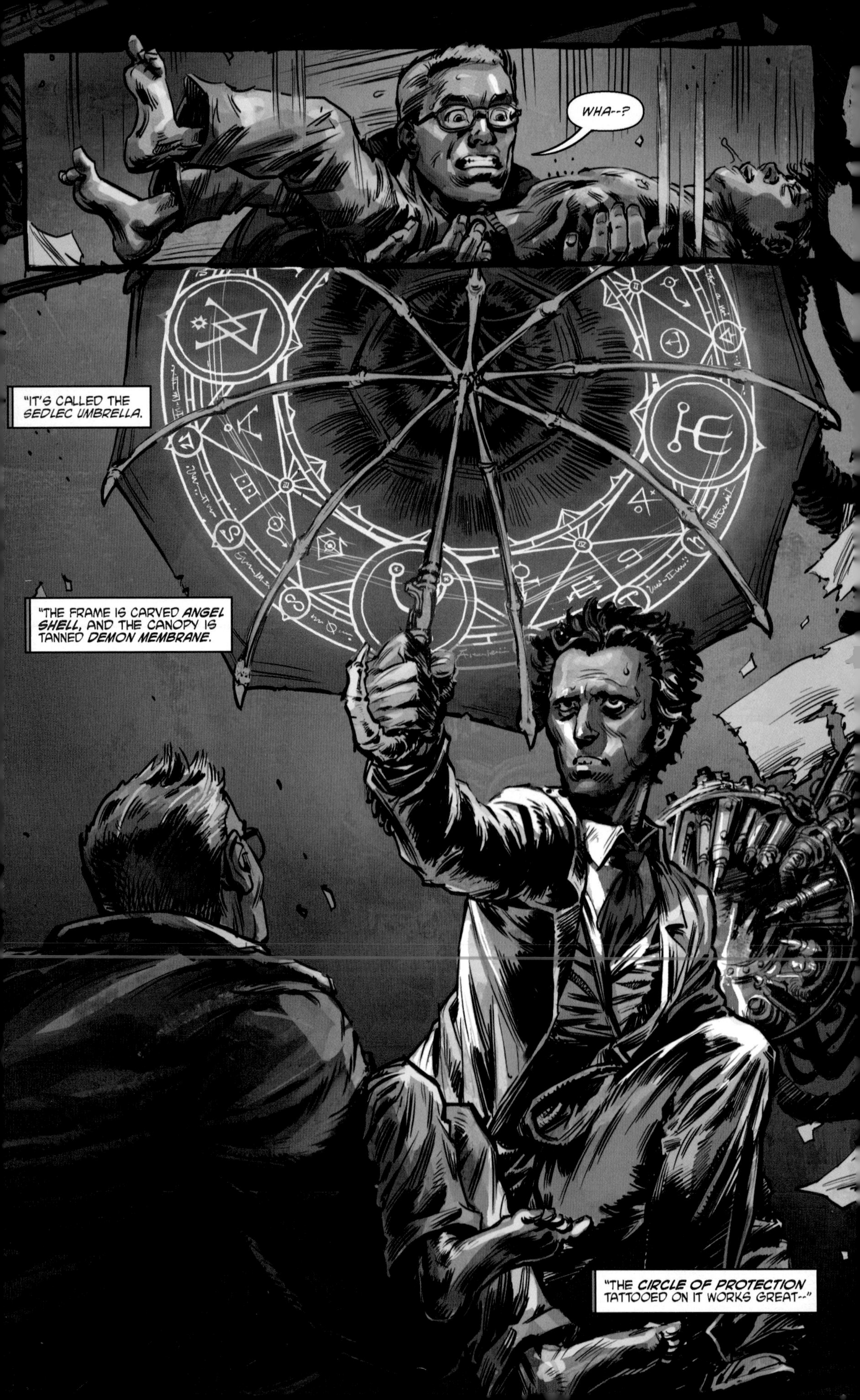
WHA--?
"IT'S CALLED THE *SEDLEC UMBRELLA*.
"THE FRAME IS CARVED *ANGEL SHELL*, AND THE CANOPY IS TANNED *DEMON MEMBRANE*.
"THE *CIRCLE OF PROTECTION* TATTOOED ON IT WORKS GREAT--"

--FOR REPELLING *BOTH* SPECIES.

THAT'S *AMAZING*. ALL THIS TIME, AND ALL THESE DOCTORS AND PRIESTS-- AND YOU *CURED* DAVID BY *HOLDING YOUR UMBRELLA* OVER HIM?

OH, HE'S NOT *CURED*. THE DEMONS ARE SEDATED, BUT THEY'LL STILL HAVE TO *COME OUT*.

BUT THEY'RE JUST AN *OPPORTUNISTIC* INFECTION.

I DON'T HAVE A WAY TO CURE HIS *REAL ILLNESS* YET -- BUT AS FOR MANAGING THE SYMPTOMS...

...EVER HEARD OF *DAVID VETTER*?

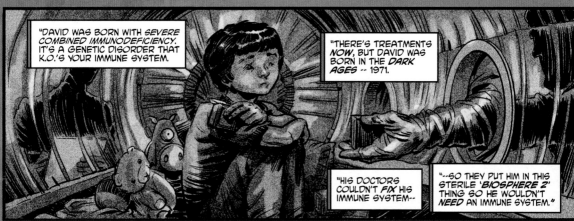

"DAVID WAS BORN WITH *SEVERE COMBINED IMMUNODEFICIENCY*. IT'S A GENETIC DISORDER THAT K.O.'S YOUR IMMUNE SYSTEM.

"THERE'S TREATMENTS *NOW*, BUT DAVID WAS BORN IN THE *DARK AGES* -- 1971.

"HIS DOCTORS COULDN'T *FIX* HIS IMMUNE SYSTEM--

"--SO THEY PUT HIM IN THIS STERILE '*BIOSPHERE 2*' THING SO HE WOULDN'T *NEED* AN IMMUNE SYSTEM."

YOU TREAT SOMEONE WITH A *BROKEN IMMUNE SYSTEM* BY *ISOLATING THEM* FROM PATHOGENS.

THE *PRINCIPLE'S* THE SAME, WHETHER THE PATHOGENS ARE GERMS--OR *SPIRITS*.

HOW'S HE GOING TO *SLEEP* UNDER THE UMBRELLA?

YOU *DON'T* GET TO KEEP MY UMBRELLA. I *NEED* IT.

BUT... I DON'T UNDER-STAND. WHAT ARE WE SUPPOSED TO *DO*?

WELL...

...I NOTICE YOUR LANDSCAPING COULD USE BETTER *FENG SHUI*...

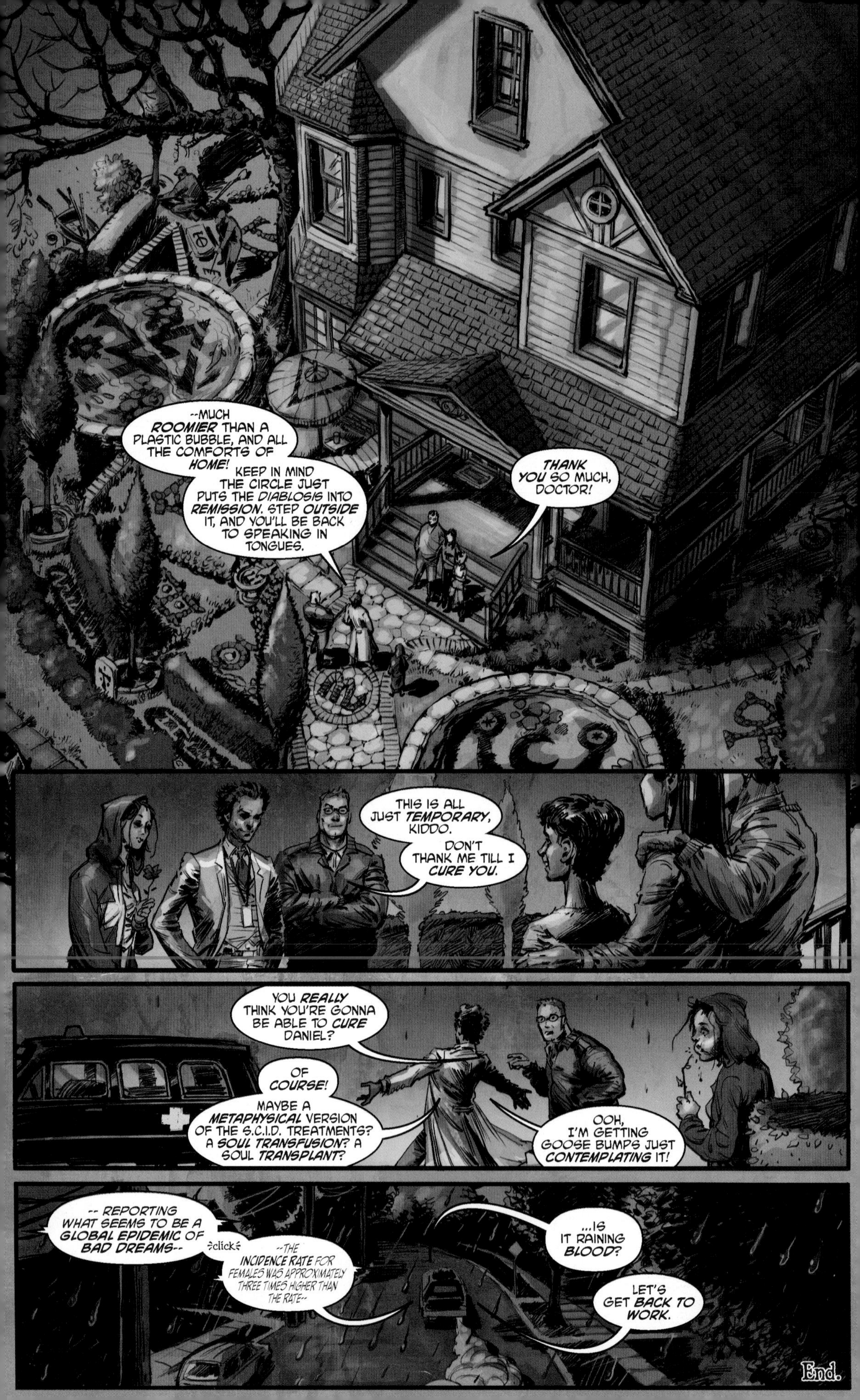
--MUCH ROOMIER THAN A PLASTIC BUBBLE, AND ALL THE COMFORTS OF HOME!
KEEP IN MIND THE CIRCLE JUST PUTS THE DIABLOSIS INTO REMISSION. STEP OUTSIDE IT, AND YOU'LL BE BACK TO SPEAKING IN TONGUES.
THANK YOU SO MUCH, DOCTOR!
THIS IS ALL JUST TEMPORARY, KIDDO.
DON'T THANK ME TILL I CURE YOU.
YOU REALLY THINK YOU'RE GONNA BE ABLE TO CURE DANIEL?
OF COURSE!
MAYBE A METAPHYSICAL VERSION OF THE S.C.I.D. TREATMENTS? A SOUL TRANSFUSION? A SOUL TRANSPLANT?
OOH, I'M GETTING GOOSE BUMPS JUST CONTEMPLATING IT!
-- REPORTING WHAT SEEMS TO BE A GLOBAL EPIDEMIC OF BAD DREAMS--
click
--THE INCIDENCE RATE FOR FEMALES WAS APPROXIMATELY THREE TIMES HIGHER THAN THE RATE--
...IS IT RAINING BLOOD?
LET'S GET BACK TO WORK.
End.

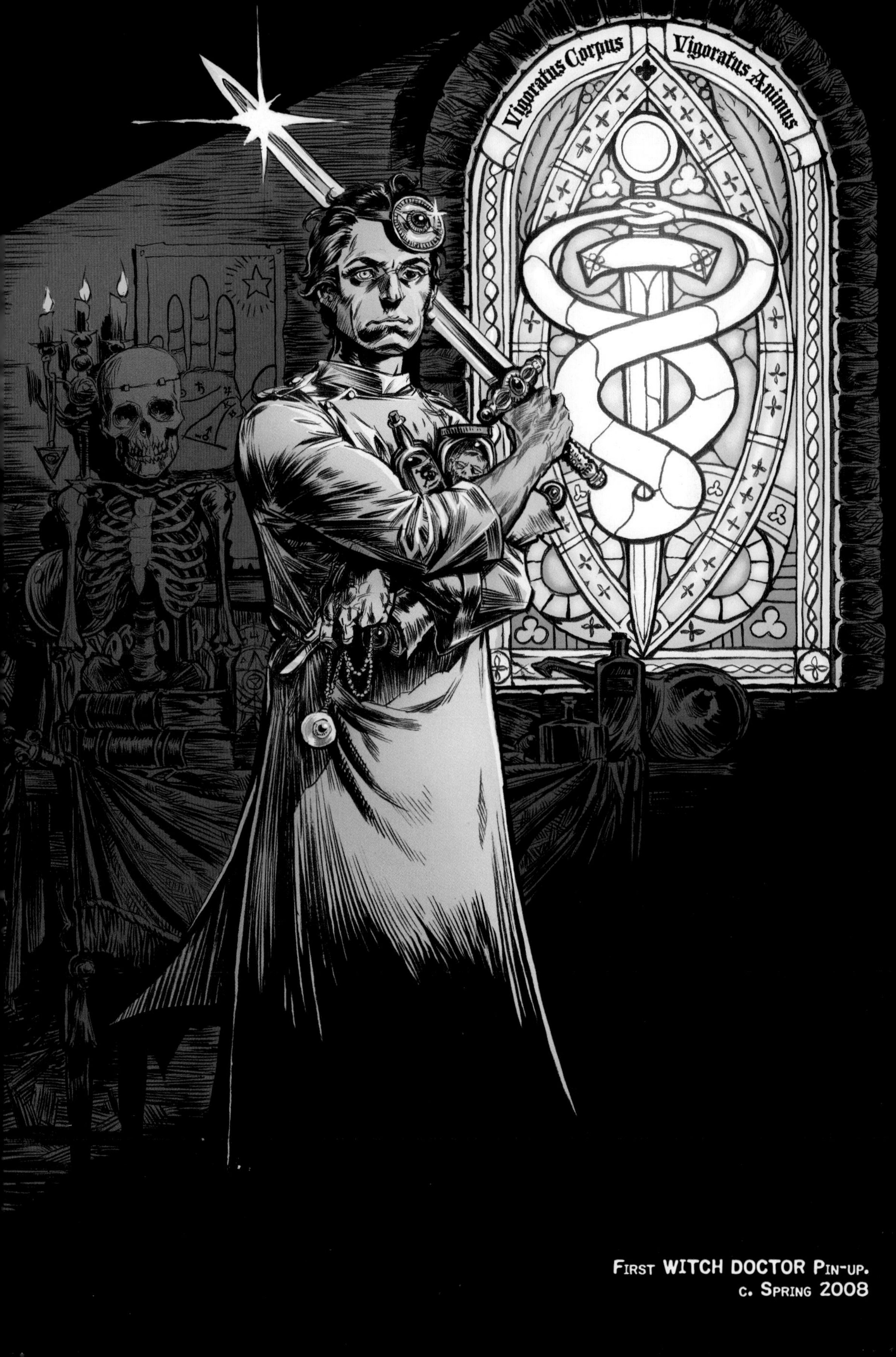
Vigoratus Corpus
Vigoratus Animus

First WITCH DOCTOR Pin-up.
c. Spring 2008

CHAPTER TWO

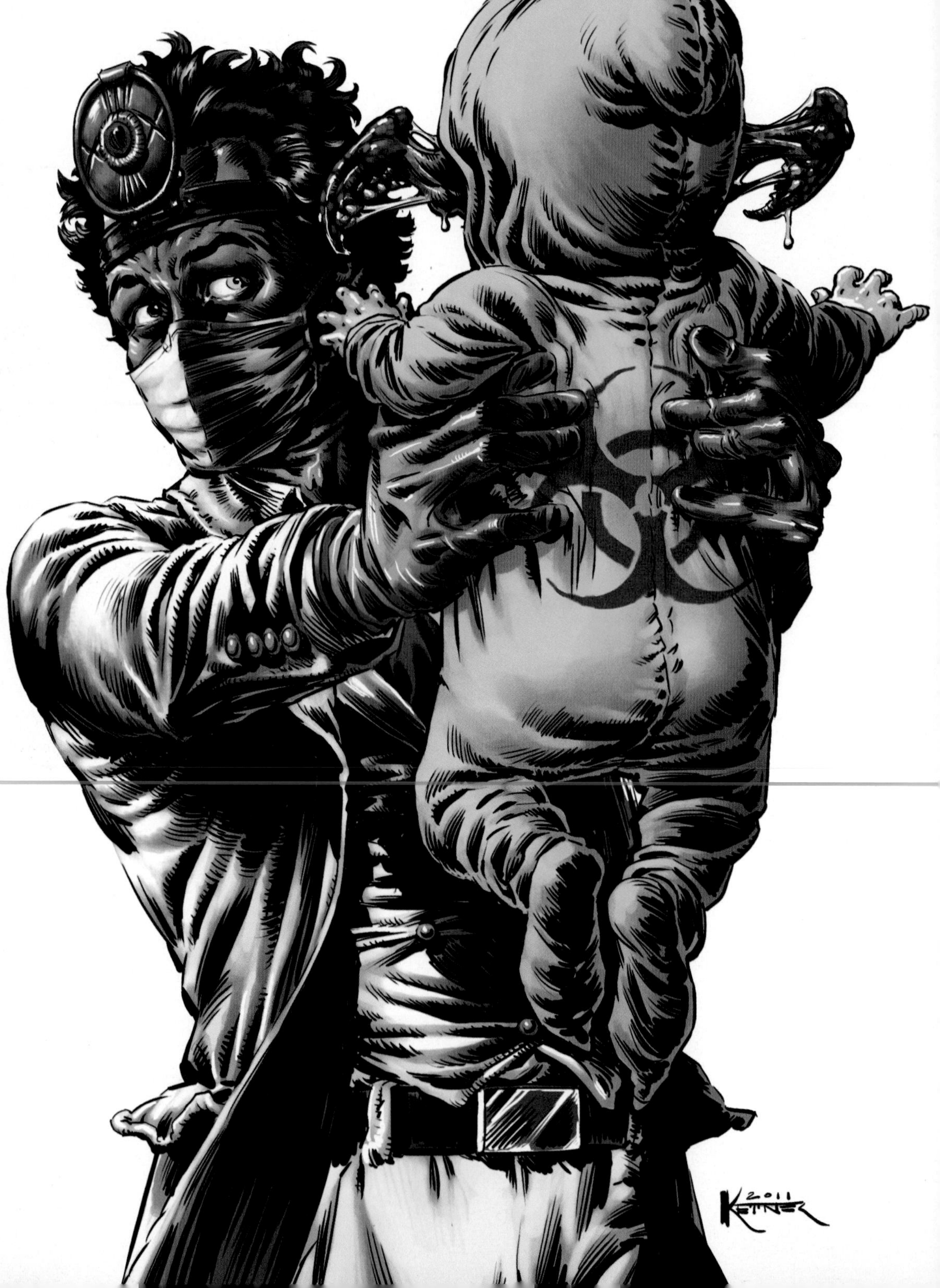

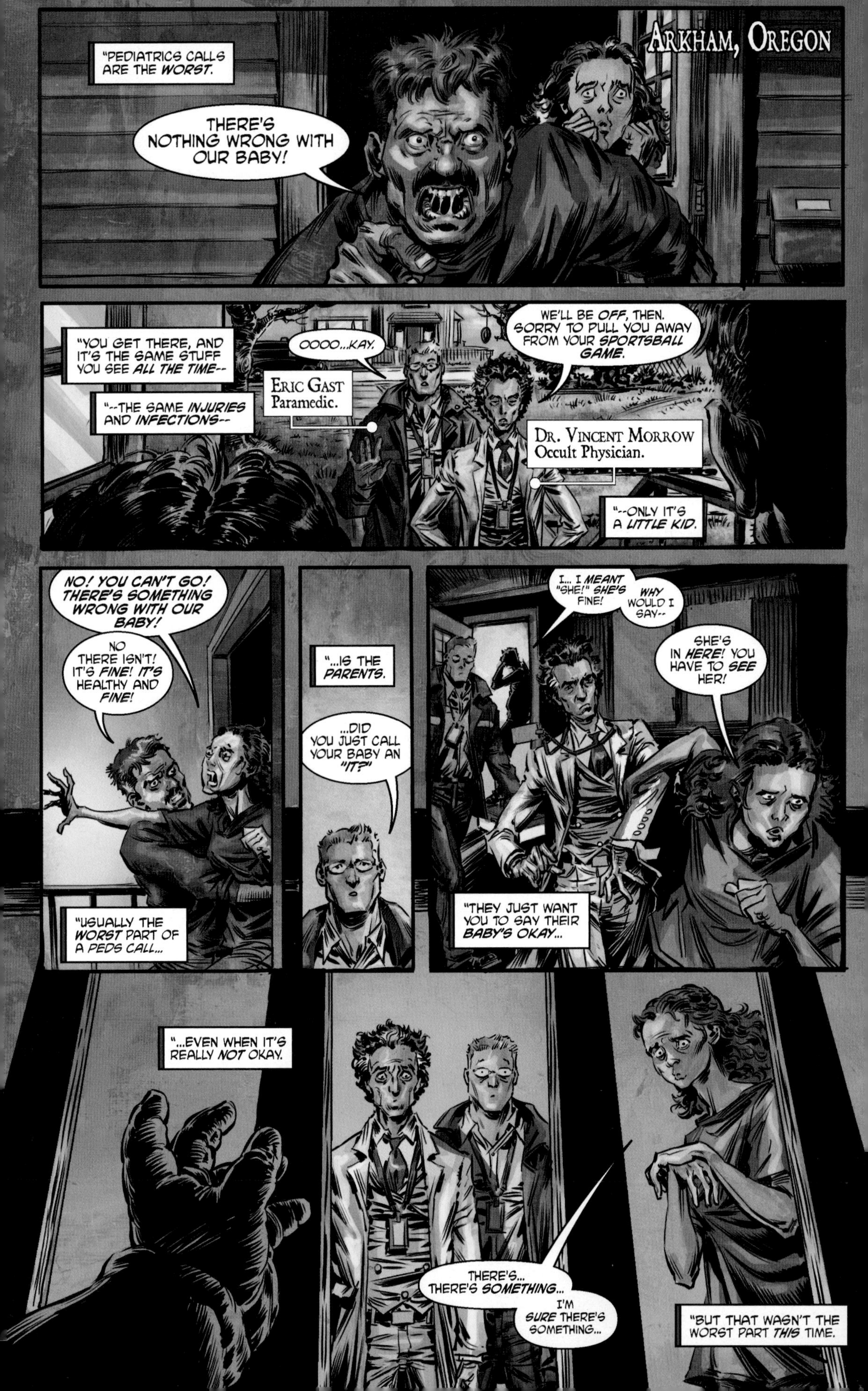
ARKHAM, OREGON
"PEDIATRICS CALLS ARE THE *WORST*.
THERE'S NOTHING WRONG WITH OUR BABY!
"YOU GET THERE, AND IT'S THE SAME STUFF YOU SEE *ALL THE TIME*--
"--THE SAME *INJURIES* AND *INFECTIONS*--
OOOO...KAY.
WE'LL BE *OFF*, THEN. SORRY TO PULL YOU AWAY FROM YOUR *SPORTSBALL GAME*.
ERIC GAST Paramedic.
DR. VINCENT MORROW Occult Physician.
"--ONLY IT'S A *LITTLE KID*.
NO! YOU CAN'T GO! THERE'S SOMETHING WRONG WITH OUR BABY!
NO THERE ISN'T! IT'S *FINE*! *IT'S* HEALTHY AND *FINE*!
"USUALLY THE *WORST* PART OF A *PEDS CALL*...
"...IS THE *PARENTS*.
...DID YOU JUST CALL YOUR BABY AN *"IT?"*
I... I *MEANT* "SHE!" *SHE'S* FINE!
WHY WOULD I SAY--
SHE'S IN *HERE*! YOU HAVE TO *SEE* HER!
"THEY JUST WANT YOU TO SAY THEIR *BABY'S OKAY*...
"...EVEN WHEN IT'S REALLY *NOT* OKAY.
THERE'S... THERE'S *SOMETHING*...
I'M *SURE* THERE'S SOMETHING...
"BUT THAT WASN'T THE WORST PART *THIS* TIME.

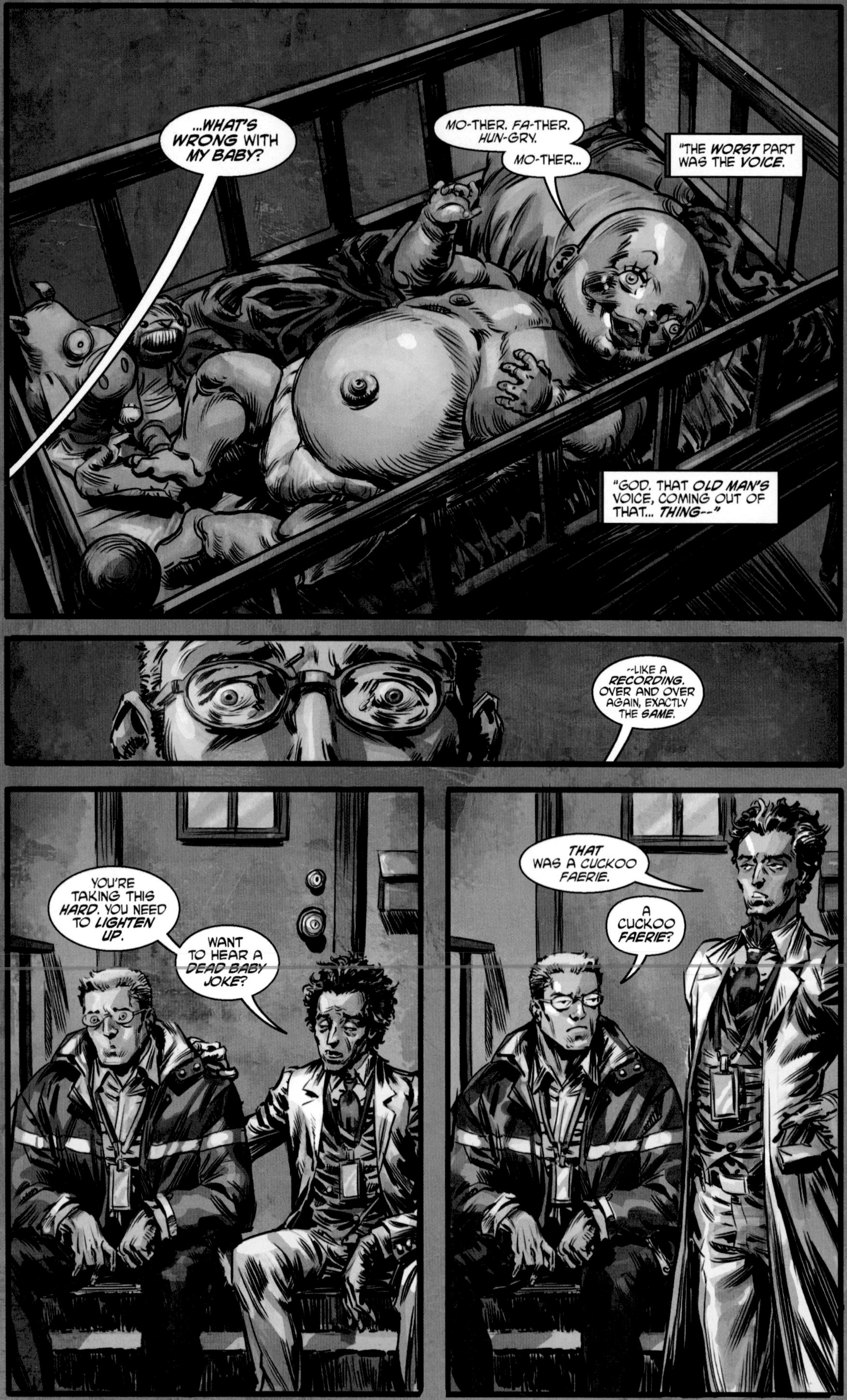
...WHAT'S WRONG WITH MY BABY?
MO-THER. FA-THER. HUN-GRY.
MO-THER...
"THE WORST PART WAS THE VOICE.
"GOD. THAT OLD MAN'S VOICE, COMING OUT OF THAT... THING--"
--LIKE A RECORDING. OVER AND OVER AGAIN, EXACTLY THE SAME.
YOU'RE TAKING THIS HARD. YOU NEED TO LIGHTEN UP.
WANT TO HEAR A DEAD BABY JOKE?
THAT WAS A CUCKOO FAERIE.
A CUCKOO FAERIE?

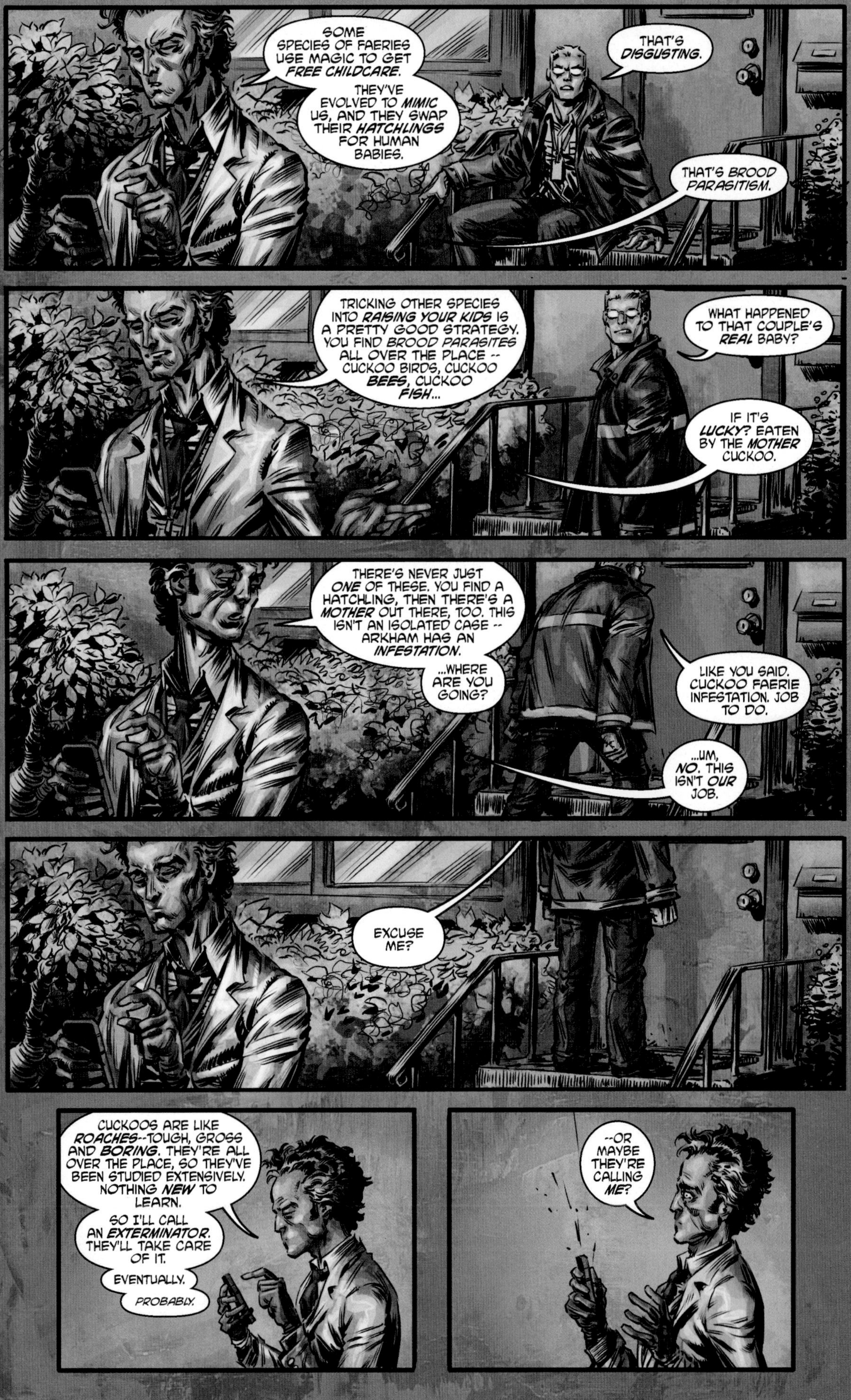
SOME SPECIES OF FAERIES USE MAGIC TO GET FREE CHILDCARE.
THEY'VE EVOLVED TO MIMIC US, AND THEY SWAP THEIR HATCHLINGS FOR HUMAN BABIES.
THAT'S DISGUSTING.
THAT'S BROOD PARASITISM.
TRICKING OTHER SPECIES INTO RAISING YOUR KIDS IS A PRETTY GOOD STRATEGY. YOU FIND BROOD PARASITES ALL OVER THE PLACE -- CUCKOO BIRDS, CUCKOO BEES, CUCKOO FISH...
WHAT HAPPENED TO THAT COUPLE'S REAL BABY?
IF IT'S LUCKY? EATEN BY THE MOTHER CUCKOO.
THERE'S NEVER JUST ONE OF THESE. YOU FIND A HATCHLING, THEN THERE'S A MOTHER OUT THERE, TOO. THIS ISN'T AN ISOLATED CASE -- ARKHAM HAS AN INFESTATION.
...WHERE ARE YOU GOING?
LIKE YOU SAID. CUCKOO FAERIE INFESTATION. JOB TO DO.
...UM, NO. THIS ISN'T OUR JOB.
EXCUSE ME?
CUCKOOS ARE LIKE ROACHES--TOUGH, GROSS AND BORING. THEY'RE ALL OVER THE PLACE, SO THEY'VE BEEN STUDIED EXTENSIVELY. NOTHING NEW TO LEARN.
SO I'LL CALL AN EXTERMINATOR. THEY'LL TAKE CARE OF IT.
EVENTUALLY.
PROBABLY.
--OR MAYBE THEY'RE CALLING ME?

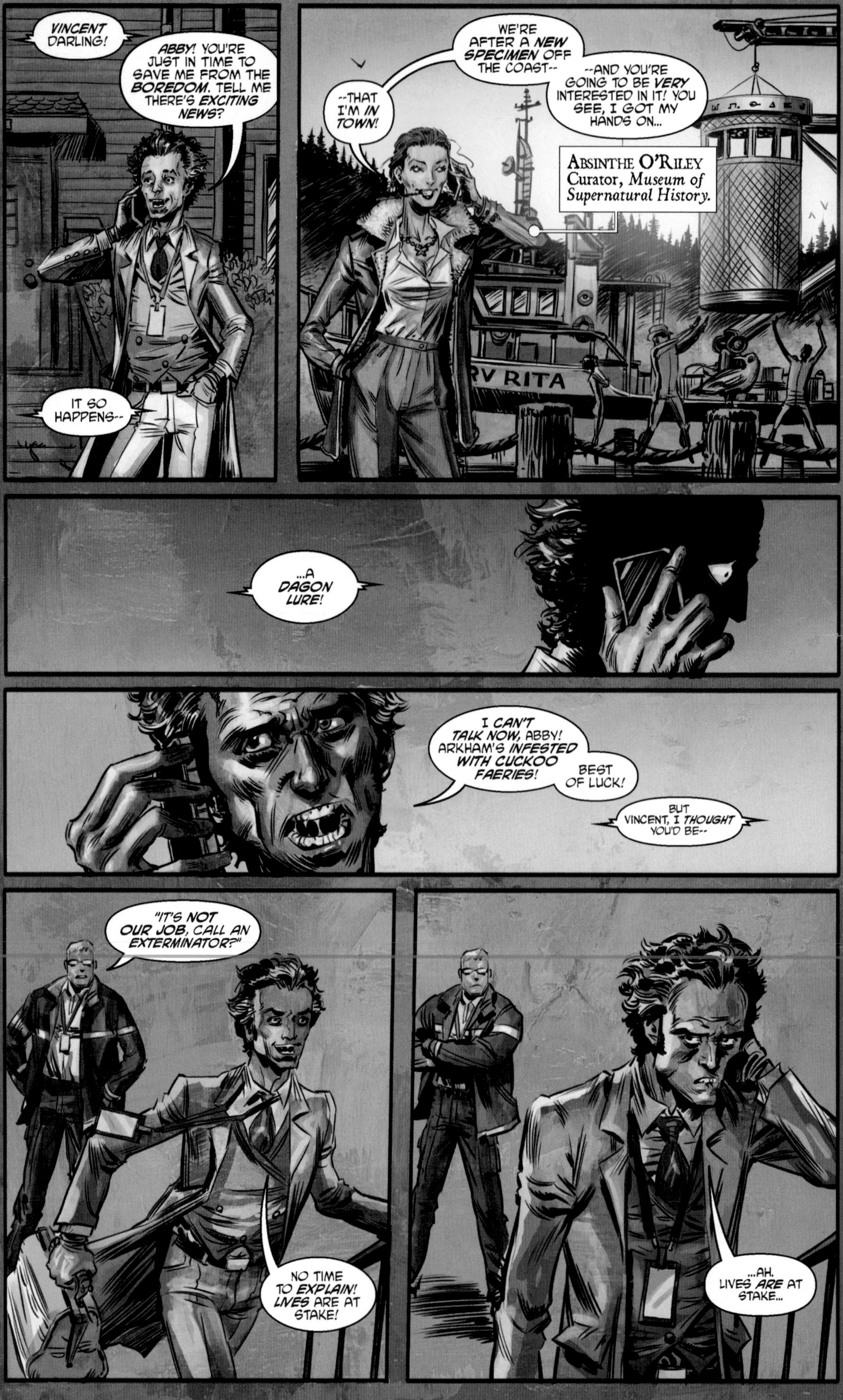
VINCENT DARLING!
ABBY! YOU'RE JUST IN TIME TO SAVE ME FROM THE BOREDOM. TELL ME THERE'S EXCITING NEWS?
IT SO HAPPENS--
--THAT I'M IN TOWN!
WE'RE AFTER A NEW SPECIMEN OFF THE COAST--
--AND YOU'RE GOING TO BE VERY INTERESTED IN IT! YOU SEE, I GOT MY HANDS ON...
ABSINTHE O'RILEY Curator, Museum of Supernatural History.
RV RITA
...A DAGON LURE!
I CAN'T TALK NOW, ABBY! ARKHAM'S INFESTED WITH CUCKOO FAERIES!
BEST OF LUCK!
BUT VINCENT, I THOUGHT YOU'D BE--
"IT'S NOT OUR JOB, CALL AN EXTERMINATOR?"
NO TIME TO EXPLAIN! LIVES ARE AT STAKE!
...AH. LIVES ARE AT STAKE...

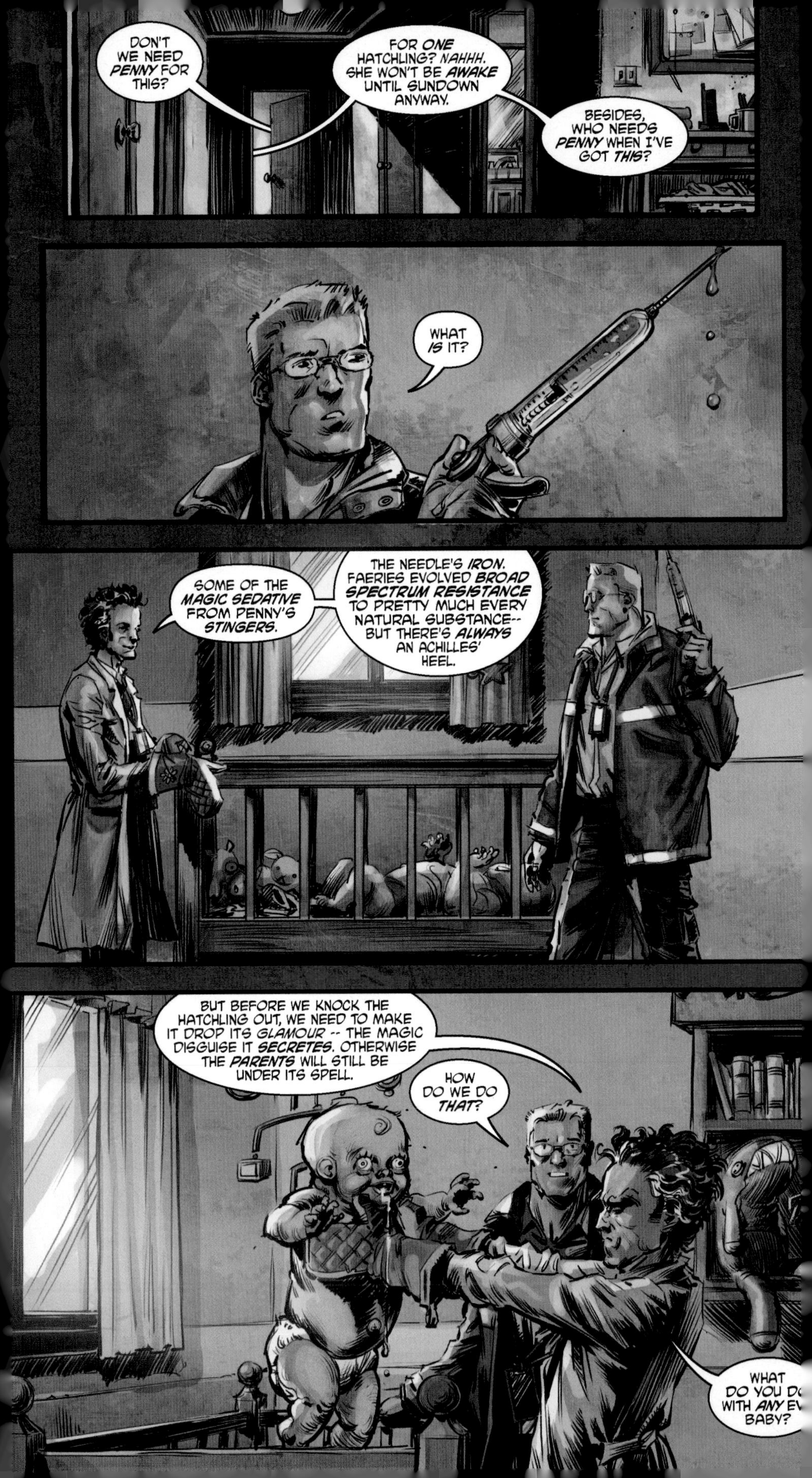
DON'T WE NEED *PENNY* FOR THIS?
FOR *ONE* HATCHLING? *NAHHH.* SHE WON'T BE *AWAKE* UNTIL SUNDOWN ANYWAY.
BESIDES, WHO NEEDS *PENNY* WHEN I'VE GOT *THIS*?
WHAT *IS* IT?
SOME OF THE *MAGIC SEDATIVE* FROM PENNY'S *STINGERS.*
THE NEEDLE'S *IRON.* FAERIES EVOLVED *BROAD SPECTRUM RESISTANCE* TO PRETTY MUCH EVERY NATURAL SUBSTANCE-- BUT THERE'S *ALWAYS* AN ACHILLES' HEEL.
BUT BEFORE WE KNOCK THE HATCHLING OUT, WE NEED TO MAKE IT DROP ITS *GLAMOUR* -- THE MAGIC DISGUISE IT *SECRETES.* OTHERWISE THE *PARENTS* WILL STILL BE UNDER ITS SPELL.
HOW DO WE DO *THAT*?

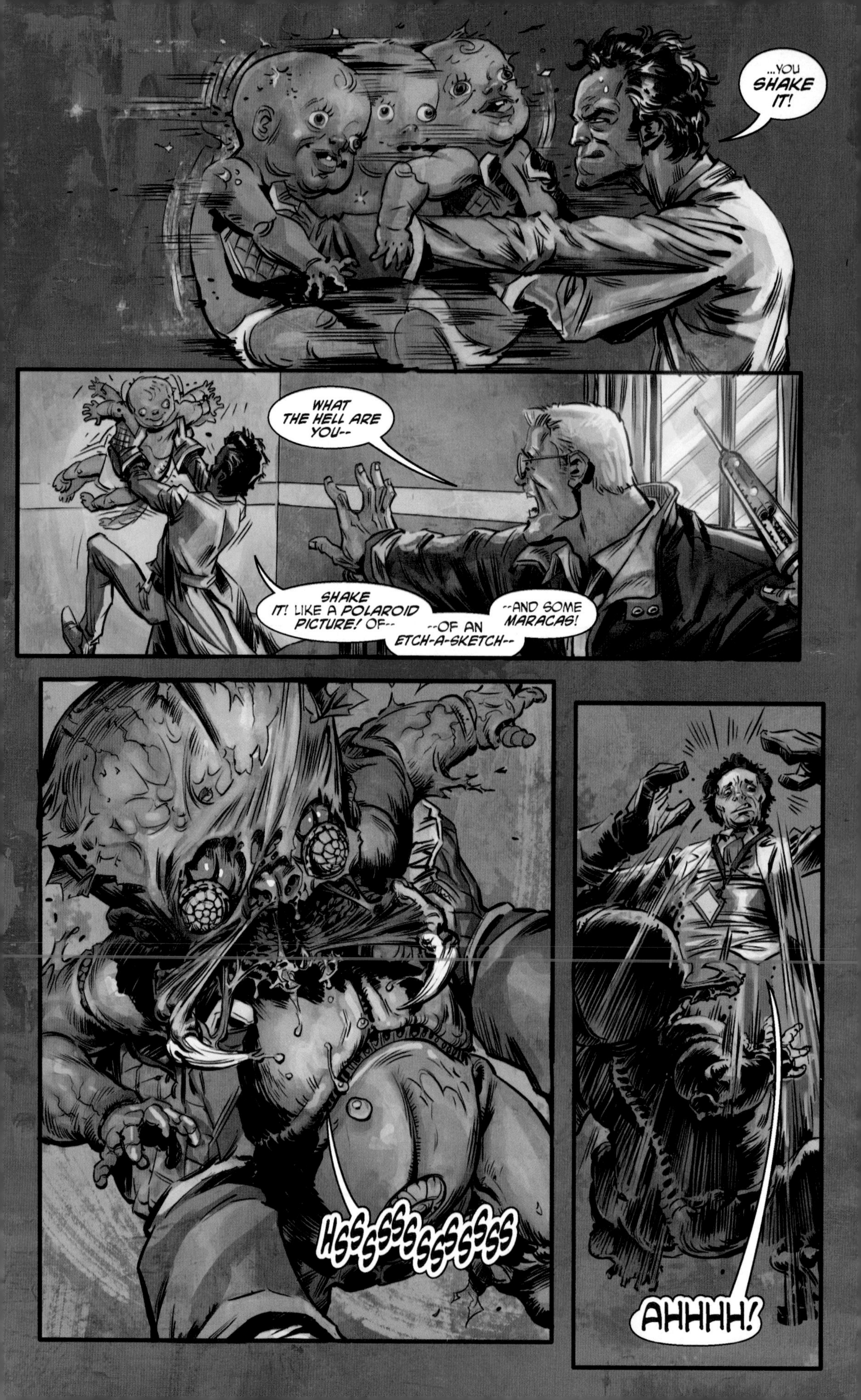
...YOU SHAKE IT!
WHAT THE HELL ARE YOU--
SHAKE IT! LIKE A POLAROID PICTURE! OF--
--OF AN ETCH-A-SKETCH--
--AND SOME MARACAS!
HSSSSSSSSSSSSSS
AHHHH!

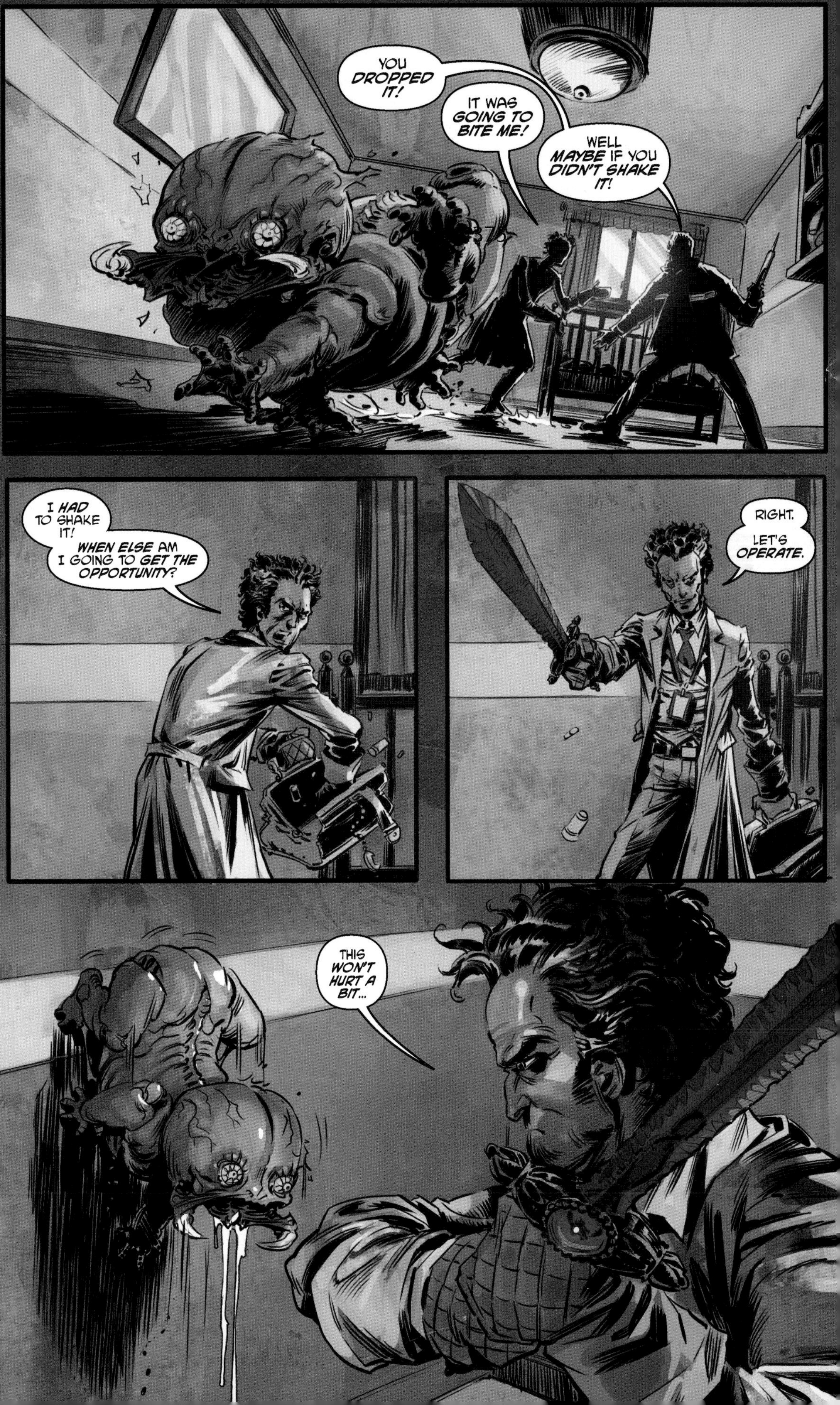
YOU DROPPED IT!
IT WAS GOING TO BITE ME!
WELL MAYBE IF YOU DIDN'T SHAKE IT!
I HAD TO SHAKE IT!
WHEN ELSE AM I GOING TO GET THE OPPORTUNITY?
RIGHT.
LET'S OPERATE.
THIS WON'T HURT A BIT...

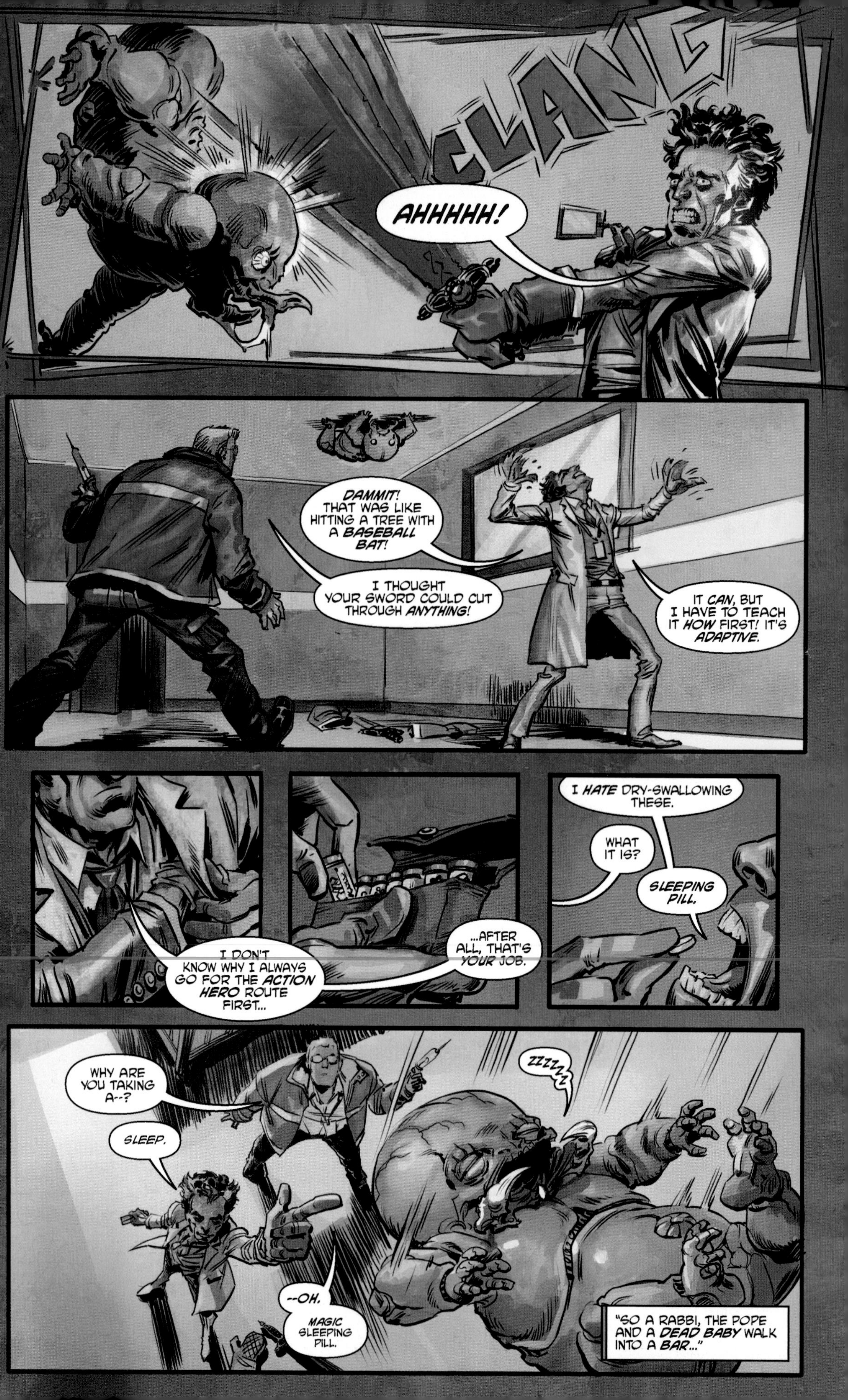
CLANG
AHHHHH!
DAMMIT! THAT WAS LIKE HITTING A TREE WITH A BASEBALL BAT!
I THOUGHT YOUR SWORD COULD CUT THROUGH ANYTHING!
IT CAN, BUT I HAVE TO TEACH IT HOW FIRST! IT'S ADAPTIVE.
I DON'T KNOW WHY I ALWAYS GO FOR THE ACTION HERO ROUTE FIRST...
...AFTER ALL, THAT'S YOUR JOB.
I HATE DRY-SWALLOWING THESE.
WHAT IT IS?
SLEEPING PILL.
WHY ARE YOU TAKING A--?
SLEEP.
ZZZZZZ
--OH.
MAGIC SLEEPING PILL.
"SO A RABBI, THE POPE AND A DEAD BABY WALK INTO A BAR..."

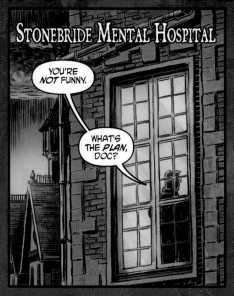

STONEBRIDE MENTAL HOSPITAL

YOU'RE *NOT* FUNNY.

WHAT'S THE *PLAN*, DOC?

WHY DON'T *YOU* TELL *ME*? YOU KNOW THE SITUATION. WHAT *NEEDS TO* HAPPEN HERE?

...WELL, THE HATCHLINGS AREN'T THE *REAL* THREAT, RIGHT?

EVEN IF WE CATCH *ALL* THE HATCHLINGS, THE *MOTHER'S* STILL OUT THERE TO *MAKE MORE.*

SO WE FIND THE *MOTHER*, AND THEN WE FIND THE OTHER HATCHLINGS ...*SOMEHOW.*

MAYBE PUT *PENNY* OUT THERE, ON THE GROUND? SHE CAN *SMELL SUPERNATURAL CREATURES* OR SOMETHING, RIGHT?

STINKY.

"PENNY DREADFUL." Morrow's patient/helper.

IF WE FIND THE HATCHLINGS, WE'LL *FIND* THE MOTHER.

A MOTHER CUCKOO LIKES TO KEEP AN *EYE* ON HER BROOD. IN A *SPOT MAP* WITH THE LOCATIONS OF THE HATCHLINGS PLOTTED ON IT -- SHE'LL BE AT THE *CENTER.*

SO WE FIRE UP MY *MAP PLOTTER*, PUT A *TISSUE BIOPSY* FROM THE HATCHLING IN IT...

...AND *ABRACA--*

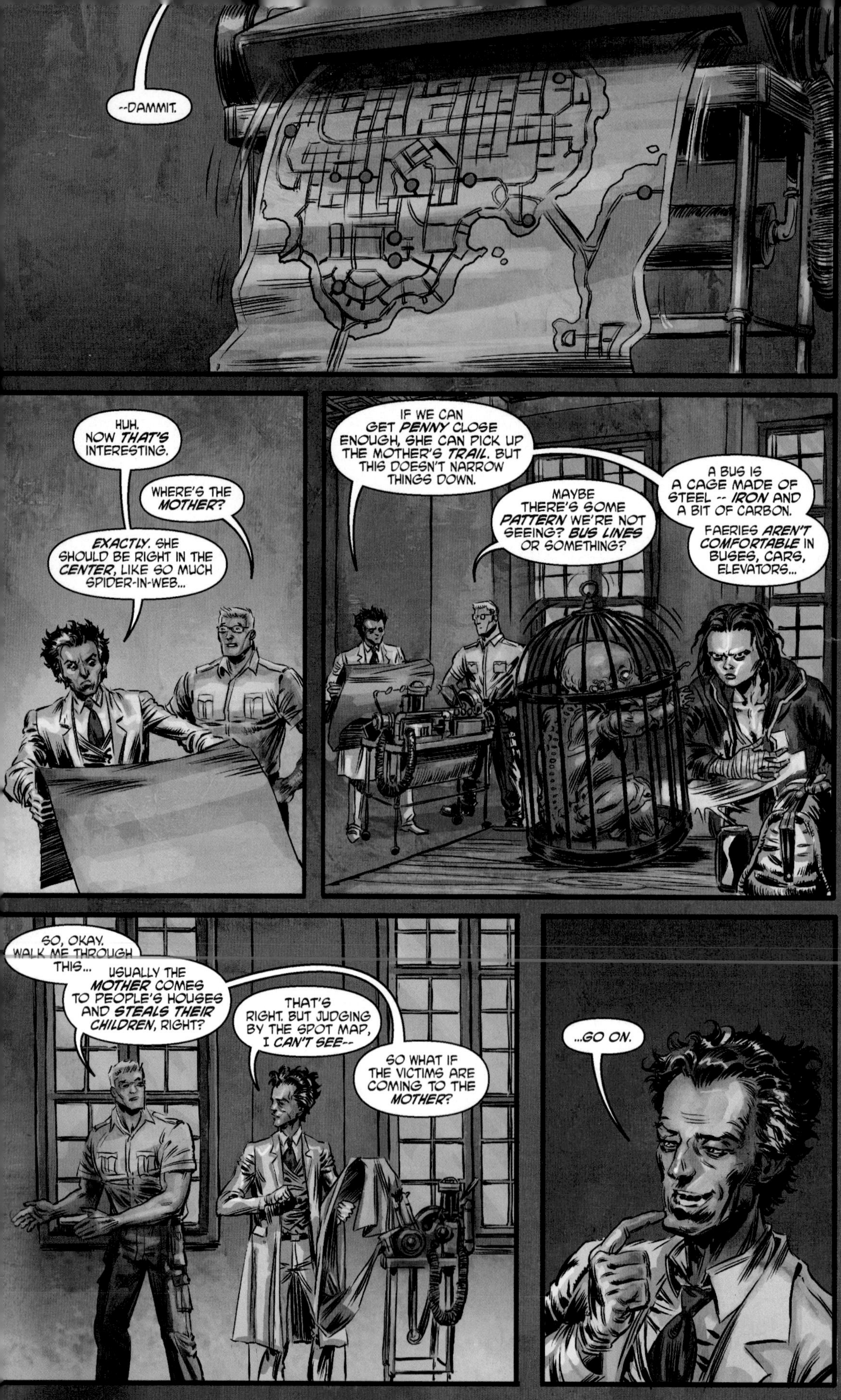
--DAMMIT.
HUH. NOW THAT'S INTERESTING.
WHERE'S THE MOTHER?
EXACTLY. SHE SHOULD BE RIGHT IN THE CENTER, LIKE SO MUCH SPIDER-IN-WEB...
IF WE CAN GET PENNY CLOSE ENOUGH, SHE CAN PICK UP THE MOTHER'S TRAIL. BUT THIS DOESN'T NARROW THINGS DOWN.
MAYBE THERE'S SOME PATTERN WE'RE NOT SEEING? BUS LINES OR SOMETHING?
A BUS IS A CAGE MADE OF STEEL -- IRON AND A BIT OF CARBON.
FAERIES AREN'T COMFORTABLE IN BUSES, CARS, ELEVATORS...
SO, OKAY. WALK ME THROUGH THIS...
USUALLY THE MOTHER COMES TO PEOPLE'S HOUSES AND STEALS THEIR CHILDREN, RIGHT?
THAT'S RIGHT. BUT JUDGING BY THE SPOT MAP, I CAN'T SEE--
SO WHAT IF THE VICTIMS ARE COMING TO THE MOTHER?
...GO ON.

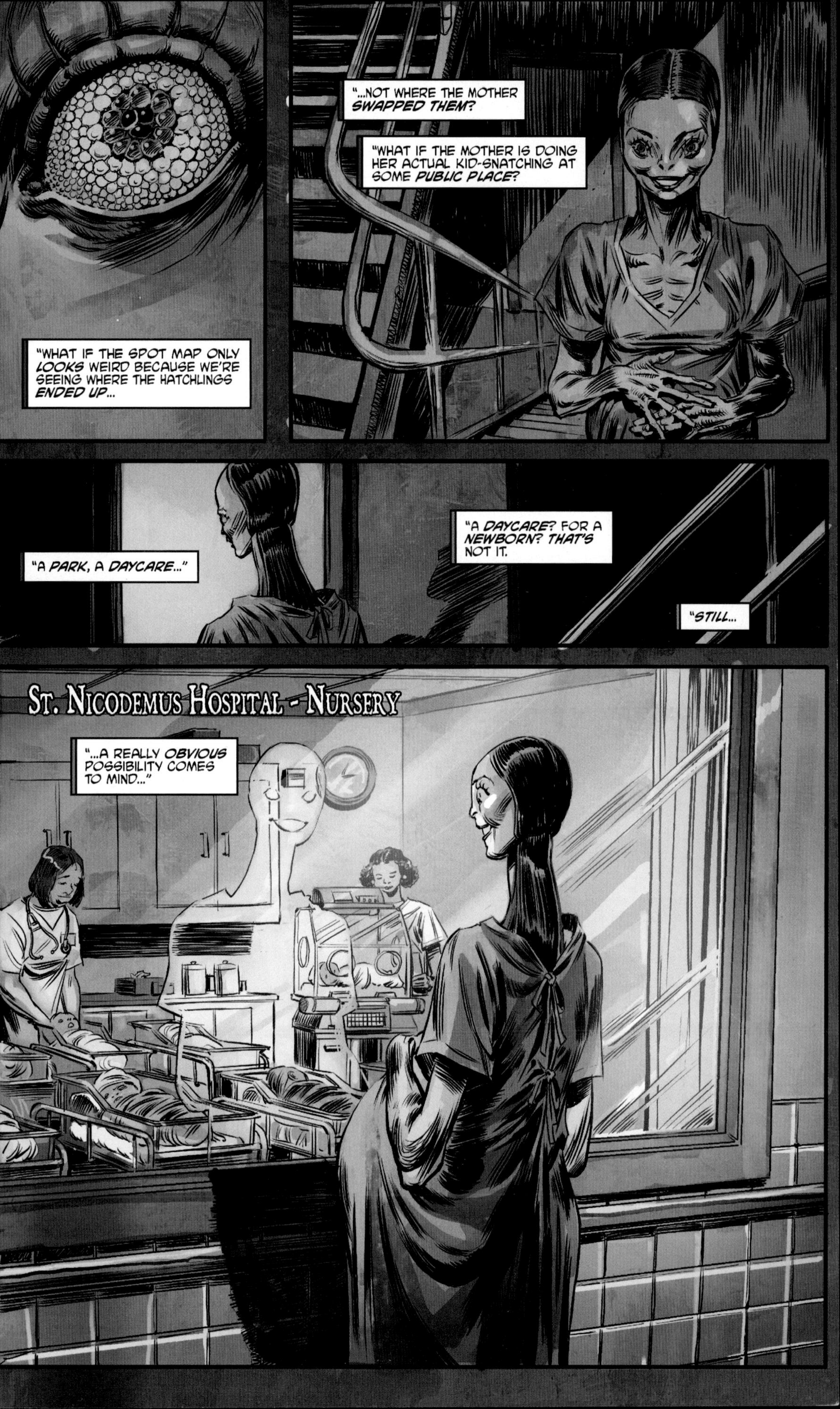
"WHAT IF THE SPOT MAP ONLY LOOKS WEIRD BECAUSE WE'RE SEEING WHERE THE HATCHLINGS ENDED UP...
"...NOT WHERE THE MOTHER SWAPPED THEM?
"WHAT IF THE MOTHER IS DOING HER ACTUAL KID-SNATCHING AT SOME PUBLIC PLACE?
"A PARK, A DAYCARE..."
"A DAYCARE? FOR A NEWBORN? THAT'S NOT IT.
"STILL...
St. Nicodemus Hospital - Nursery
"...A REALLY OBVIOUS POSSIBILITY COMES TO MIND..."

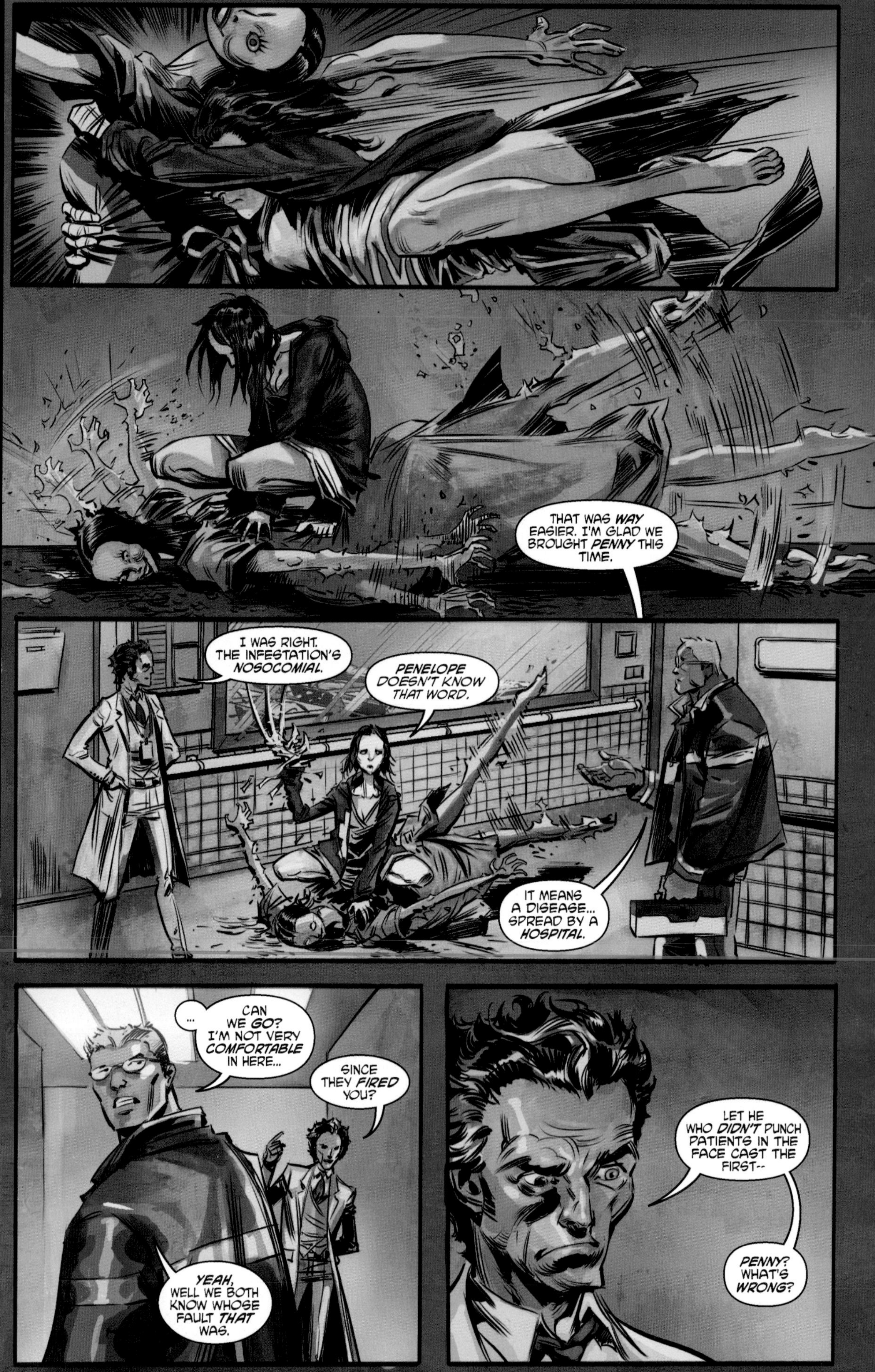
THAT WAS WAY EASIER. I'M GLAD WE BROUGHT PENNY THIS TIME.
I WAS RIGHT. THE INFESTATION'S NOSOCOMIAL.
PENELOPE DOESN'T KNOW THAT WORD.
IT MEANS A DISEASE... SPREAD BY A HOSPITAL.
...
CAN WE GO? I'M NOT VERY COMFORTABLE IN HERE...
SINCE THEY FIRED YOU?
YEAH, WELL WE BOTH KNOW WHOSE FAULT THAT WAS.
LET HE WHO DIDN'T PUNCH PATIENTS IN THE FACE CAST THE FIRST--
PENNY? WHAT'S WRONG?

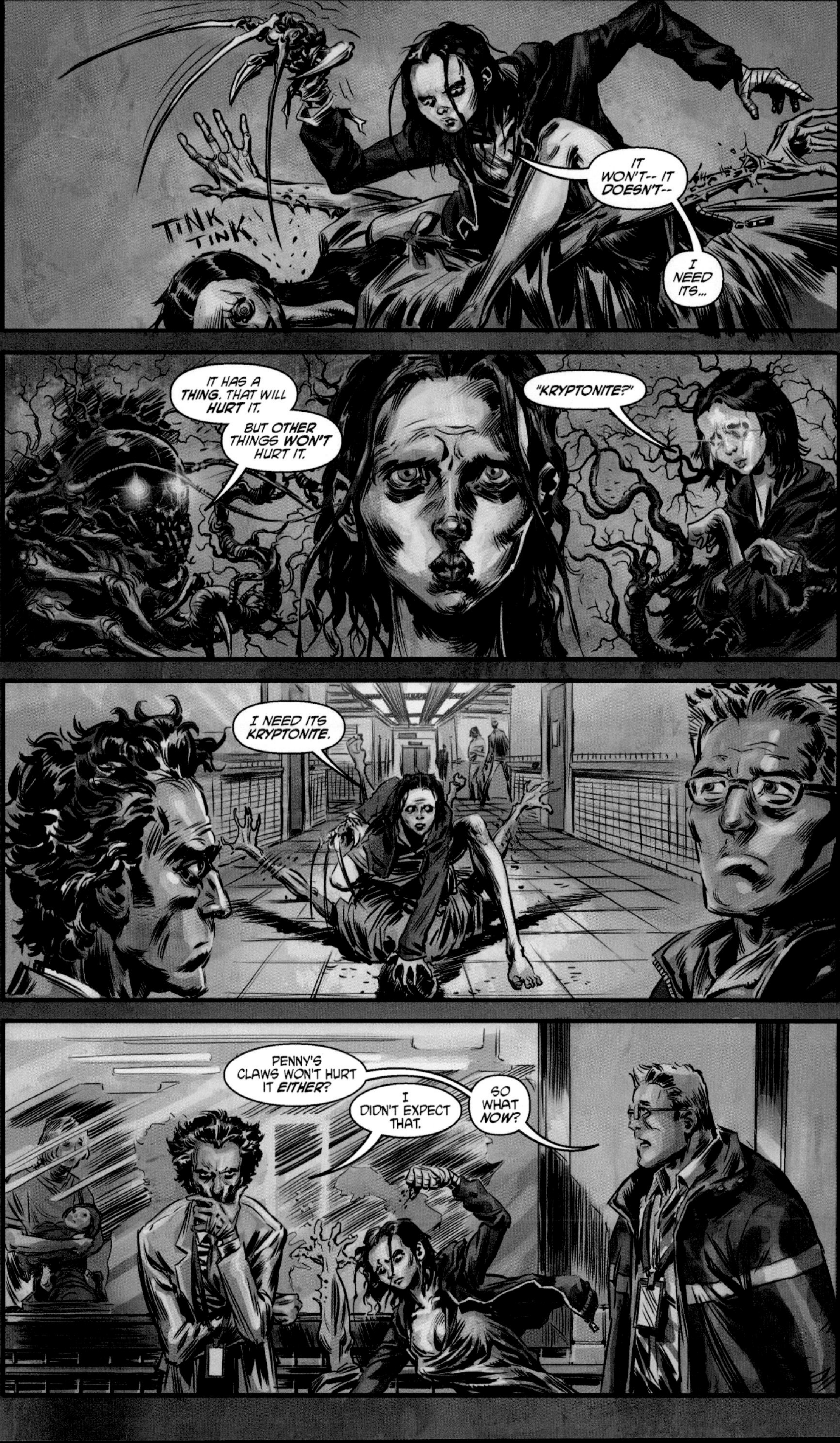
TINK TINK
IT WON'T-- IT DOESN'T--
I NEED ITS...
IT HAS A THING. THAT WILL HURT IT.
BUT OTHER THINGS WON'T HURT IT.
"KRYPTONITE?"
I NEED ITS KRYPTONITE.
PENNY'S CLAWS WON'T HURT IT EITHER?
I DIDN'T EXPECT THAT.
SO WHAT NOW?

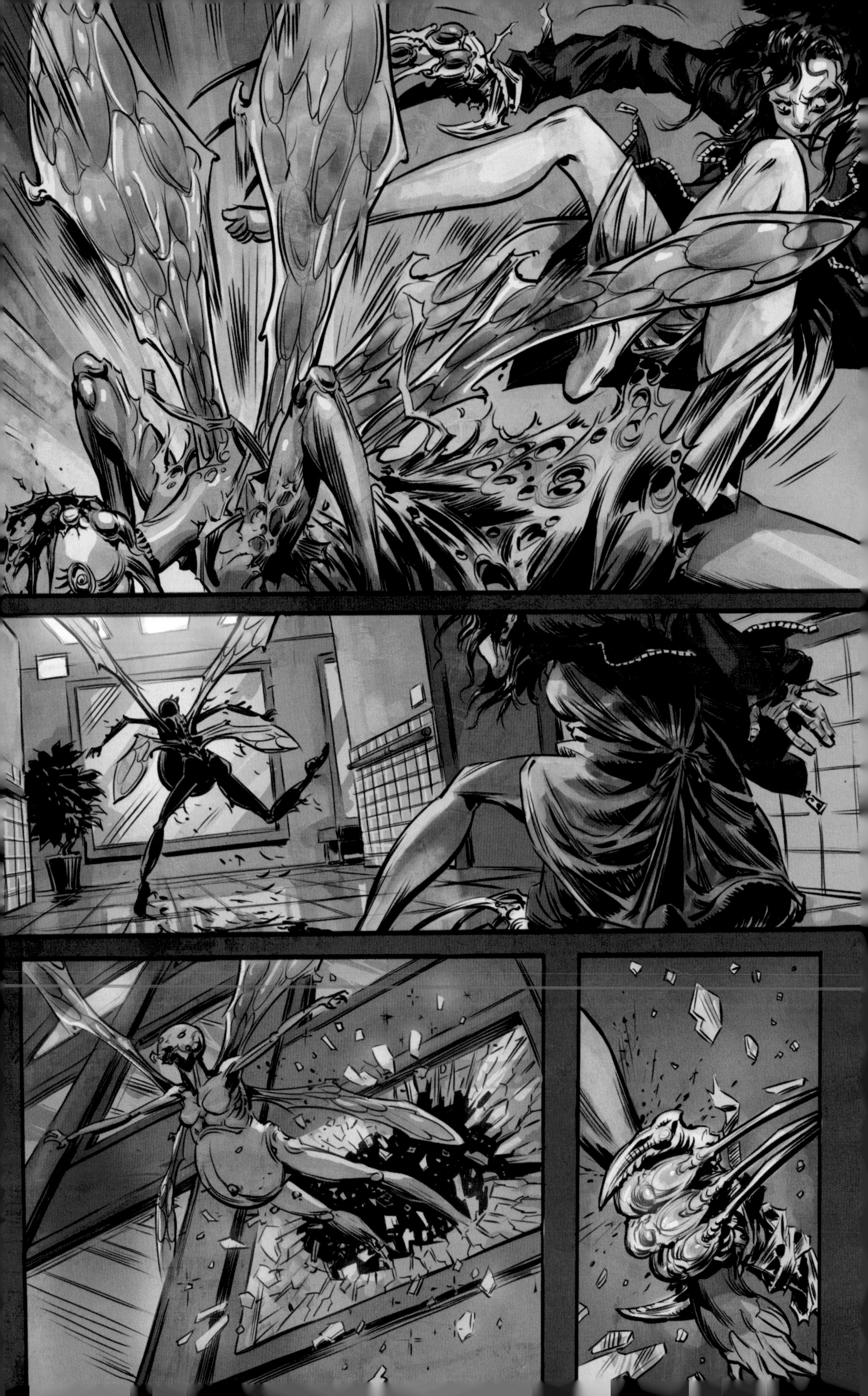

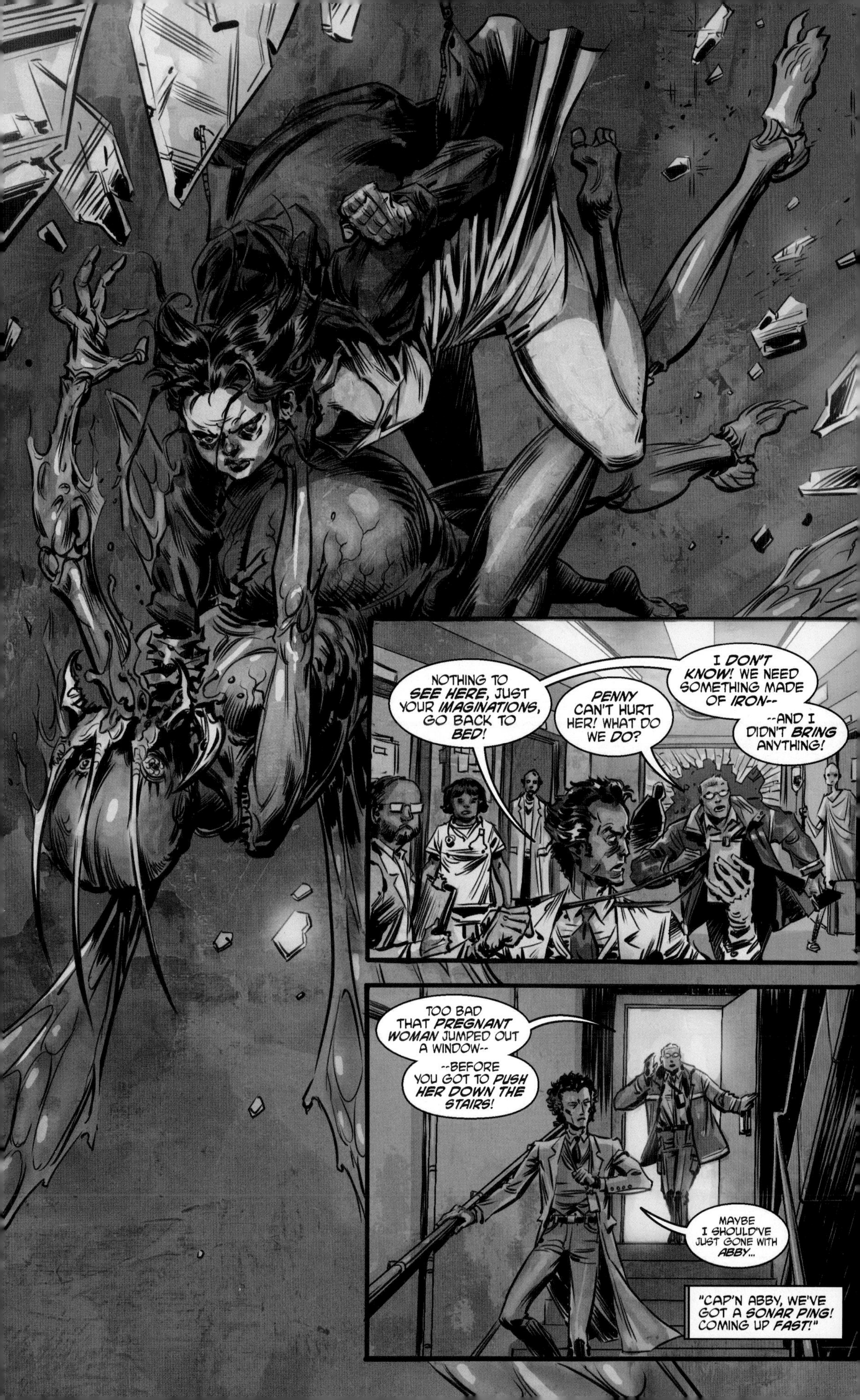
NOTHING TO SEE HERE, JUST YOUR IMAGINATIONS, GO BACK TO BED!
PENNY CAN'T HURT HER! WHAT DO WE DO?
I DON'T KNOW! WE NEED SOMETHING MADE OF IRON--
--AND I DIDN'T BRING ANYTHING!
TOO BAD THAT PREGNANT WOMAN JUMPED OUT A WINDOW--
--BEFORE YOU GOT TO PUSH HER DOWN THE STAIRS!
MAYBE I SHOULD'VE JUST GONE WITH ABBY...
"CAP'N ABBY, WE'VE GOT A SONAR PING! COMING UP FAST!"

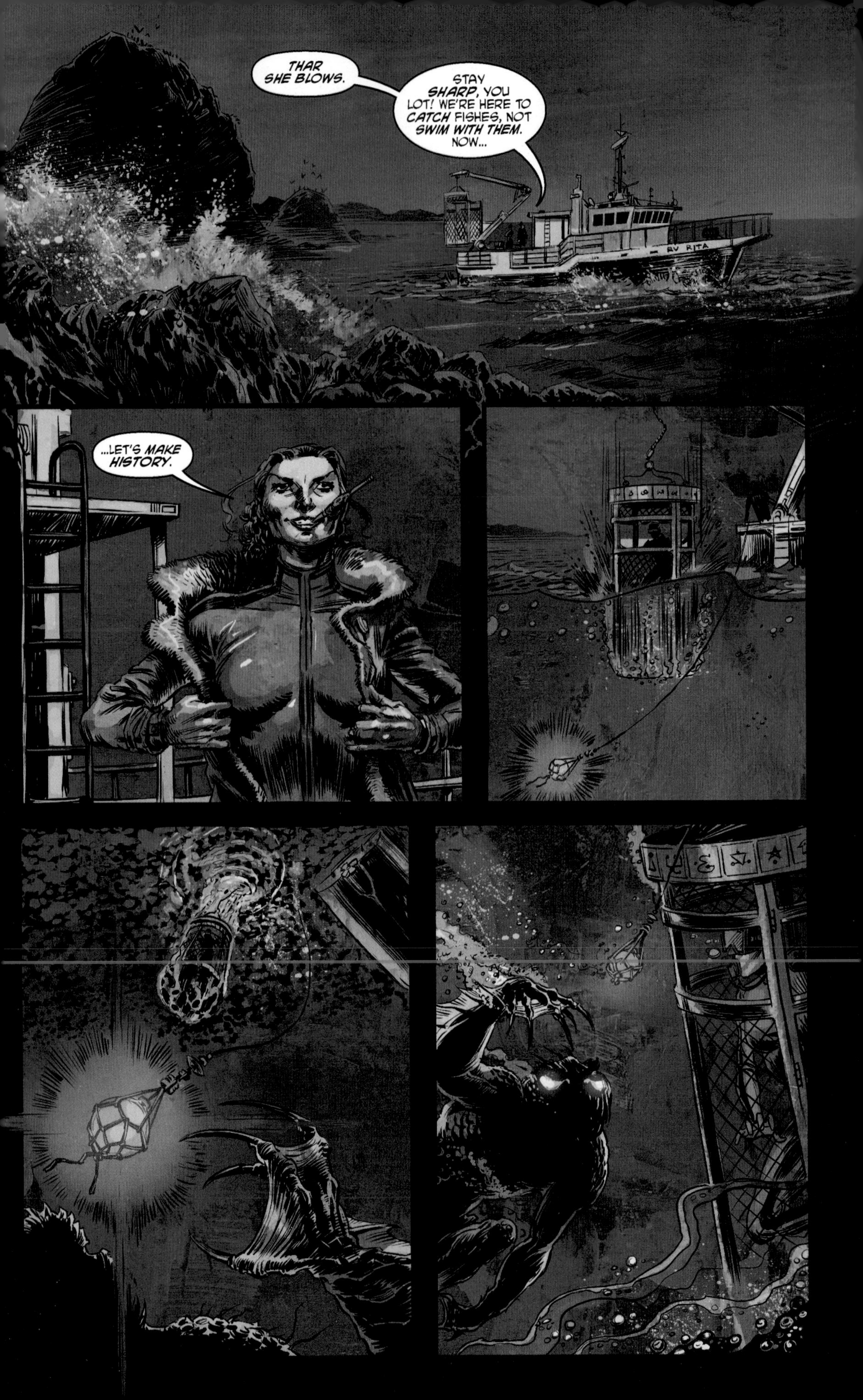
THAR SHE BLOWS.
STAY SHARP, YOU LOT! WE'RE HERE TO CATCH FISHES, NOT SWIM WITH THEM. NOW...
RV RITA
...LET'S MAKE HISTORY.

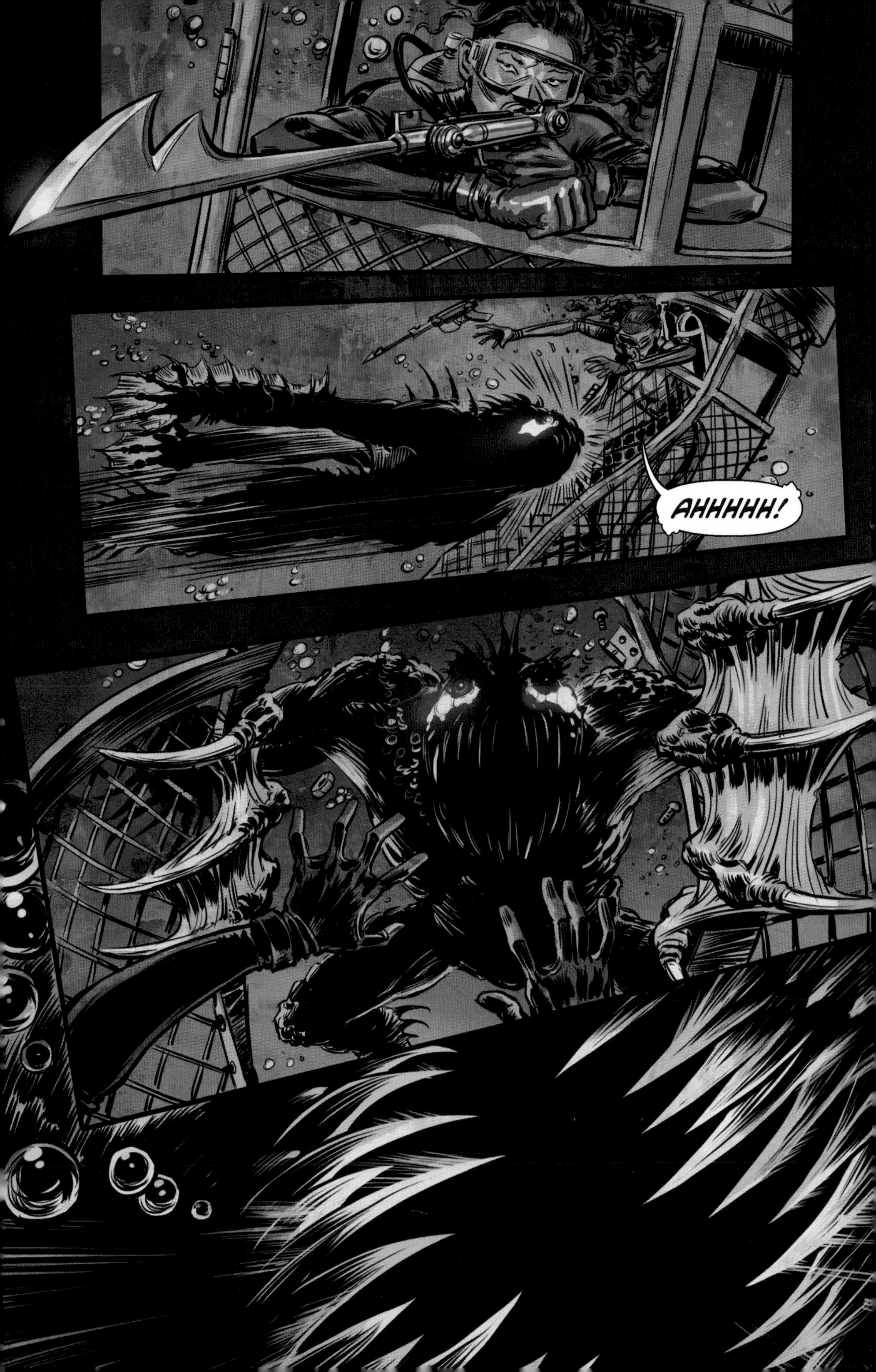
AHHHHH!

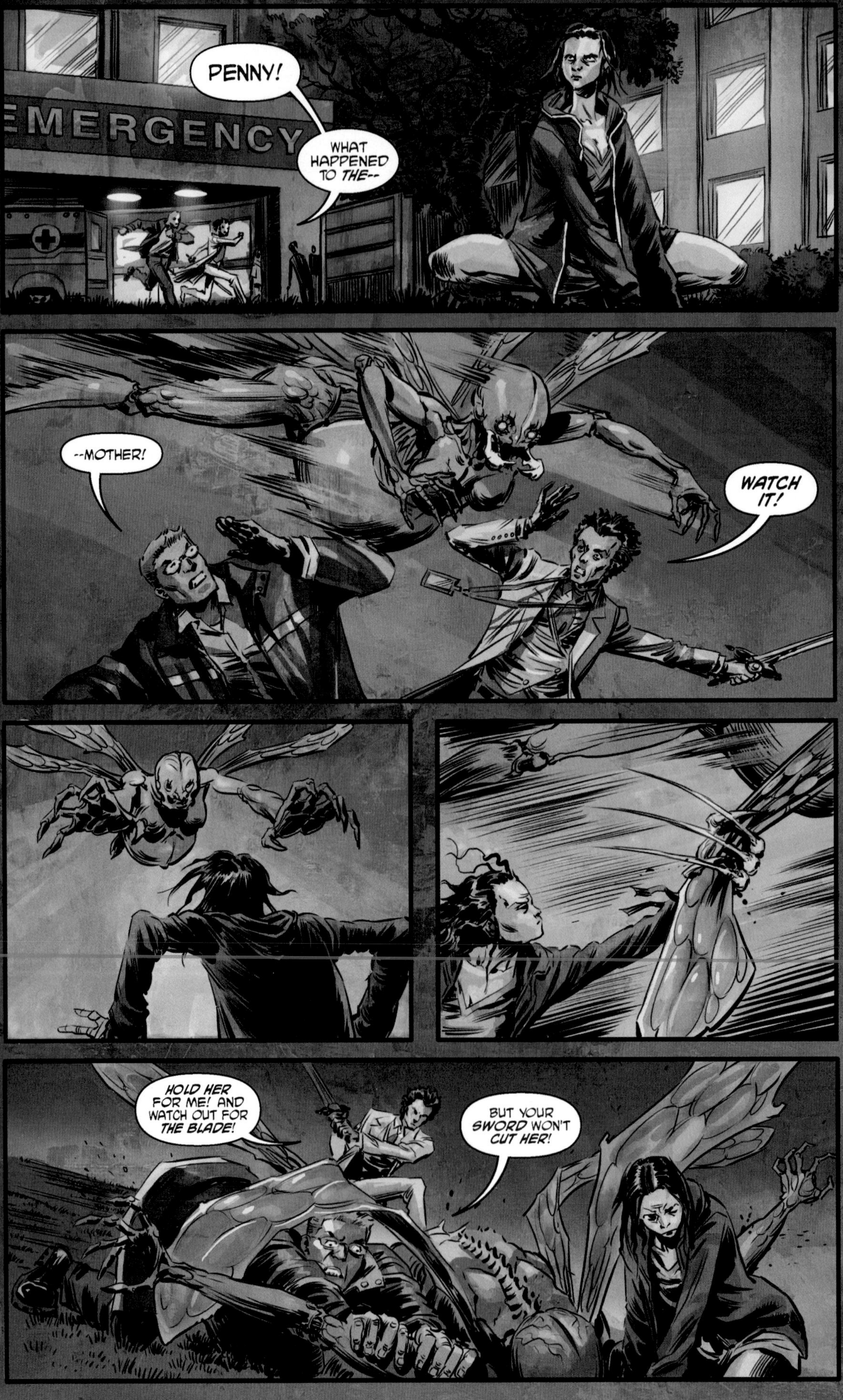

EMERGENCY
PENNY!
WHAT HAPPENED TO THE--
--MOTHER!
WATCH IT!
HOLD HER FOR ME! AND WATCH OUT FOR THE BLADE!
BUT YOUR SWORD WON'T CUT HER!

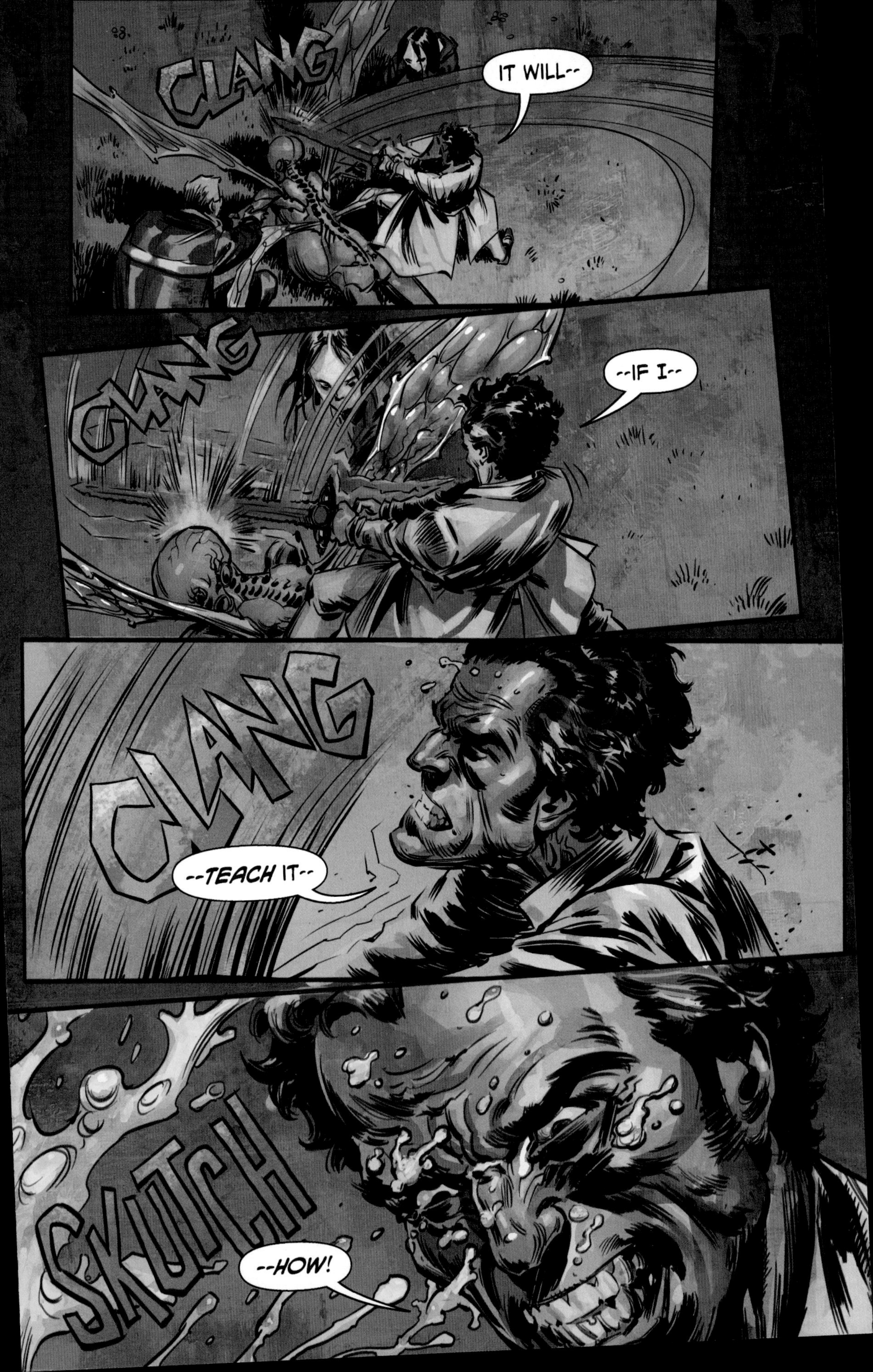
CLANG
IT WILL--
CLANG
--IF I--
CLANG
--TEACH IT--
SKLUTCH
--HOW!

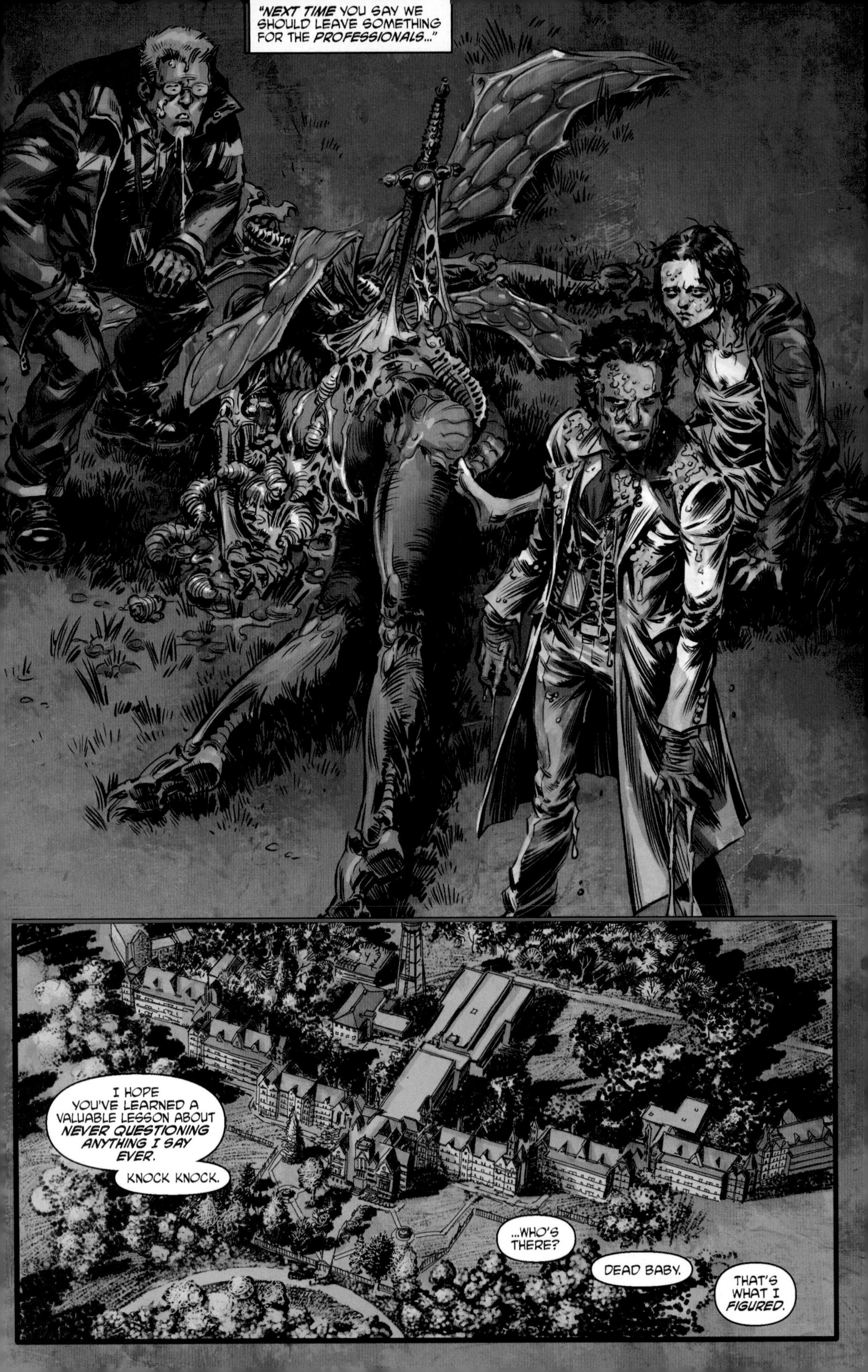
"NEXT TIME YOU SAY WE SHOULD LEAVE SOMETHING FOR THE PROFESSIONALS..."
I HOPE YOU'VE LEARNED A VALUABLE LESSON ABOUT NEVER QUESTIONING ANYTHING I SAY EVER.
KNOCK KNOCK.
...WHO'S THERE?
DEAD BABY.
THAT'S WHAT I FIGURED.

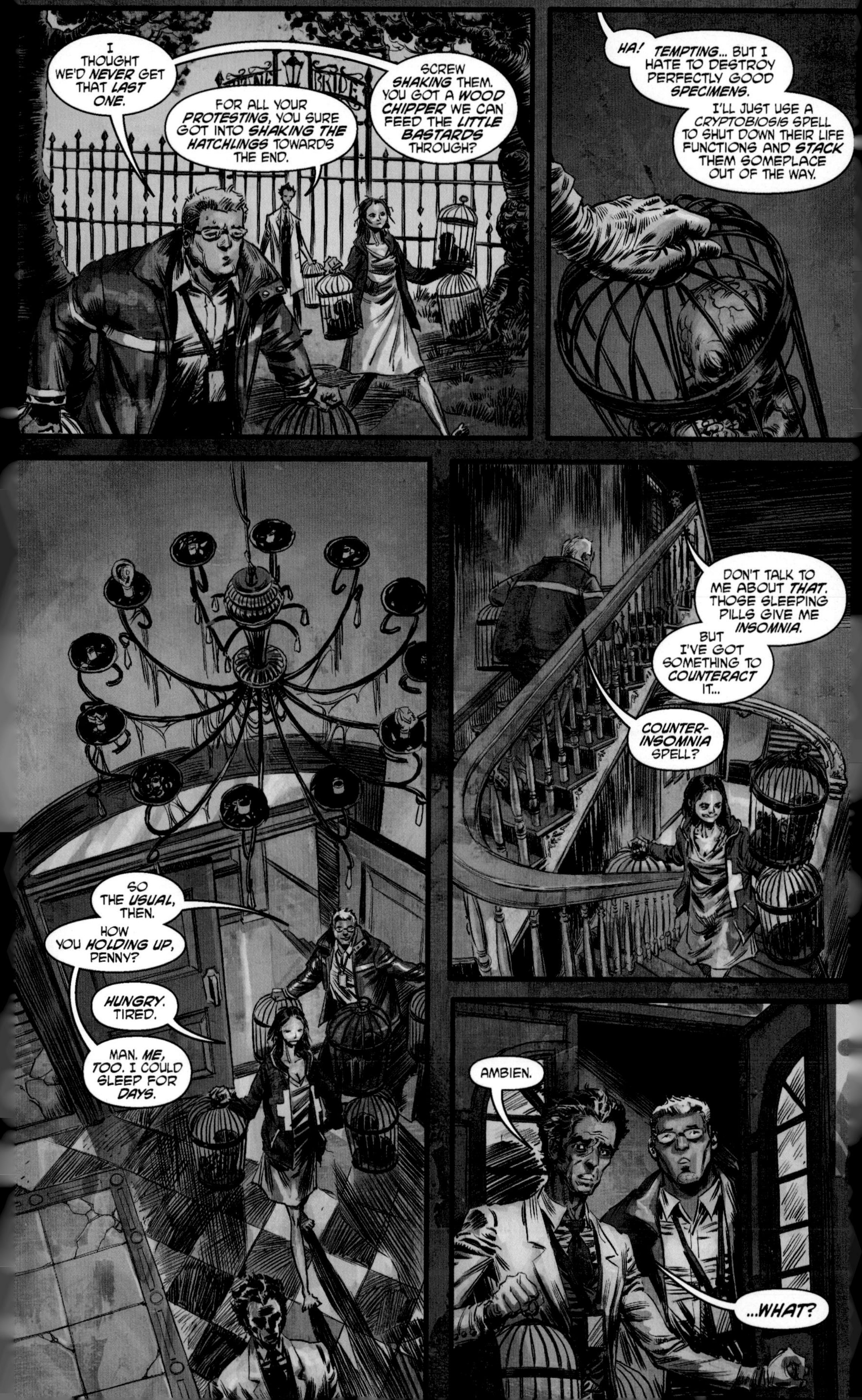
I THOUGHT WE'D NEVER GET THAT LAST ONE.
FOR ALL YOUR PROTESTING, YOU SURE GOT INTO SHAKING THE HATCHLINGS TOWARDS THE END.
SCREW SHAKING THEM. YOU GOT A WOOD CHIPPER WE CAN FEED THE LITTLE BASTARDS THROUGH?
HA! TEMPTING... BUT I HATE TO DESTROY PERFECTLY GOOD SPECIMENS.
I'LL JUST USE A CRYPTOBIOSIS SPELL TO SHUT DOWN THEIR LIFE FUNCTIONS AND STACK THEM SOMEPLACE OUT OF THE WAY.
SO THE USUAL, THEN.
HOW YOU HOLDING UP, PENNY?
HUNGRY. TIRED.
MAN. ME, TOO. I COULD SLEEP FOR DAYS.
DON'T TALK TO ME ABOUT THAT. THOSE SLEEPING PILLS GIVE ME INSOMNIA.
BUT I'VE GOT SOMETHING TO COUNTERACT IT...
COUNTER-INSOMNIA SPELL?
AMBIEN.
...WHAT?

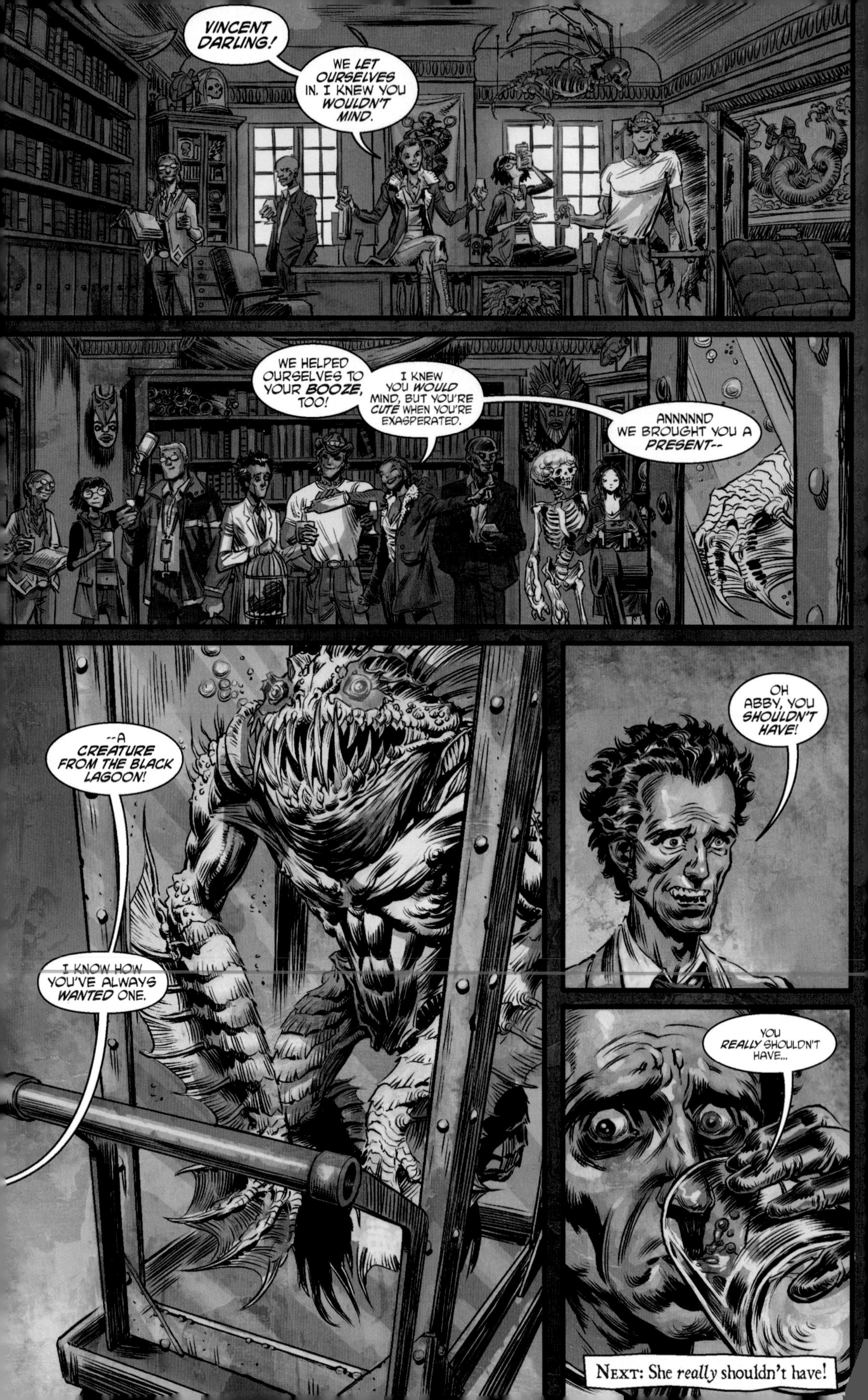
VINCENT DARLING!
WE LET OURSELVES IN. I KNEW YOU WOULDN'T MIND.
WE HELPED OURSELVES TO YOUR BOOZE, TOO!
I KNEW YOU WOULD MIND, BUT YOU'RE CUTE WHEN YOU'RE EXASPERATED.
ANNNNND WE BROUGHT YOU A PRESENT--
--A CREATURE FROM THE BLACK LAGOON!
I KNOW HOW YOU'VE ALWAYS WANTED ONE.
OH ABBY, YOU SHOULDN'T HAVE!
YOU REALLY SHOULDN'T HAVE...
NEXT: She really shouldn't have!

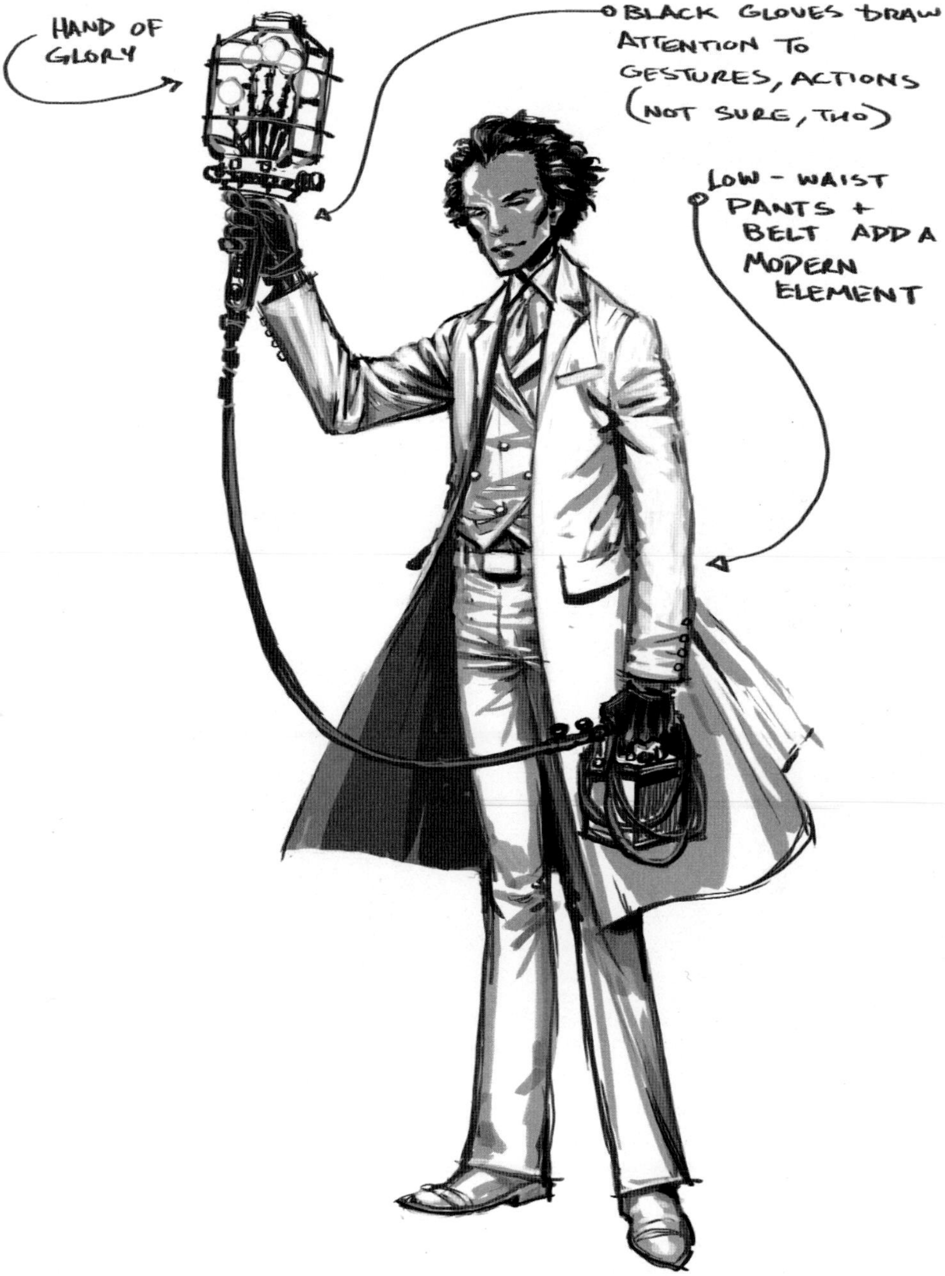
HAND OF GLORY
BLACK GLOVES DRAW ATTENTION TO GESTURES, ACTIONS (NOT SURE, THO)
LOW - WAIST PANTS + BELT ADD A MODERN ELEMENT

FIRST SKETCH OF DR. MORROW'S CURRENT LOOK.
c. LATE 2008

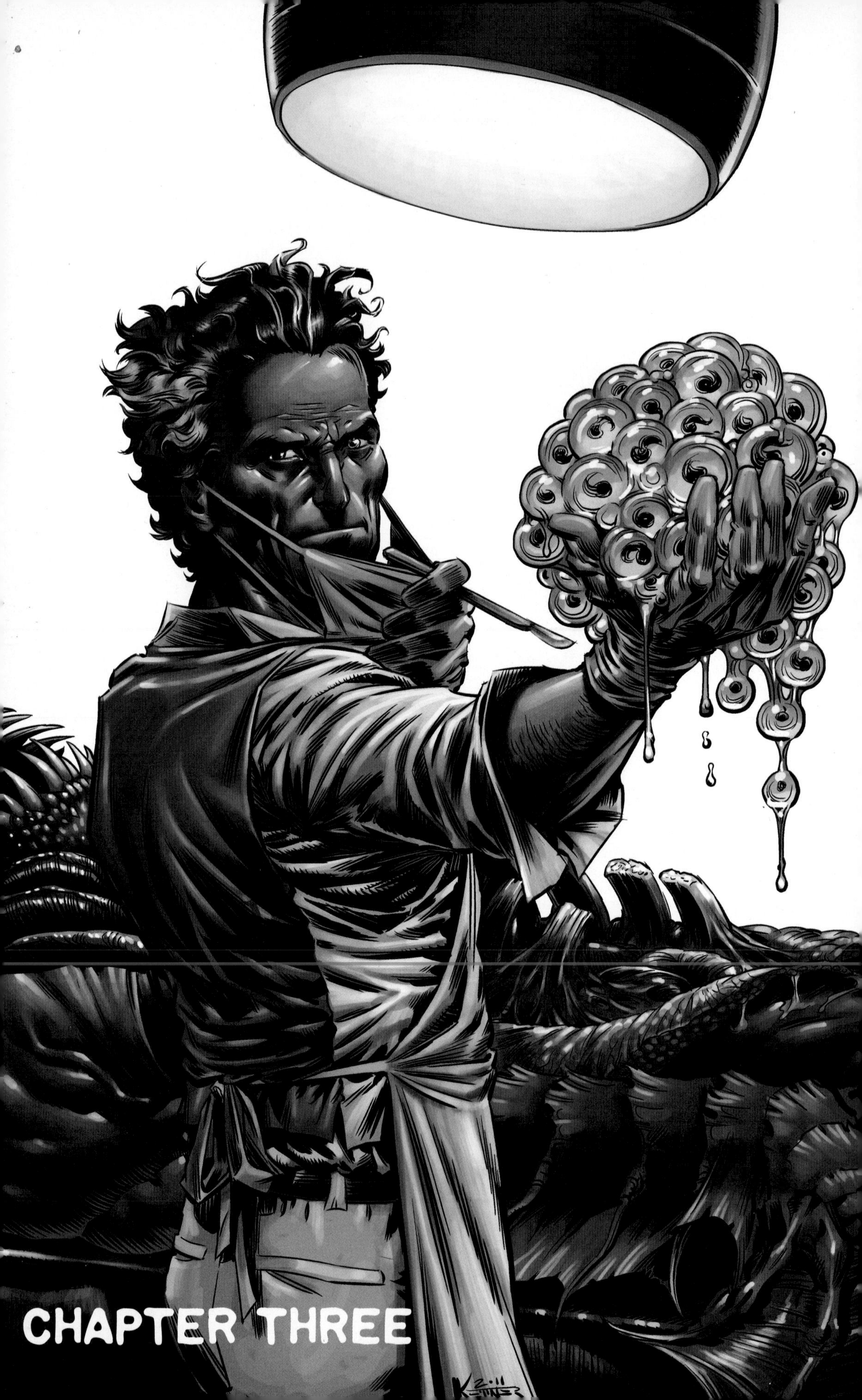
CHAPTER THREE

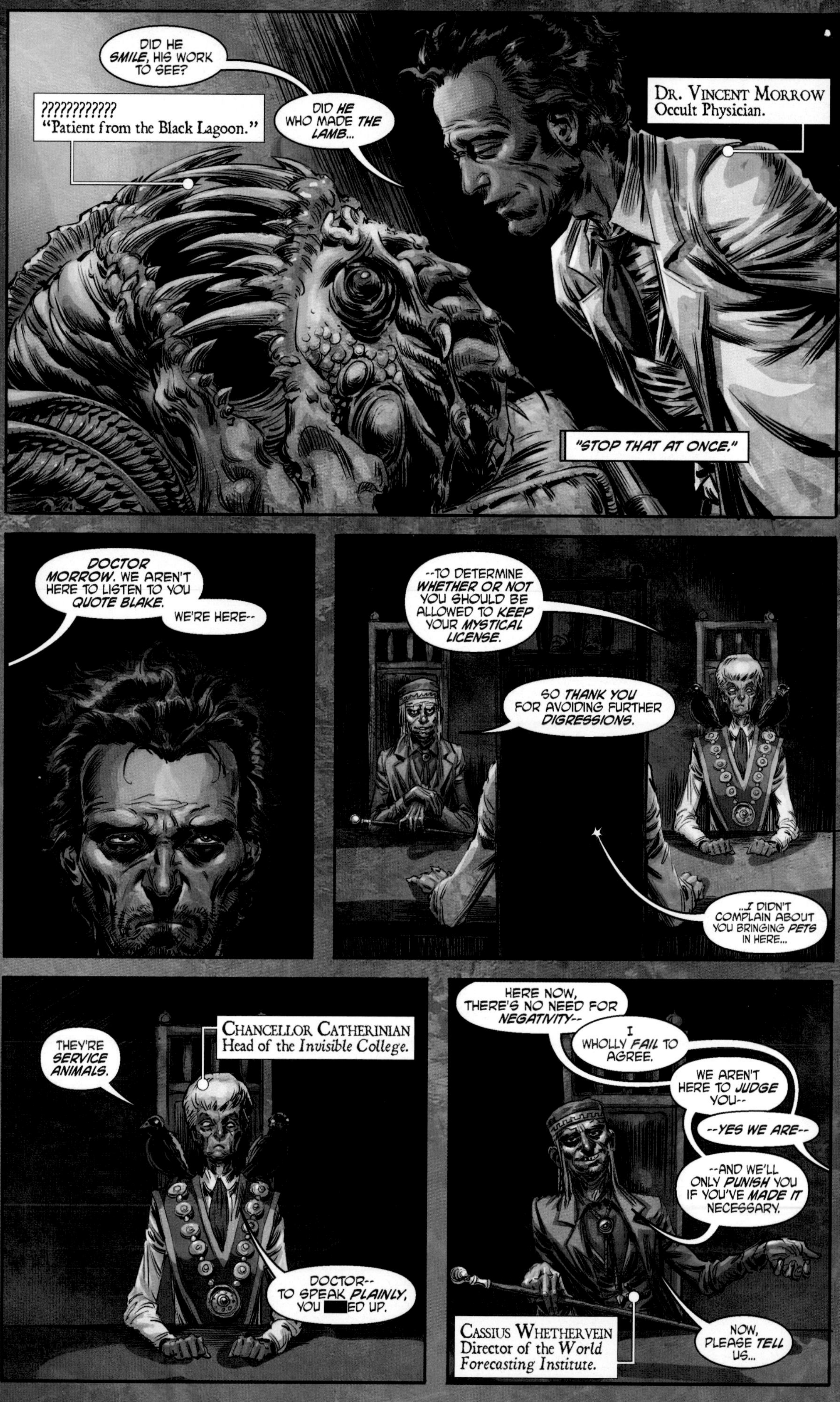
DID HE SMILE, HIS WORK TO SEE?
????????????
"Patient from the Black Lagoon."
DID HE WHO MADE THE LAMB...
DR. VINCENT MORROW
Occult Physician.
"STOP THAT AT ONCE."
DOCTOR MORROW. WE AREN'T HERE TO LISTEN TO YOU QUOTE BLAKE.
WE'RE HERE--
--TO DETERMINE WHETHER OR NOT YOU SHOULD BE ALLOWED TO KEEP YOUR MYSTICAL LICENSE.
SO THANK YOU FOR AVOIDING FURTHER DIGRESSIONS.
...I DIDN'T COMPLAIN ABOUT YOU BRINGING PETS IN HERE...
THEY'RE SERVICE ANIMALS.
CHANCELLOR CATHERINIAN
Head of the Invisible College.
DOCTOR-- TO SPEAK PLAINLY, YOU [redacted]ED UP.
HERE NOW, THERE'S NO NEED FOR NEGATIVITY--
I WHOLLY FAIL TO AGREE.
WE AREN'T HERE TO JUDGE YOU--
--YES WE ARE--
--AND WE'LL ONLY PUNISH YOU IF YOU'VE MADE IT NECESSARY.
CASSIUS WHETHERVEIN
Director of the World Forecasting Institute.
NOW, PLEASE TELL US...

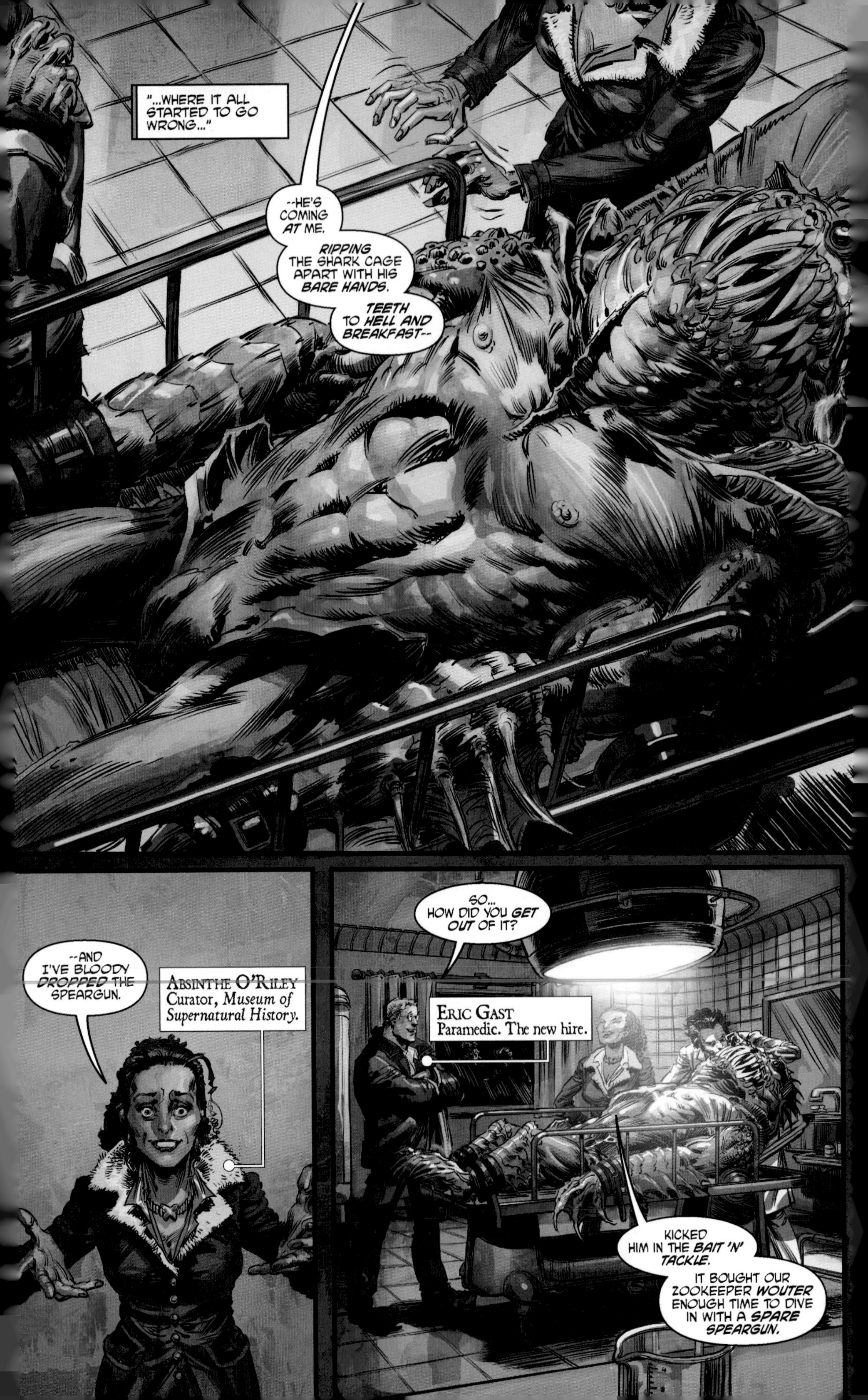
"...WHERE IT ALL STARTED TO GO WRONG..."
--HE'S COMING AT ME.
RIPPING THE SHARK CAGE APART WITH HIS BARE HANDS.
TEETH TO HELL AND BREAKFAST--
--AND I'VE BLOODY DROPPED THE SPEARGUN.
ABSINTHE O'RILEY Curator, Museum of Supernatural History.
SO... HOW DID YOU GET OUT OF IT?
ERIC GAST Paramedic. The new hire.
KICKED HIM IN THE BAIT 'N' TACKLE.
IT BOUGHT OUR ZOOKEEPER WOUTER ENOUGH TIME TO DIVE IN WITH A SPARE SPEARGUN.

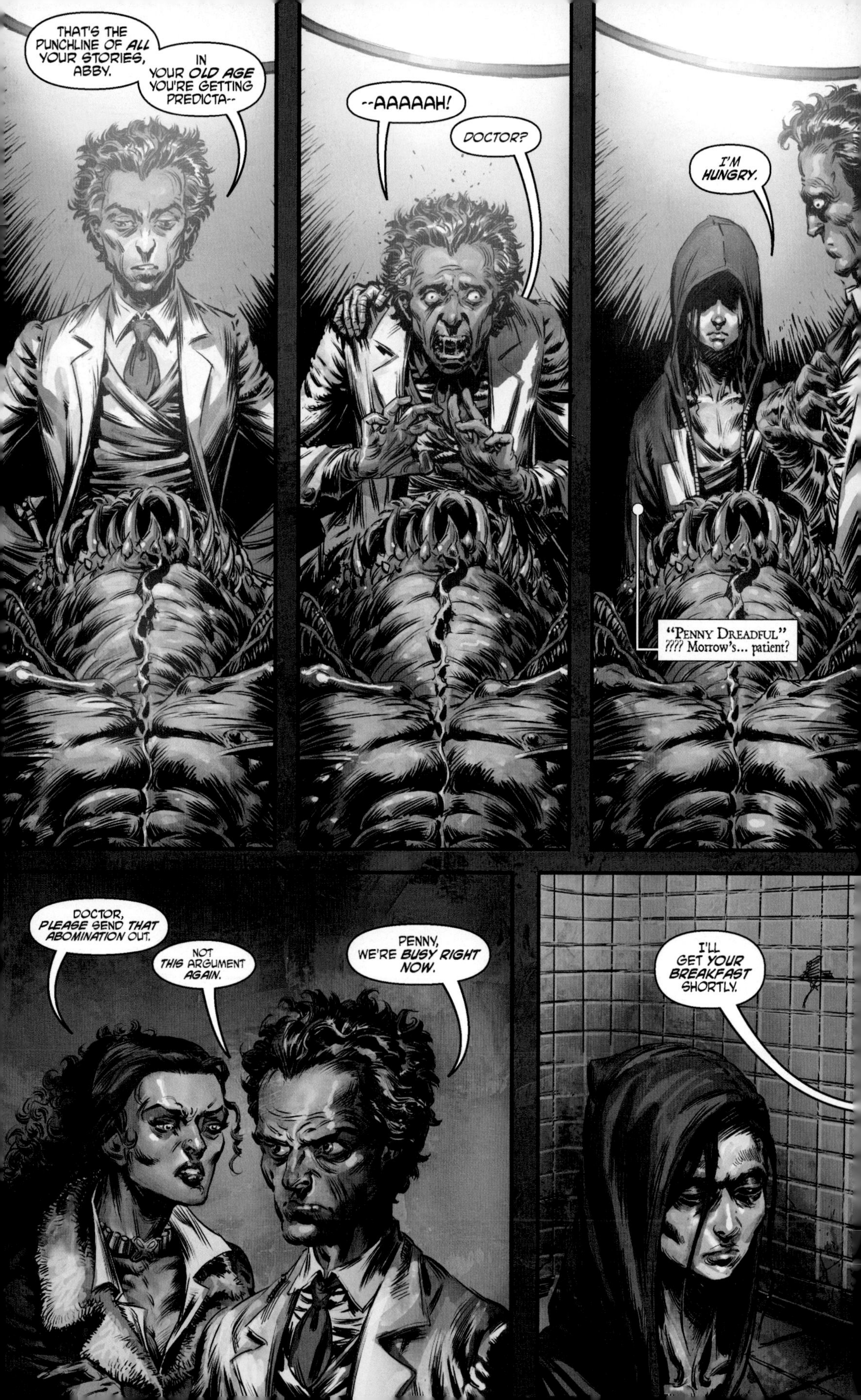
THAT'S THE PUNCHLINE OF ALL YOUR STORIES, ABBY.
IN YOUR OLD AGE YOU'RE GETTING PREDICTA--
--AAAAAH!
DOCTOR?
I'M HUNGRY.
"PENNY DREADFUL" ???? Morrow's... patient?
DOCTOR, PLEASE SEND THAT ABOMINATION OUT.
NOT THIS ARGUMENT AGAIN.
PENNY, WE'RE BUSY RIGHT NOW.
I'LL GET YOUR BREAKFAST SHORTLY.

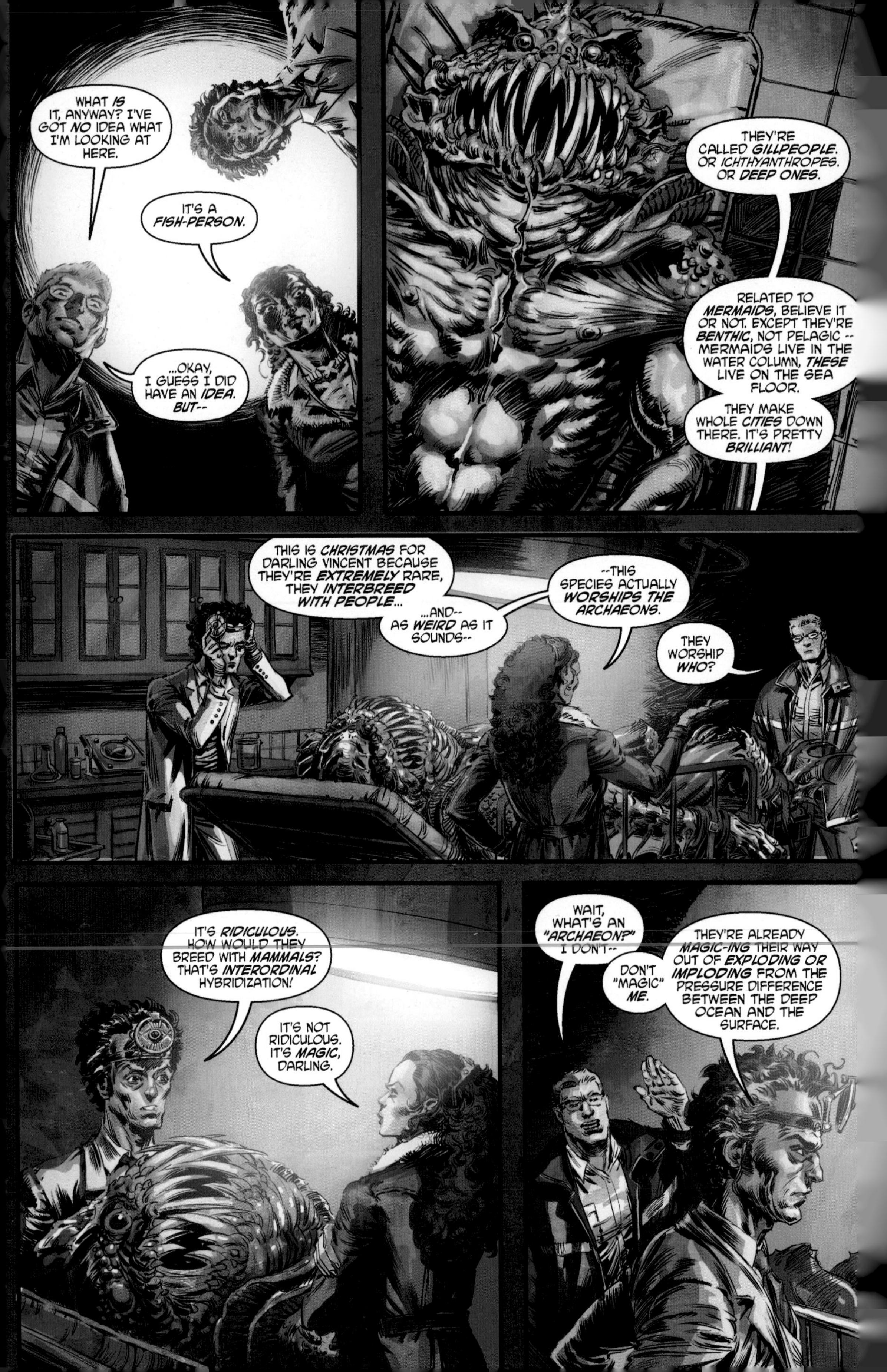
WHAT IS IT, ANYWAY? I'VE GOT NO IDEA WHAT I'M LOOKING AT HERE.
IT'S A FISH-PERSON.
...OKAY, I GUESS I DID HAVE AN IDEA. BUT--
THEY'RE CALLED GILLPEOPLE. OR ICHTHYANTHROPES. OR DEEP ONES.
RELATED TO MERMAIDS, BELIEVE IT OR NOT. EXCEPT THEY'RE BENTHIC, NOT PELAGIC -- MERMAIDS LIVE IN THE WATER COLUMN, THESE LIVE ON THE SEA FLOOR.
THEY MAKE WHOLE CITIES DOWN THERE. IT'S PRETTY BRILLIANT!
THIS IS CHRISTMAS FOR DARLING VINCENT BECAUSE THEY'RE EXTREMELY RARE, THEY INTERBREED WITH PEOPLE...
...AND-- AS WEIRD AS IT SOUNDS--
--THIS SPECIES ACTUALLY WORSHIPS THE ARCHAEONS.
THEY WORSHIP WHO?
IT'S RIDICULOUS. HOW WOULD THEY BREED WITH MAMMALS? THAT'S INTERORDINAL HYBRIDIZATION!
IT'S NOT RIDICULOUS. IT'S MAGIC, DARLING.
WAIT, WHAT'S AN "ARCHAEON?" I DON'T--
DON'T "MAGIC" ME.
THEY'RE ALREADY MAGIC-ING THEIR WAY OUT OF EXPLODING OR IMPLODING FROM THE PRESSURE DIFFERENCE BETWEEN THE DEEP OCEAN AND THE SURFACE.

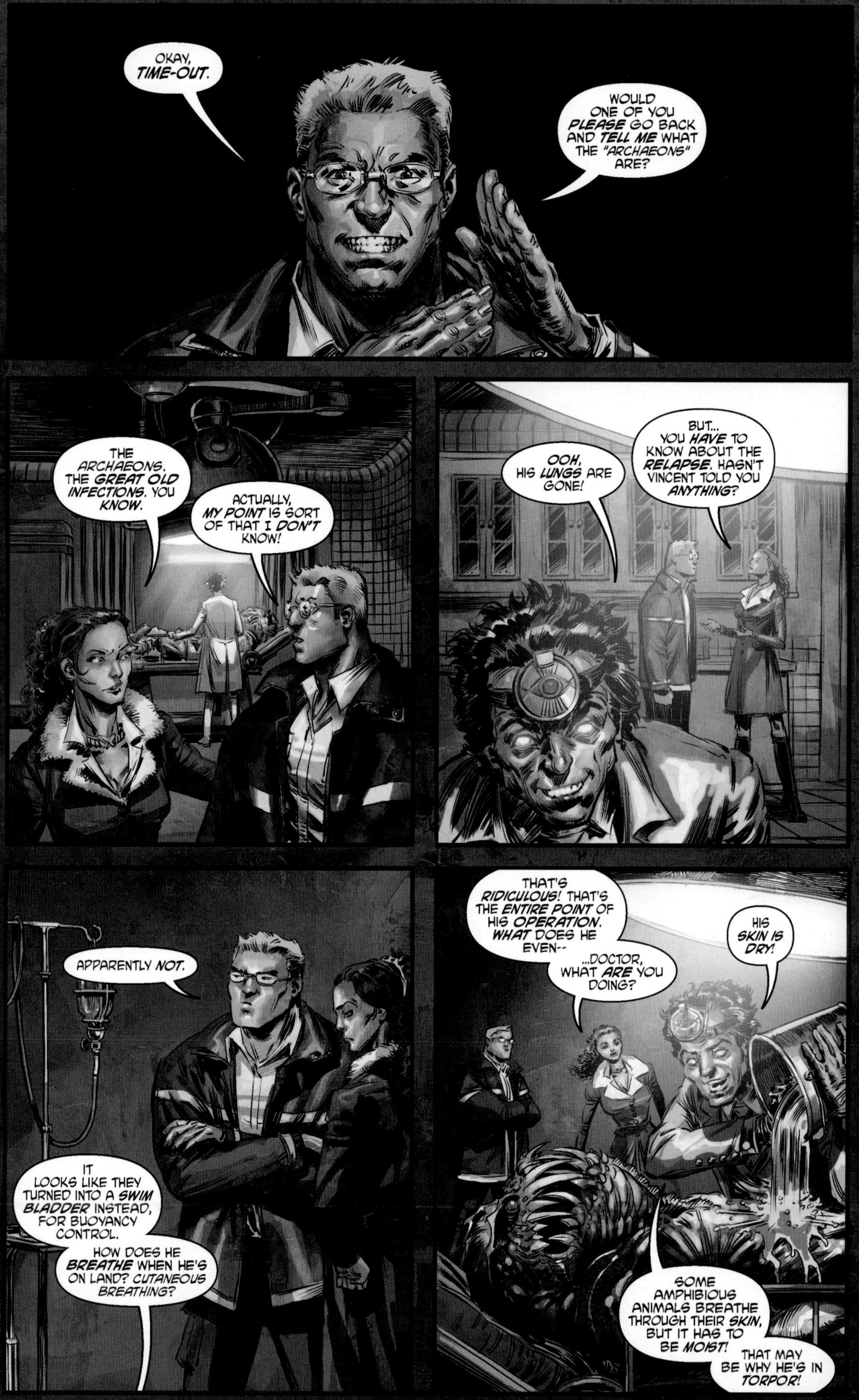
OKAY, TIME-OUT.
WOULD ONE OF YOU PLEASE GO BACK AND TELL ME WHAT THE "ARCHAEONS" ARE?
THE ARCHAEONS. THE GREAT OLD INFECTIONS. YOU KNOW.
ACTUALLY, MY POINT IS SORT OF THAT I DON'T KNOW!
OOH, HIS LUNGS ARE GONE!
BUT... YOU HAVE TO KNOW ABOUT THE RELAPSE. HASN'T VINCENT TOLD YOU ANYTHING?
APPARENTLY NOT.
IT LOOKS LIKE THEY TURNED INTO A SWIM BLADDER INSTEAD, FOR BUOYANCY CONTROL.
HOW DOES HE BREATHE WHEN HE'S ON LAND? CUTANEOUS BREATHING?
THAT'S RIDICULOUS! THAT'S THE ENTIRE POINT OF HIS OPERATION. WHAT DOES HE EVEN--
...DOCTOR, WHAT ARE YOU DOING?
HIS SKIN IS DRY!
SOME AMPHIBIOUS ANIMALS BREATHE THROUGH THEIR SKIN, BUT IT HAS TO BE MOIST!
THAT MAY BE WHY HE'S IN TORPOR!

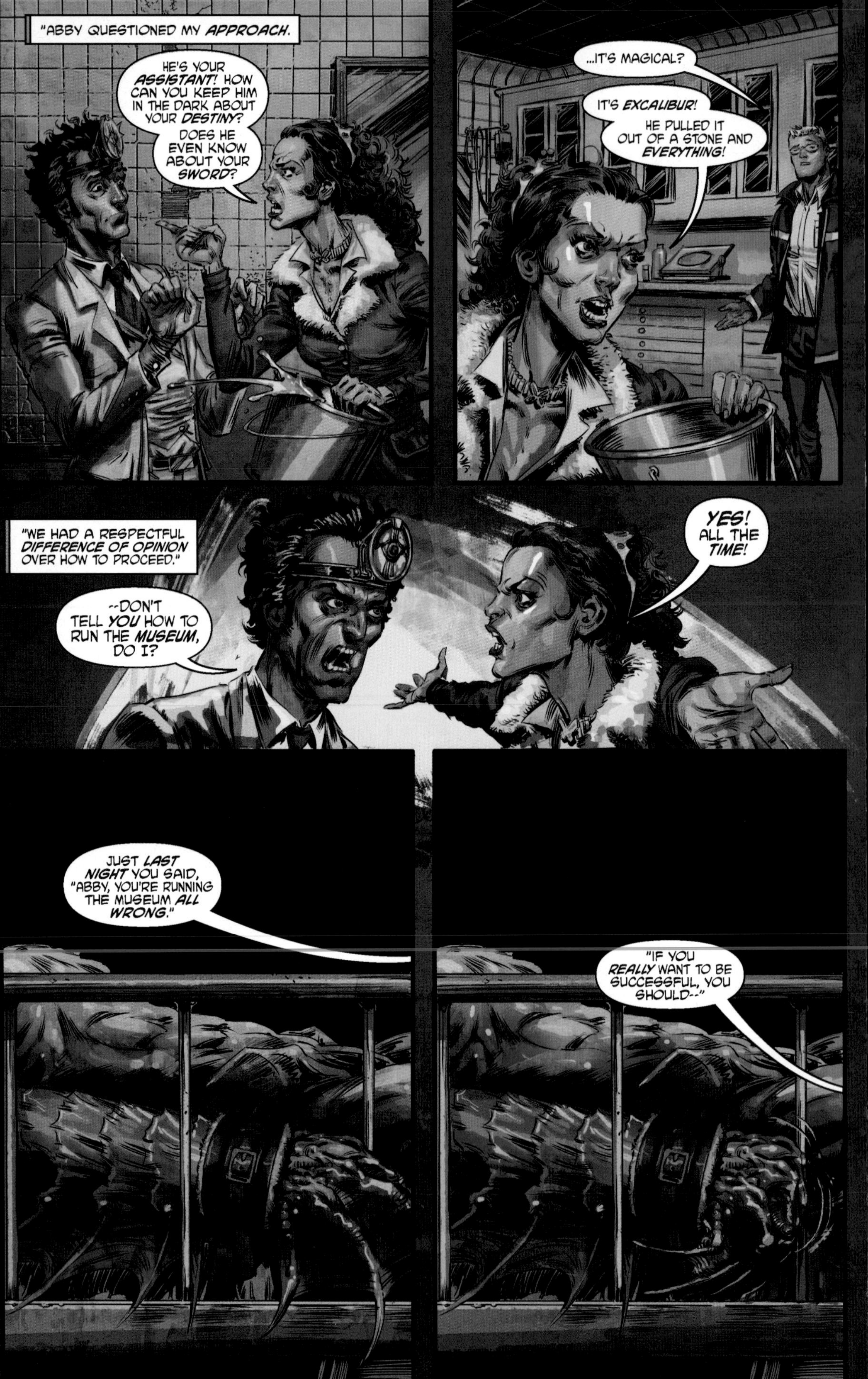
"ABBY QUESTIONED MY APPROACH.
HE'S YOUR ASSISTANT! HOW CAN YOU KEEP HIM IN THE DARK ABOUT YOUR DESTINY?
DOES HE EVEN KNOW ABOUT YOUR SWORD?
...IT'S MAGICAL?
IT'S EXCALIBUR!
HE PULLED IT OUT OF A STONE AND EVERYTHING!
"WE HAD A RESPECTFUL DIFFERENCE OF OPINION OVER HOW TO PROCEED."
--DON'T TELL YOU HOW TO RUN THE MUSEUM, DO I?
YES! ALL THE TIME!
JUST LAST NIGHT YOU SAID, "ABBY, YOU'RE RUNNING THE MUSEUM ALL WRONG."
"IF YOU REALLY WANT TO BE SUCCESSFUL, YOU SHOULD--"

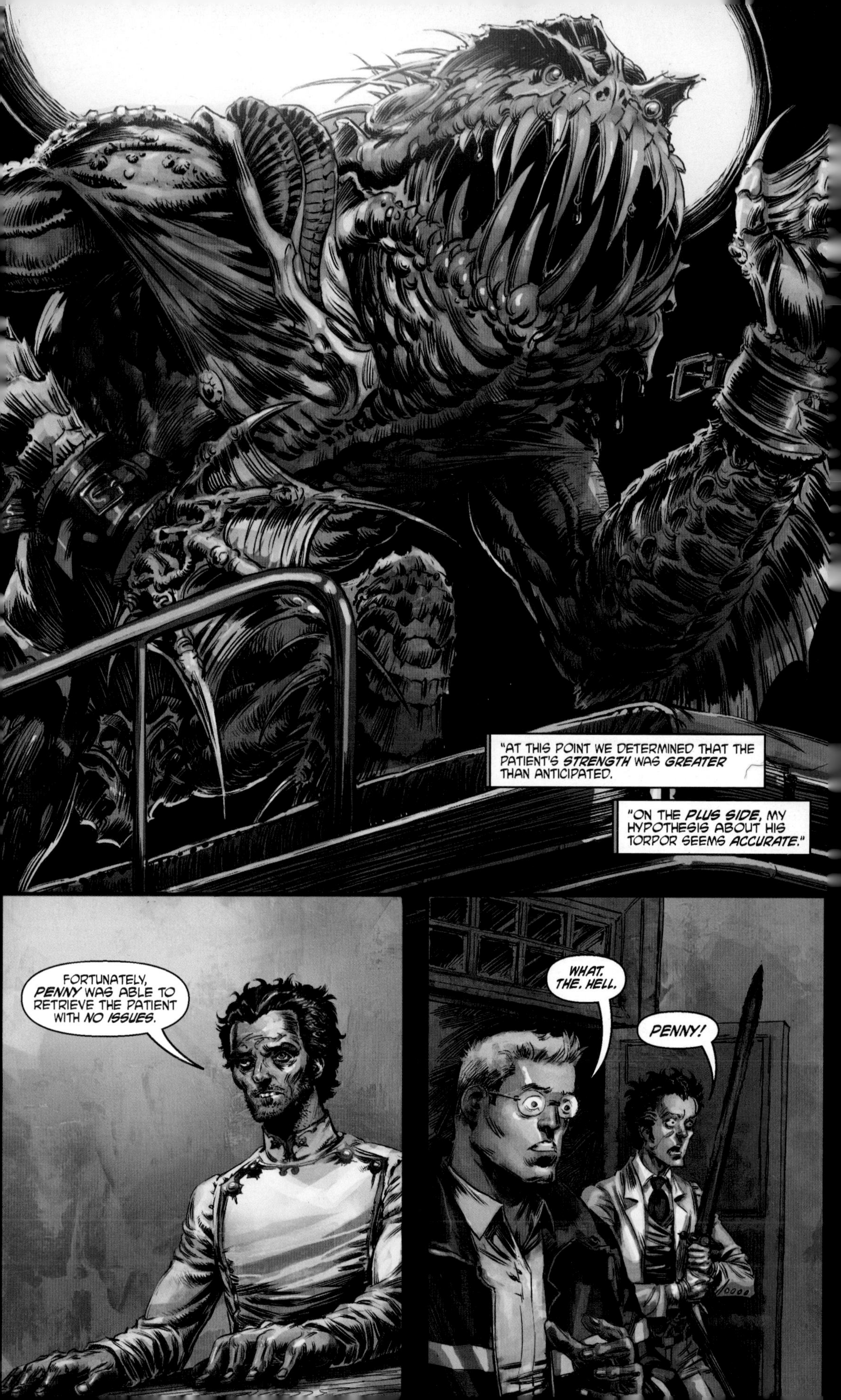
"AT THIS POINT WE DETERMINED THAT THE PATIENT'S STRENGTH WAS GREATER THAN ANTICIPATED.
"ON THE PLUS SIDE, MY HYPOTHESIS ABOUT HIS TORPOR SEEMS ACCURATE."
FORTUNATELY, PENNY WAS ABLE TO RETRIEVE THE PATIENT WITH NO ISSUES.
WHAT. THE. HELL.
PENNY!

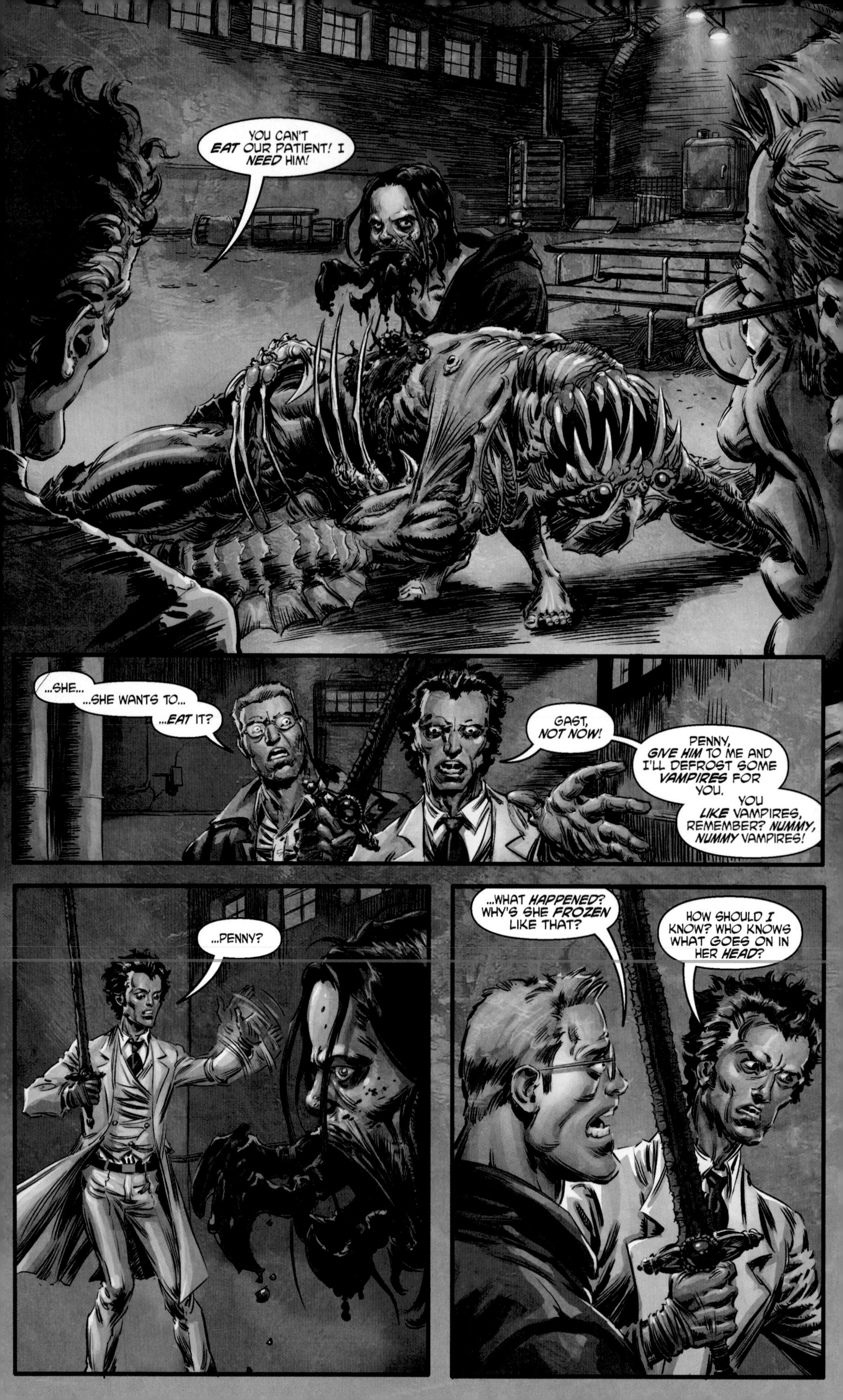
YOU CAN'T EAT OUR PATIENT! I NEED HIM!
...SHE... ...SHE WANTS TO... ...EAT IT?
GAST, NOT NOW!
PENNY, GIVE HIM TO ME AND I'LL DEFROST SOME VAMPIRES FOR YOU.
YOU LIKE VAMPIRES, REMEMBER? NUMMY, NUMMY VAMPIRES!
...PENNY?
...WHAT HAPPENED? WHY'S SHE FROZEN LIKE THAT?
HOW SHOULD I KNOW? WHO KNOWS WHAT GOES ON IN HER HEAD?

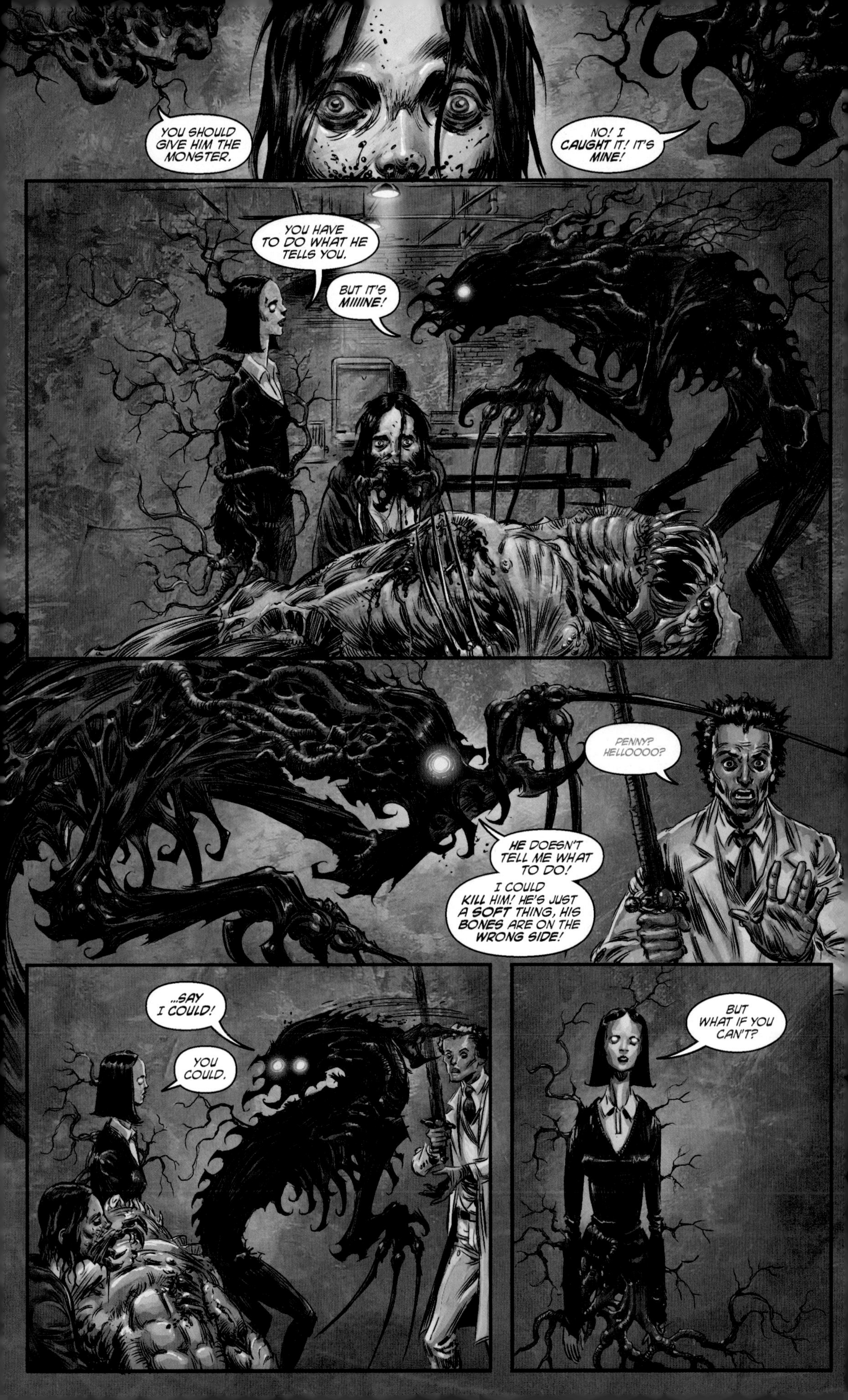
YOU SHOULD GIVE HIM THE MONSTER.
NO! I CAUGHT IT! IT'S MINE!
YOU HAVE TO DO WHAT HE TELLS YOU.
BUT IT'S MIIIINE!
PENNY? HELLOOOO?
HE DOESN'T TELL ME WHAT TO DO!
I COULD KILL HIM! HE'S JUST A SOFT THING, HIS BONES ARE ON THE WRONG SIDE!
...SAY I COULD!
YOU COULD.
BUT WHAT IF YOU CAN'T?

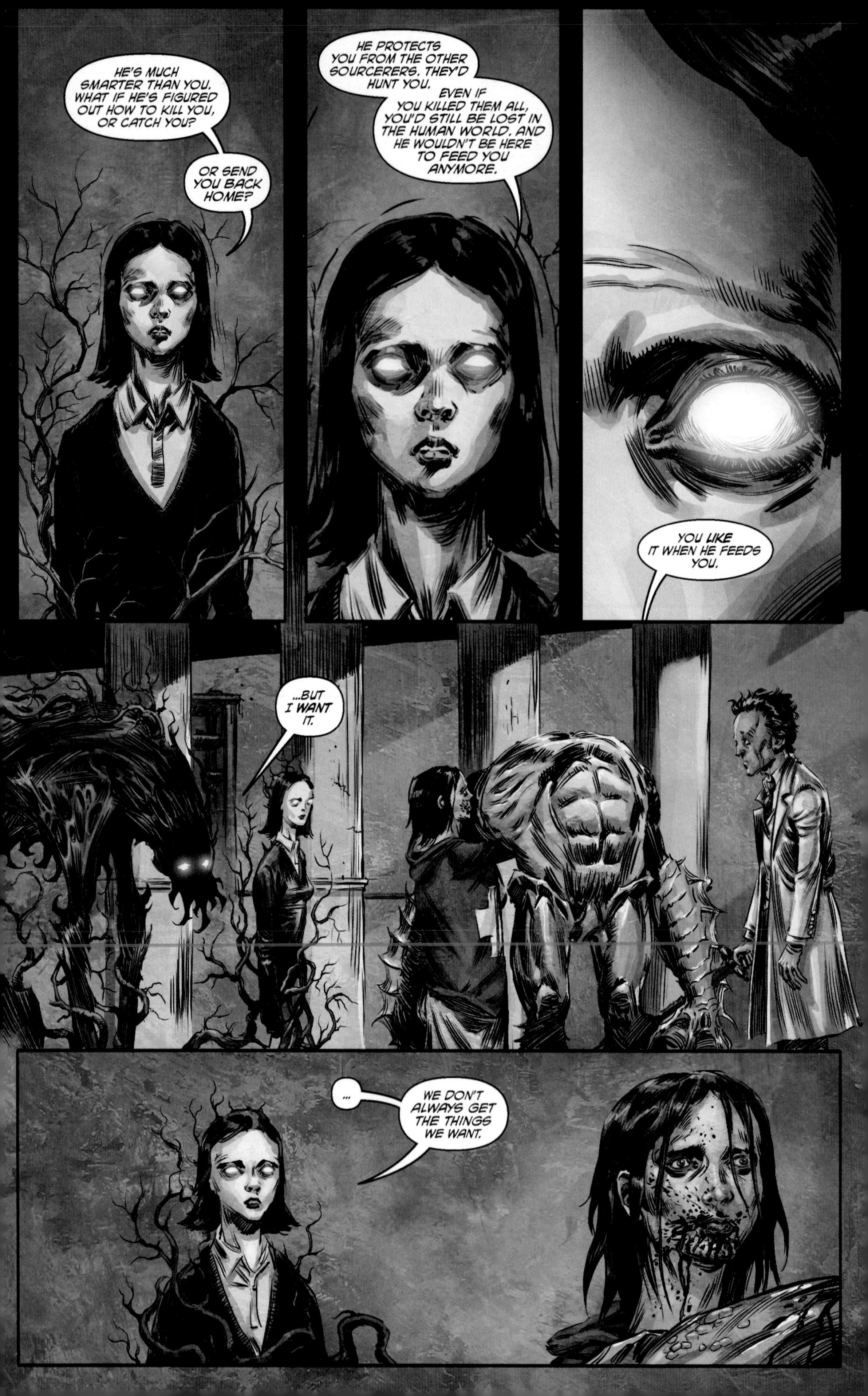
HE'S MUCH SMARTER THAN YOU. WHAT IF HE'S FIGURED OUT HOW TO KILL YOU, OR CATCH YOU?
OR SEND YOU BACK HOME?
HE PROTECTS YOU FROM THE OTHER SOURCERERS. THEY'D HUNT YOU.
EVEN IF YOU KILLED THEM ALL, YOU'D STILL BE LOST IN THE HUMAN WORLD. AND HE WOULDN'T BE HERE TO FEED YOU ANYMORE.
YOU LIKE IT WHEN HE FEEDS YOU.
...BUT I WANT IT.
...
WE DON'T ALWAYS GET THE THINGS WE WANT.

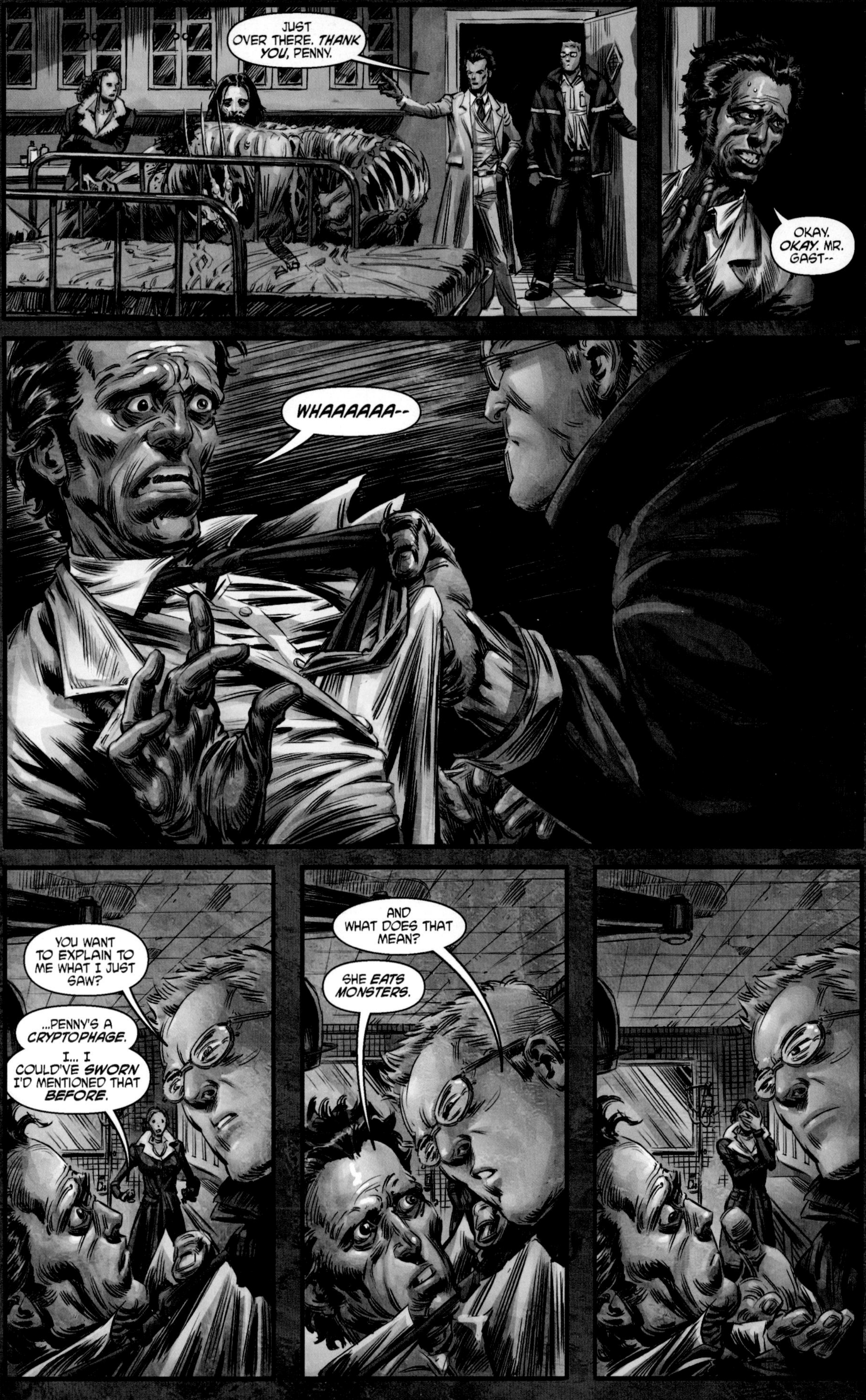
JUST OVER THERE. THANK YOU, PENNY.
OKAY. OKAY. MR. GAST--
WHAAAAAA--
YOU WANT TO EXPLAIN TO ME WHAT I JUST SAW?
...PENNY'S A CRYPTOPHAGE.
I... I COULD'VE SWORN I'D MENTIONED THAT BEFORE.
AND WHAT DOES THAT MEAN?
SHE EATS MONSTERS.

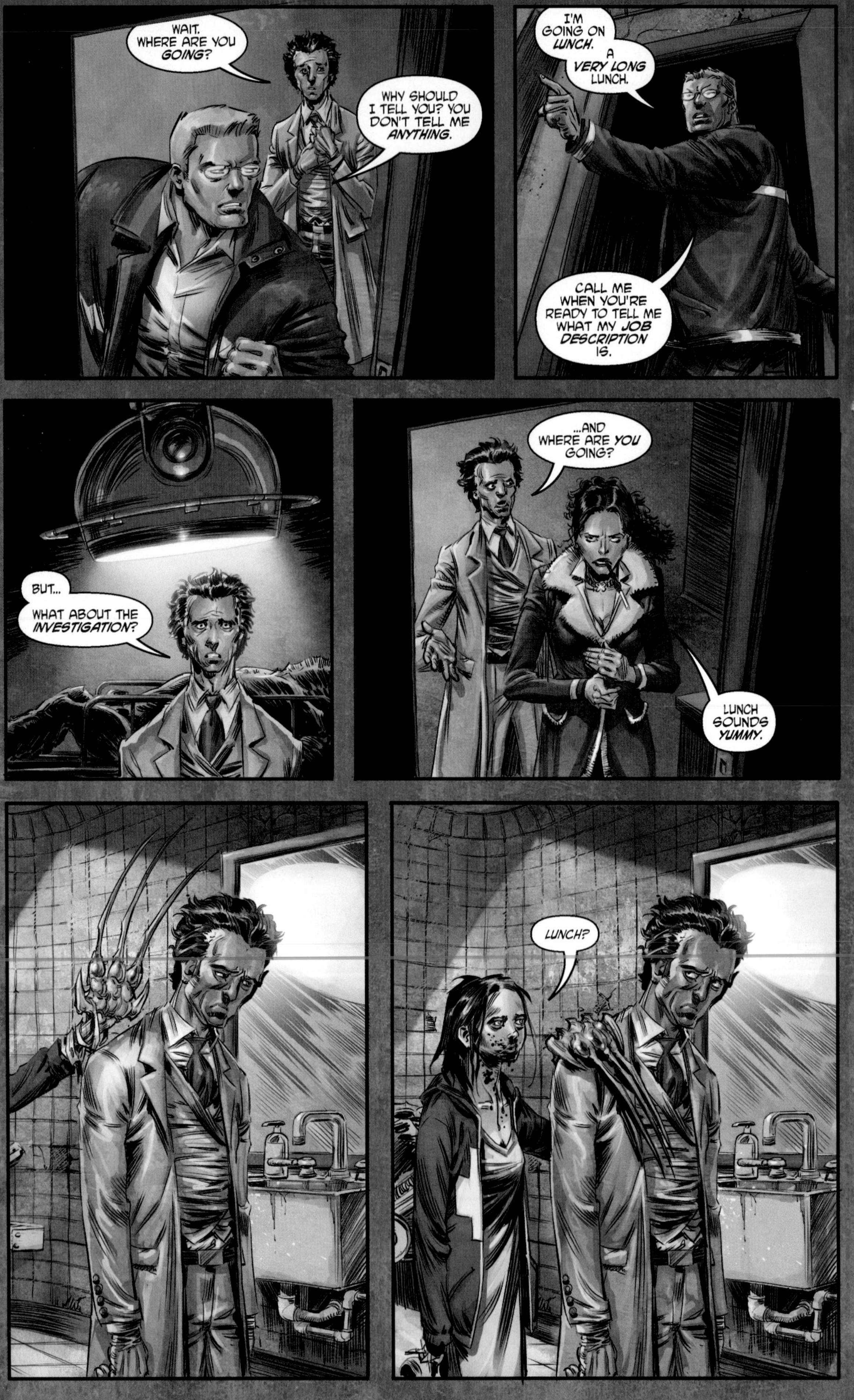
WAIT. WHERE ARE YOU GOING?
WHY SHOULD I TELL YOU? YOU DON'T TELL ME ANYTHING.
I'M GOING ON LUNCH. A VERY LONG LUNCH.
CALL ME WHEN YOU'RE READY TO TELL ME WHAT MY JOB DESCRIPTION IS.
BUT...
WHAT ABOUT THE INVESTIGATION?
...AND WHERE ARE YOU GOING?
LUNCH SOUNDS YUMMY.
LUNCH?

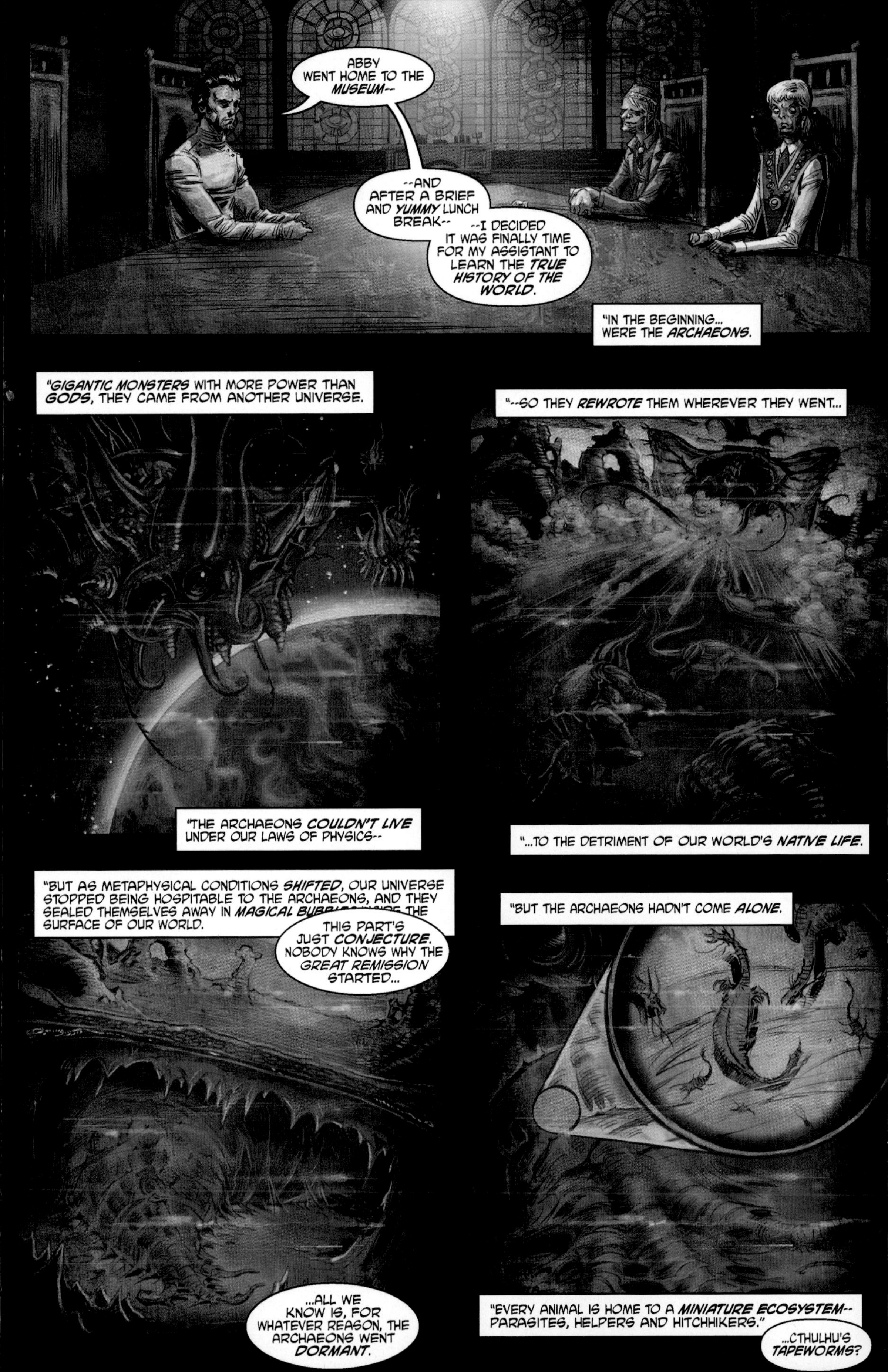

ABBY WENT HOME TO THE MUSEUM--
--AND AFTER A BRIEF AND YUMMY LUNCH BREAK--
--I DECIDED IT WAS FINALLY TIME FOR MY ASSISTANT TO LEARN THE TRUE HISTORY OF THE WORLD.
"IN THE BEGINNING... WERE THE ARCHAEONS.
"GIGANTIC MONSTERS WITH MORE POWER THAN GODS, THEY CAME FROM ANOTHER UNIVERSE.
"THE ARCHAEONS COULDN'T LIVE UNDER OUR LAWS OF PHYSICS--
"--SO THEY REWROTE THEM WHEREVER THEY WENT...
"...TO THE DETRIMENT OF OUR WORLD'S NATIVE LIFE.
"BUT AS METAPHYSICAL CONDITIONS SHIFTED, OUR UNIVERSE STOPPED BEING HOSPITABLE TO THE ARCHAEONS, AND THEY SEALED THEMSELVES AWAY IN MAGICAL BUBB THE SURFACE OF OUR WORLD.
THIS PART'S JUST CONJECTURE. NOBODY KNOWS WHY THE GREAT REMISSION STARTED...
...ALL WE KNOW IS, FOR WHATEVER REASON, THE ARCHAEONS WENT DORMANT.
"BUT THE ARCHAEONS HADN'T COME ALONE.
"EVERY ANIMAL IS HOME TO A MINIATURE ECOSYSTEM-- PARASITES, HELPERS AND HITCHHIKERS."
...CTHULHU'S TAPEWORMS?

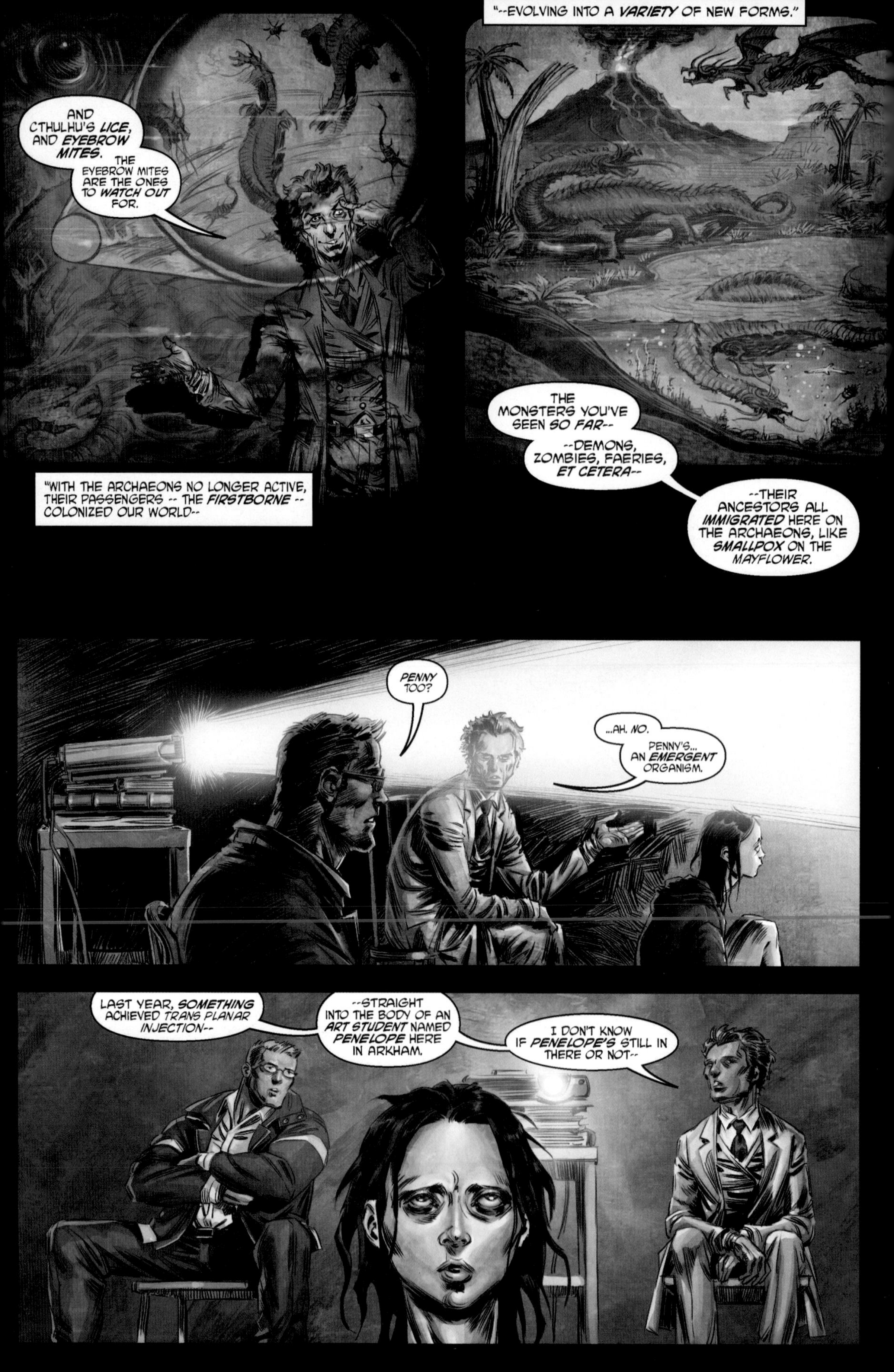
AND CTHULHU'S LICE, AND EYEBROW MITES.
THE EYEBROW MITES ARE THE ONES TO WATCH OUT FOR.
"WITH THE ARCHAEONS NO LONGER ACTIVE, THEIR PASSENGERS -- THE FIRSTBORNE -- COLONIZED OUR WORLD--
"--EVOLVING INTO A VARIETY OF NEW FORMS."
THE MONSTERS YOU'VE SEEN SO FAR--
--DEMONS, ZOMBIES, FAERIES, ET CETERA--
--THEIR ANCESTORS ALL IMMIGRATED HERE ON THE ARCHAEONS, LIKE SMALLPOX ON THE MAYFLOWER.
PENNY TOO?
...AH. NO.
PENNY'S... AN EMERGENT ORGANISM.
LAST YEAR, SOMETHING ACHIEVED TRANS PLANAR INJECTION--
--STRAIGHT INTO THE BODY OF AN ART STUDENT NAMED PENELOPE HERE IN ARKHAM.
I DON'T KNOW IF PENELOPE'S STILL IN THERE OR NOT--

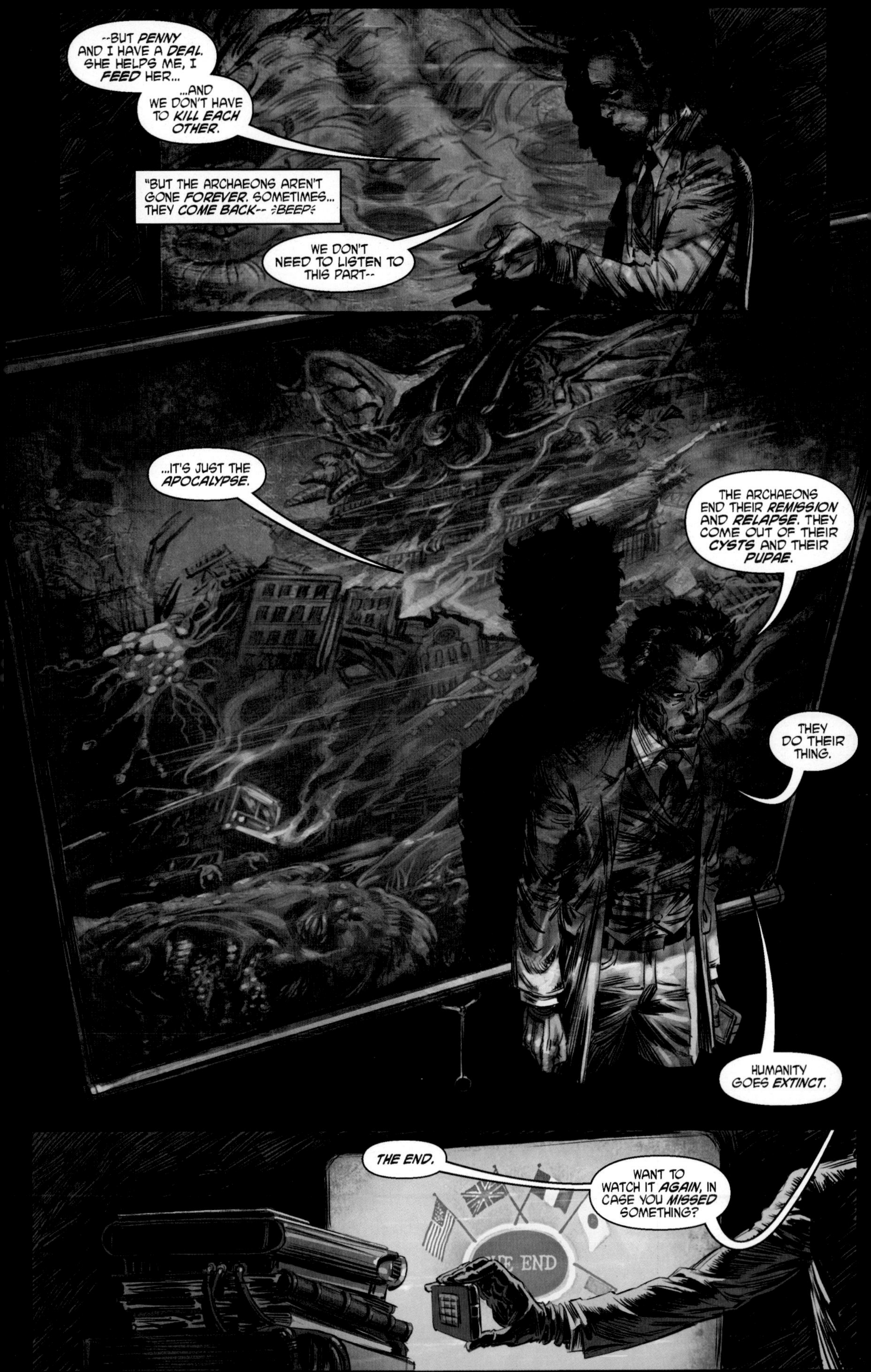
--BUT PENNY AND I HAVE A DEAL. SHE HELPS ME, I FEED HER...
...AND WE DON'T HAVE TO KILL EACH OTHER.
"BUT THE ARCHAEONS AREN'T GONE FOREVER. SOMETIMES... THEY COME BACK-- ≷BEEP≶
WE DON'T NEED TO LISTEN TO THIS PART--
...IT'S JUST THE APOCALYPSE.
THE ARCHAEONS END THEIR REMISSION AND RELAPSE. THEY COME OUT OF THEIR CYSTS AND THEIR PUPAE.
THEY DO THEIR THING.
HUMANITY GOES EXTINCT.
THE END.
WANT TO WATCH IT AGAIN, IN CASE YOU MISSED SOMETHING?

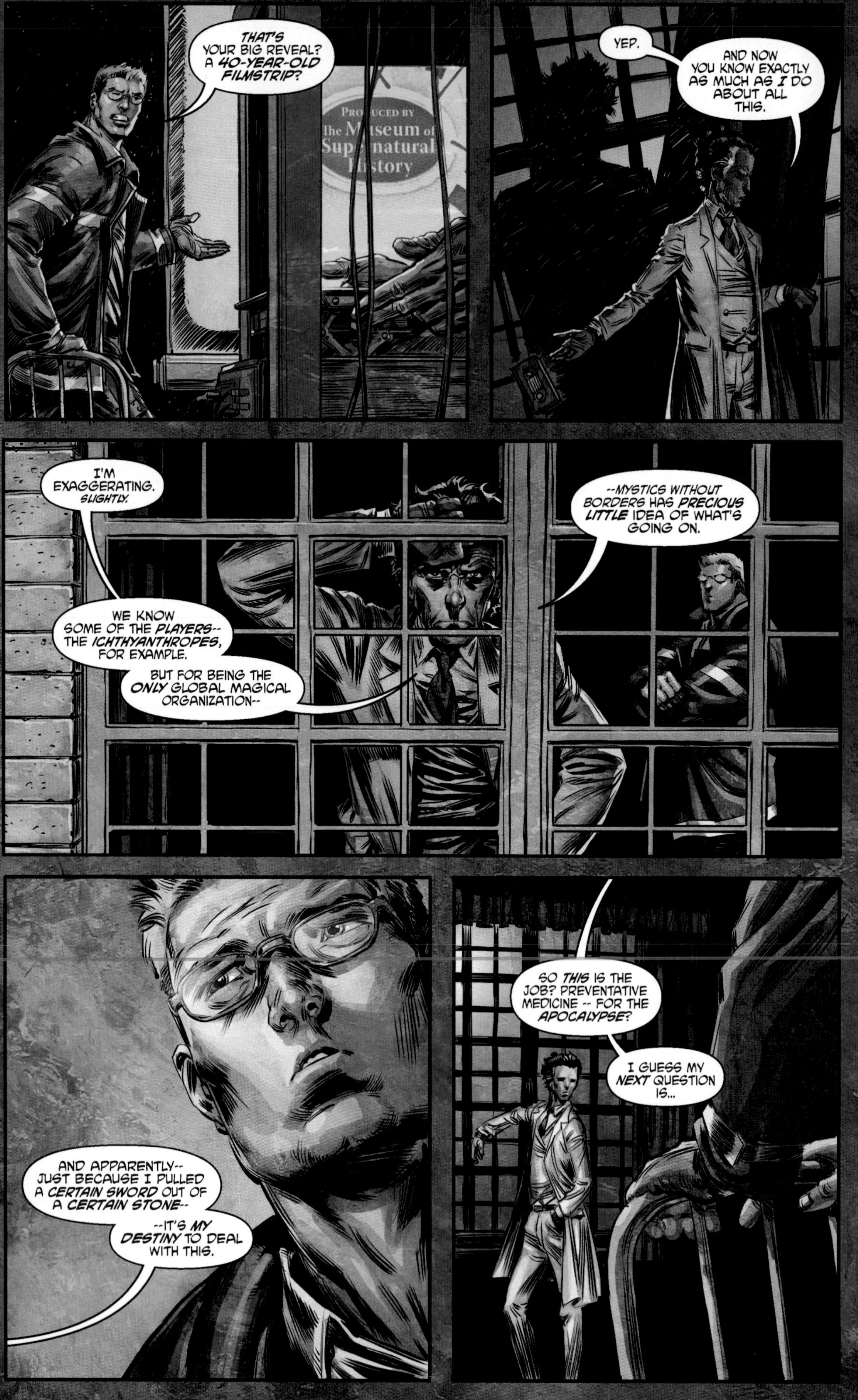
THAT'S YOUR BIG REVEAL? A 40-YEAR-OLD FILMSTRIP?
PRODUCED BY The Museum of Supernatural History
YEP.
AND NOW YOU KNOW EXACTLY AS MUCH AS I DO ABOUT ALL THIS.
I'M EXAGGERATING. SLIGHTLY.
WE KNOW SOME OF THE PLAYERS-- THE ICHTHYANTHROPES, FOR EXAMPLE.
BUT FOR BEING THE ONLY GLOBAL MAGICAL ORGANIZATION--
--MYSTICS WITHOUT BORDERS HAS PRECIOUS LITTLE IDEA OF WHAT'S GOING ON.
AND APPARENTLY-- JUST BECAUSE I PULLED A CERTAIN SWORD OUT OF A CERTAIN STONE--
--IT'S MY DESTINY TO DEAL WITH THIS.
SO THIS IS THE JOB? PREVENTATIVE MEDICINE -- FOR THE APOCALYPSE?
I GUESS MY NEXT QUESTION IS...

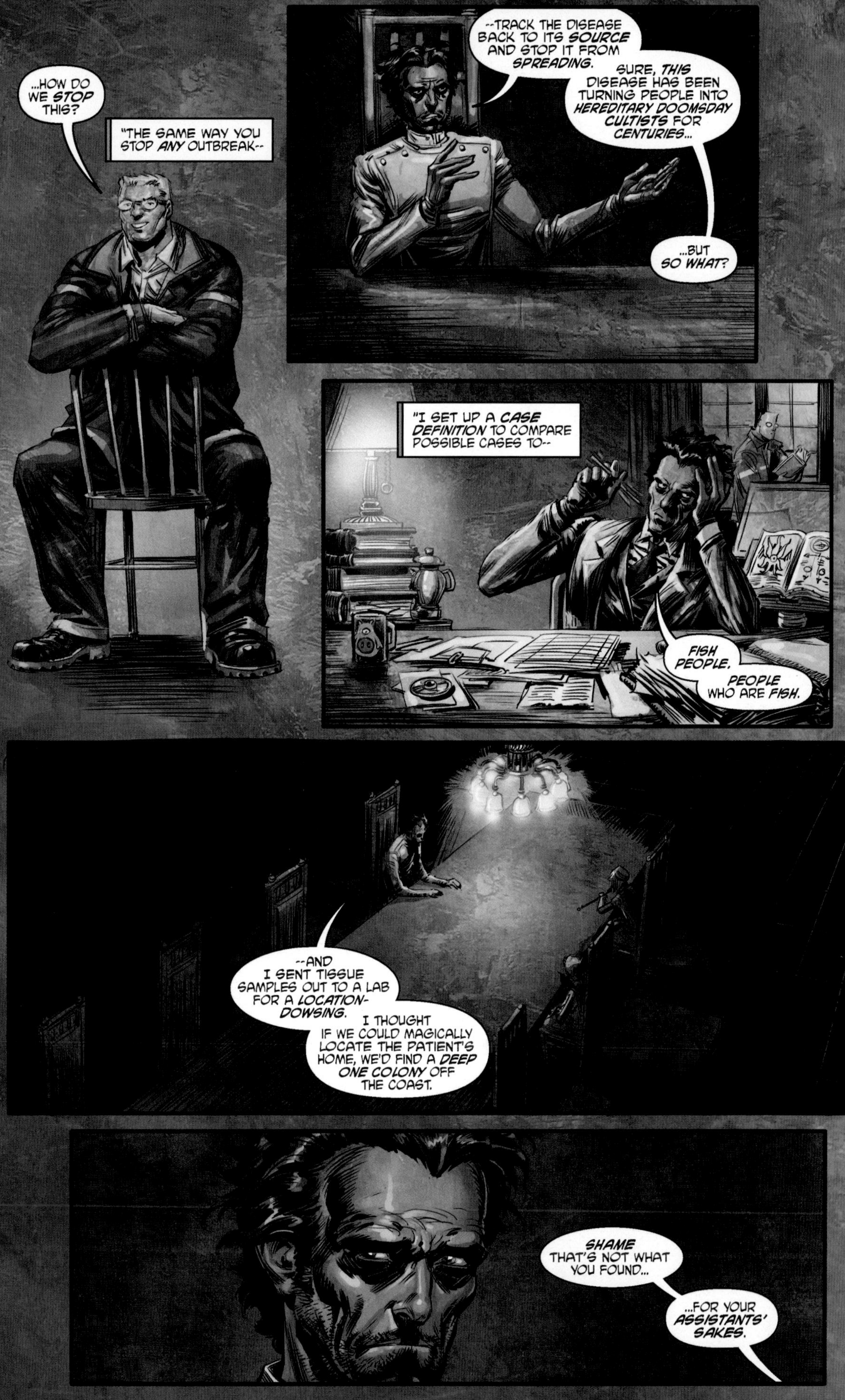

...HOW DO WE STOP THIS?
"THE SAME WAY YOU STOP ANY OUTBREAK--
--TRACK THE DISEASE BACK TO ITS SOURCE AND STOP IT FROM SPREADING.
SURE, THIS DISEASE HAS BEEN TURNING PEOPLE INTO HEREDITARY DOOMSDAY CULTISTS FOR CENTURIES...
...BUT SO WHAT?
"I SET UP A CASE DEFINITION TO COMPARE POSSIBLE CASES TO--
FISH PEOPLE.
PEOPLE WHO ARE FISH.
--AND I SENT TISSUE SAMPLES OUT TO A LAB FOR A LOCATION-DOWSING.
I THOUGHT IF WE COULD MAGICALLY LOCATE THE PATIENT'S HOME, WE'D FIND A DEEP ONE COLONY OFF THE COAST.
SHAME THAT'S NOT WHAT YOU FOUND...
...FOR YOUR ASSISTANTS' SAKES.

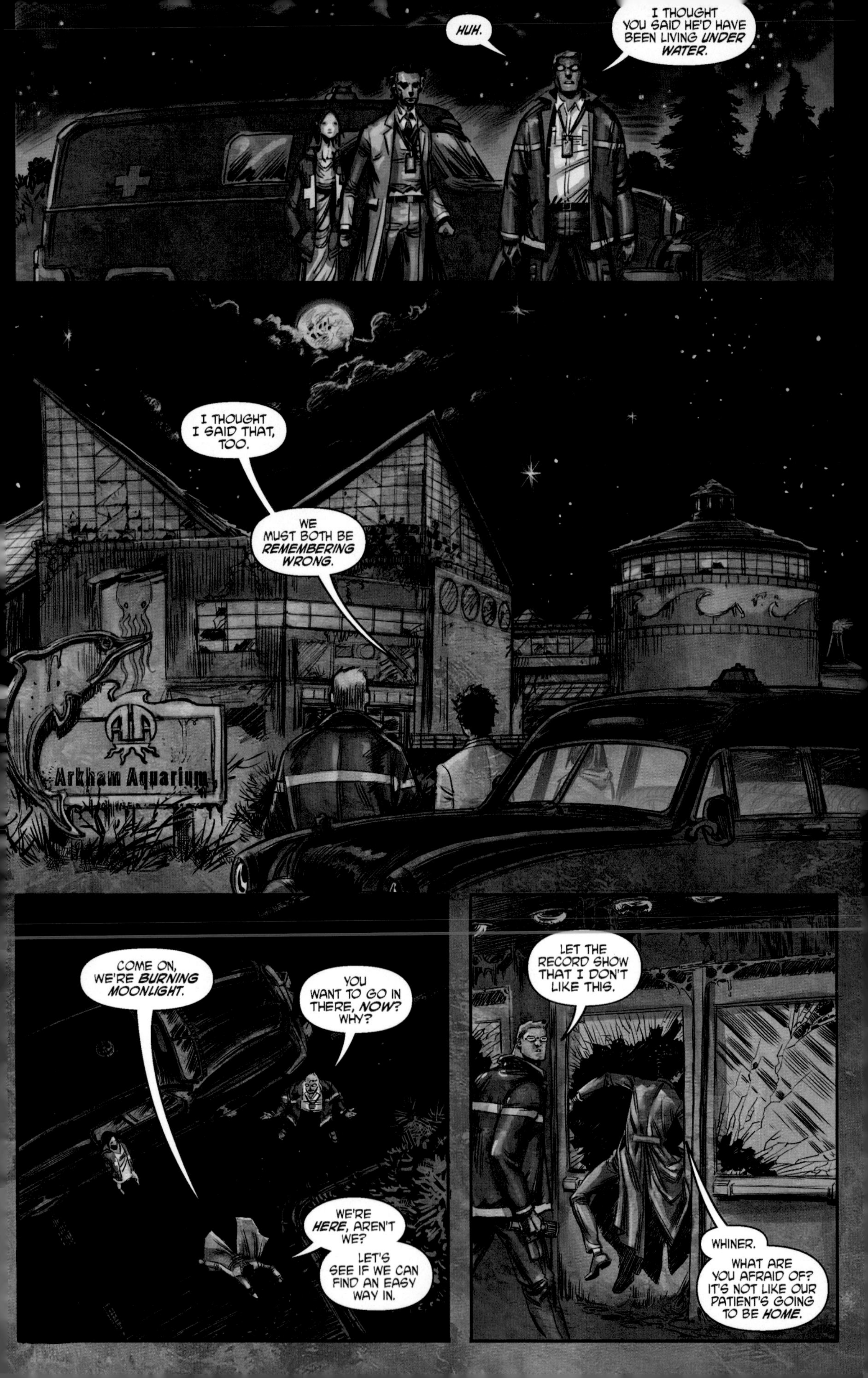
HUH.
I THOUGHT YOU SAID HE'D HAVE BEEN LIVING *UNDER WATER*.
I THOUGHT I SAID THAT, TOO.
WE MUST BOTH BE *REMEMBERING WRONG*.
Arkham Aquarium
COME ON, WE'RE *BURNING MOONLIGHT*.
YOU WANT TO GO IN THERE, *NOW*? WHY?
WE'RE *HERE*, AREN'T WE?
LET'S SEE IF WE CAN FIND AN EASY WAY IN.
LET THE RECORD SHOW THAT I DON'T LIKE THIS.
WHINER.
WHAT ARE YOU AFRAID OF? IT'S NOT LIKE OUR PATIENT'S GOING TO BE *HOME*.

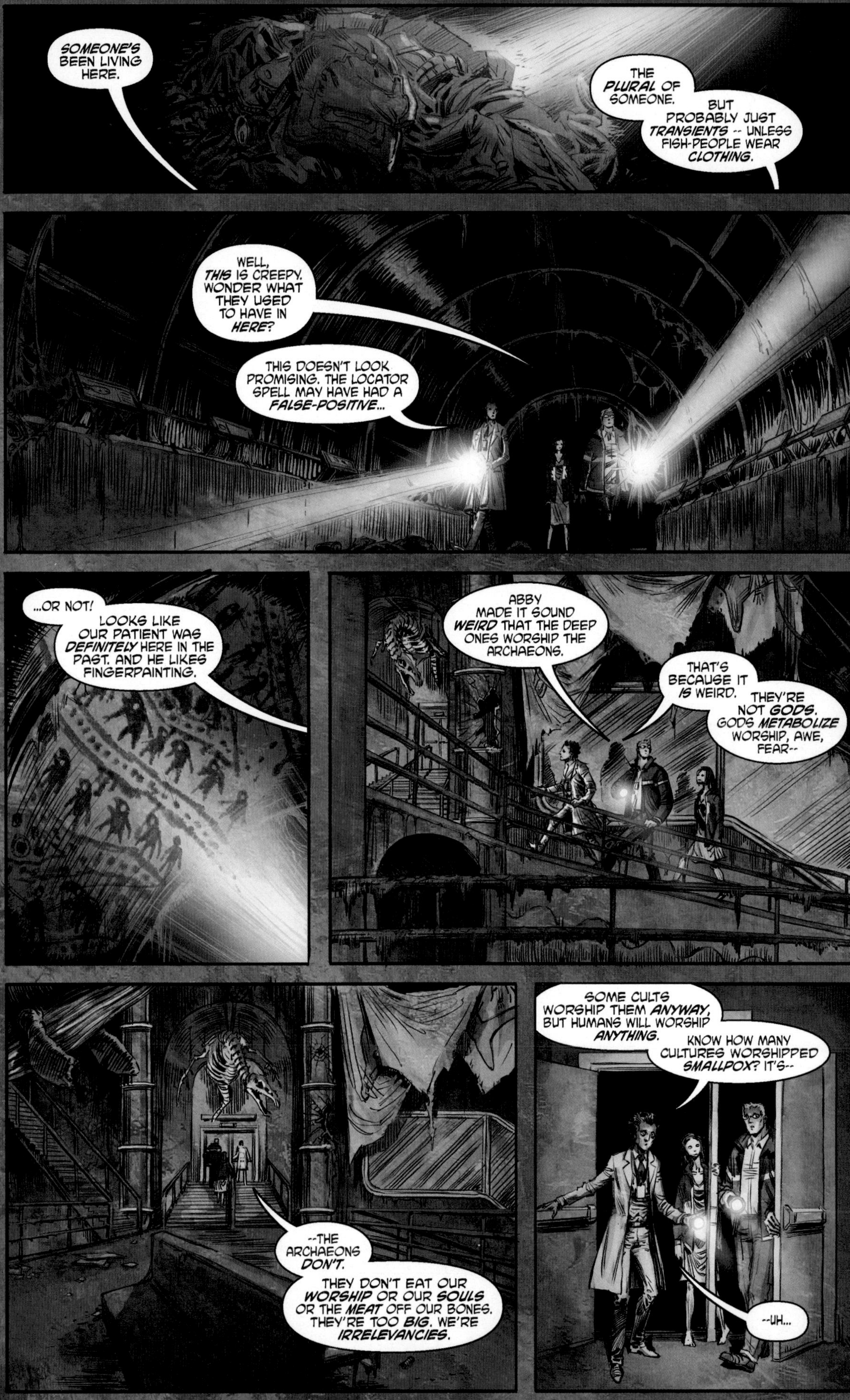
SOMEONE'S BEEN LIVING HERE.
THE PLURAL OF SOMEONE.
BUT PROBABLY JUST TRANSIENTS -- UNLESS FISH-PEOPLE WEAR CLOTHING.
WELL, THIS IS CREEPY. WONDER WHAT THEY USED TO HAVE IN HERE?
THIS DOESN'T LOOK PROMISING. THE LOCATOR SPELL MAY HAVE HAD A FALSE-POSITIVE...
...OR NOT!
LOOKS LIKE OUR PATIENT WAS DEFINITELY HERE IN THE PAST. AND HE LIKES FINGERPAINTING.
ABBY MADE IT SOUND WEIRD THAT THE DEEP ONES WORSHIP THE ARCHAEONS.
THAT'S BECAUSE IT IS WEIRD.
THEY'RE NOT GODS. GODS METABOLIZE WORSHIP, AWE, FEAR--
--THE ARCHAEONS DON'T.
THEY DON'T EAT OUR WORSHIP OR OUR SOULS OR THE MEAT OFF OUR BONES. THEY'RE TOO BIG. WE'RE IRRELEVANCIES.
SOME CULTS WORSHIP THEM ANYWAY, BUT HUMANS WILL WORSHIP ANYTHING.
KNOW HOW MANY CULTURES WORSHIPPED SMALLPOX? IT'S--
--UH...

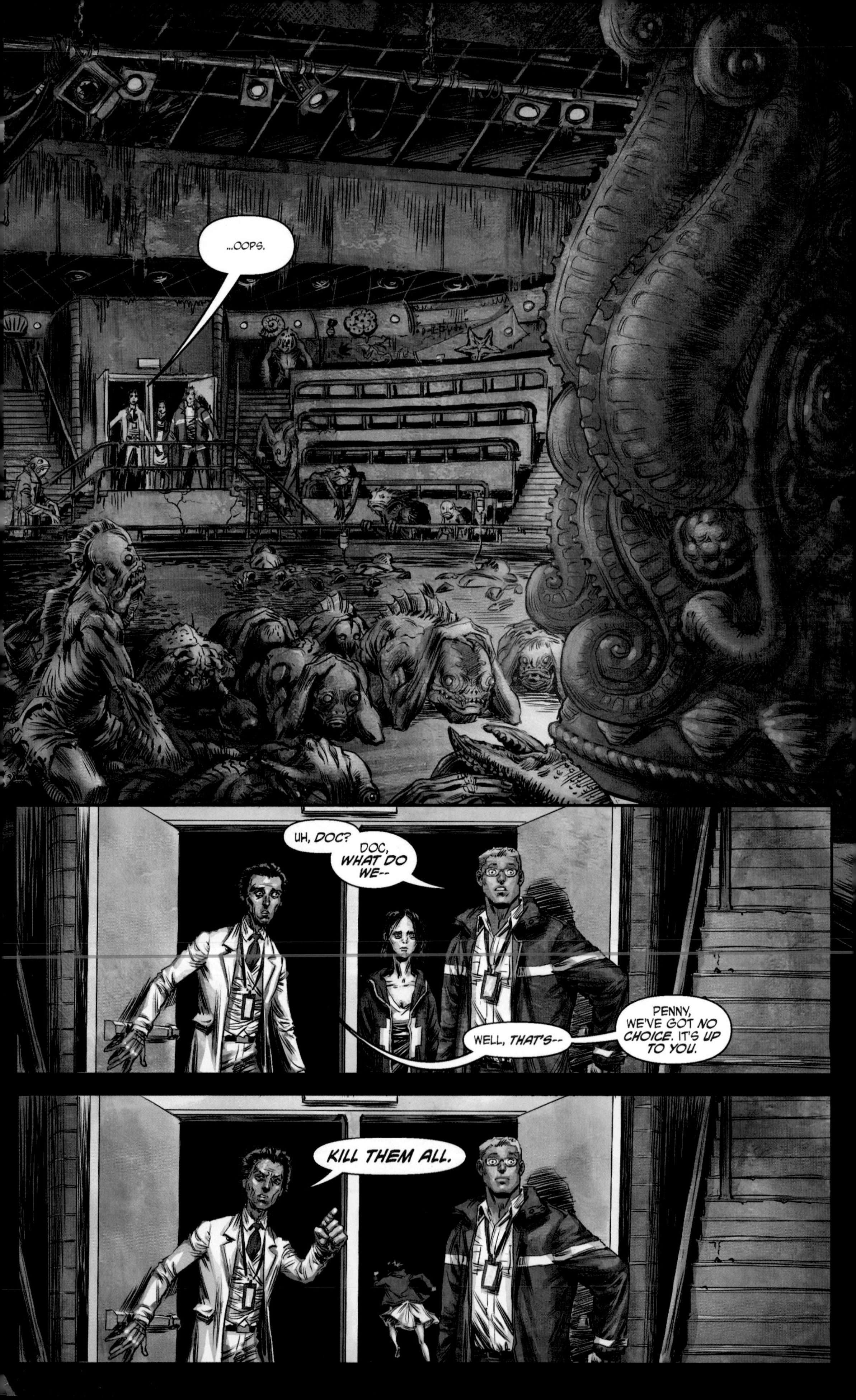
...OOPS.
UH, DOC?
DOC, WHAT DO WE--
WELL, THAT'S--
PENNY, WE'VE GOT NO CHOICE. IT'S UP TO YOU.
KILL THEM ALL.

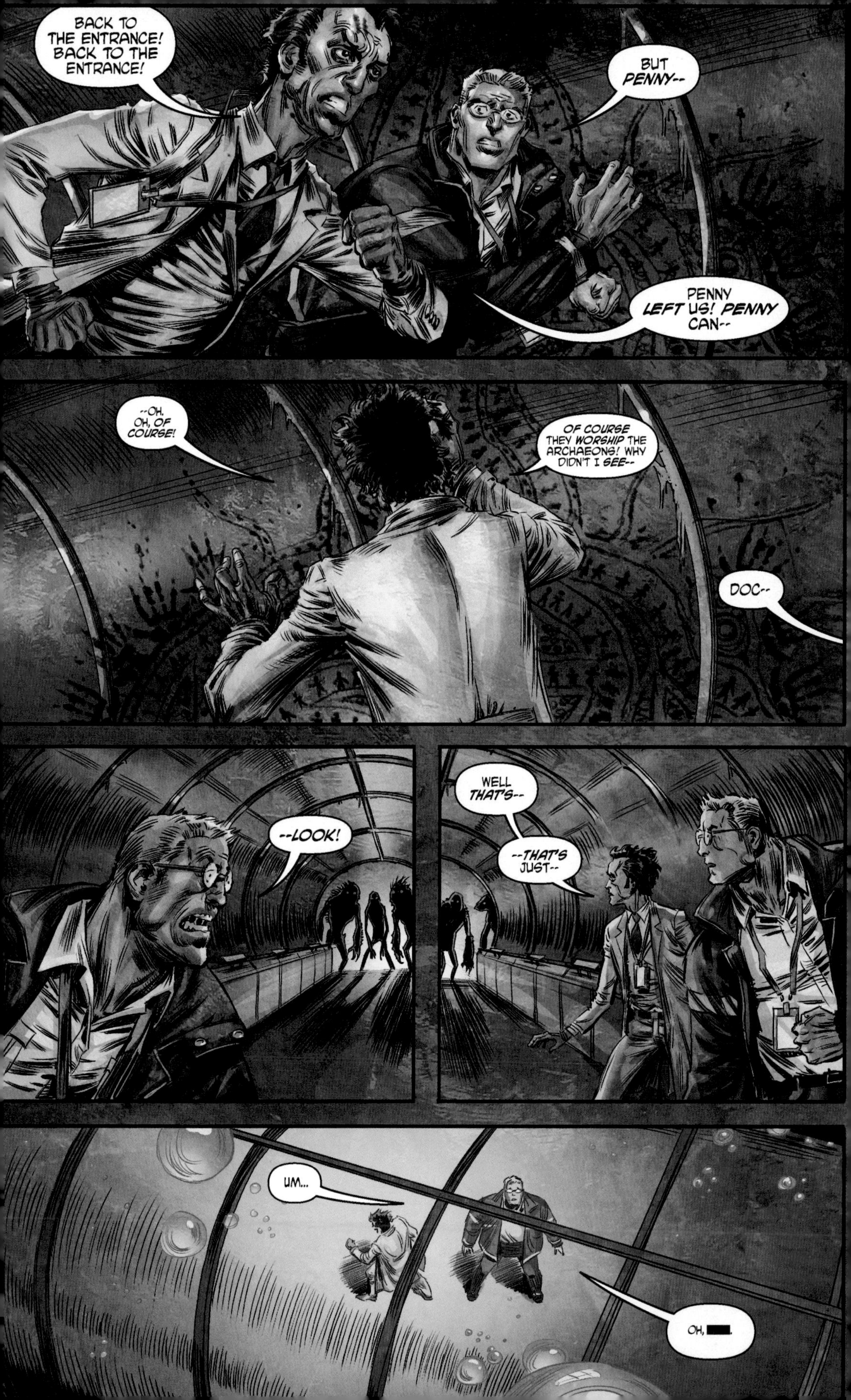
BACK TO THE ENTRANCE! BACK TO THE ENTRANCE!
BUT PENNY--
PENNY LEFT US! PENNY CAN--
--OH. OH, OF COURSE!
OF COURSE THEY WORSHIP THE ARCHAEONS! WHY DIDN'T I SEE--
DOC--
--LOOK!
WELL THAT'S--
--THAT'S JUST--
UM...
OH, [redacted].

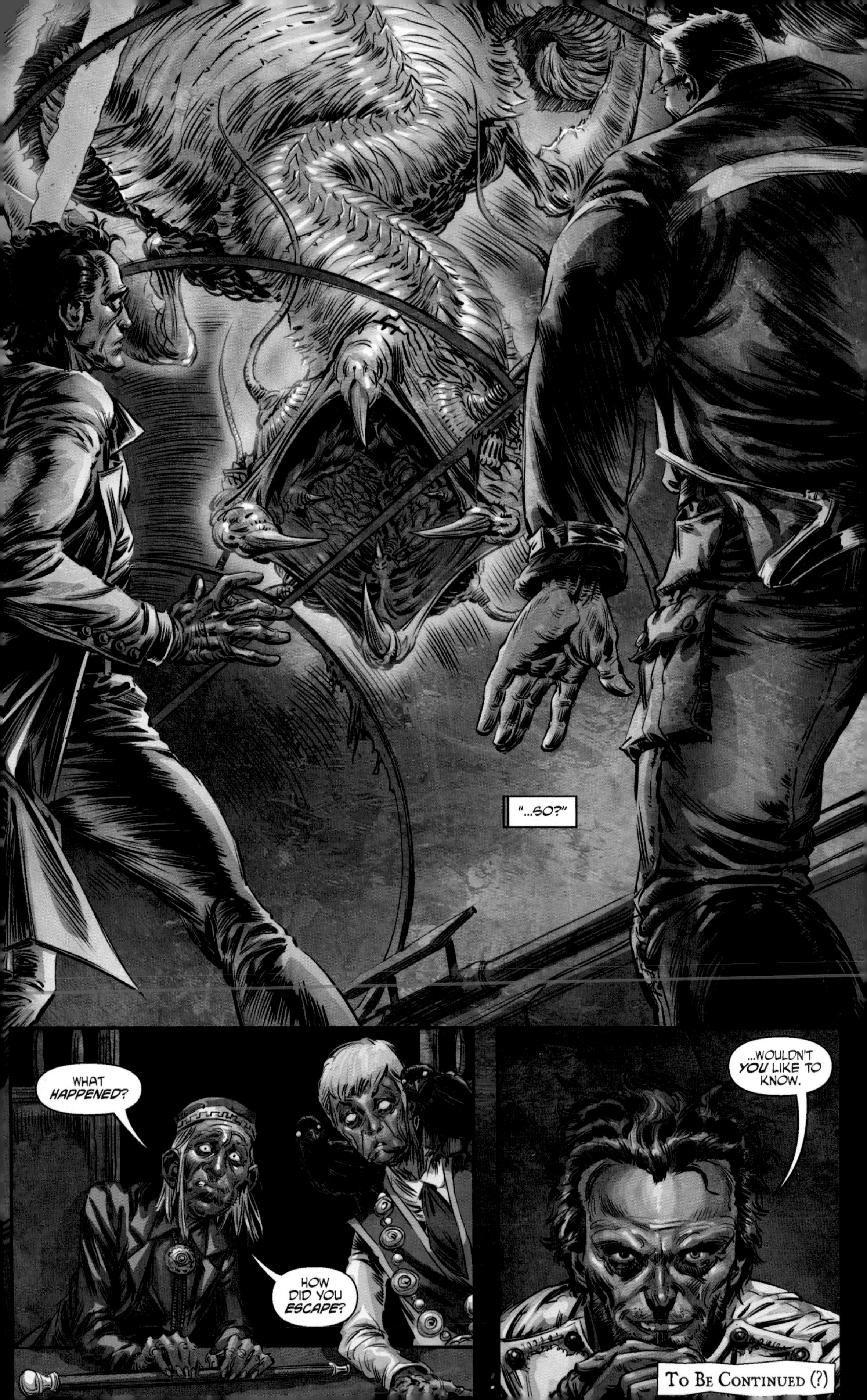
"...SO?"
WHAT HAPPENED?
HOW DID YOU ESCAPE?
...WOULDN'T YOU LIKE TO KNOW.
To Be Continued (?)

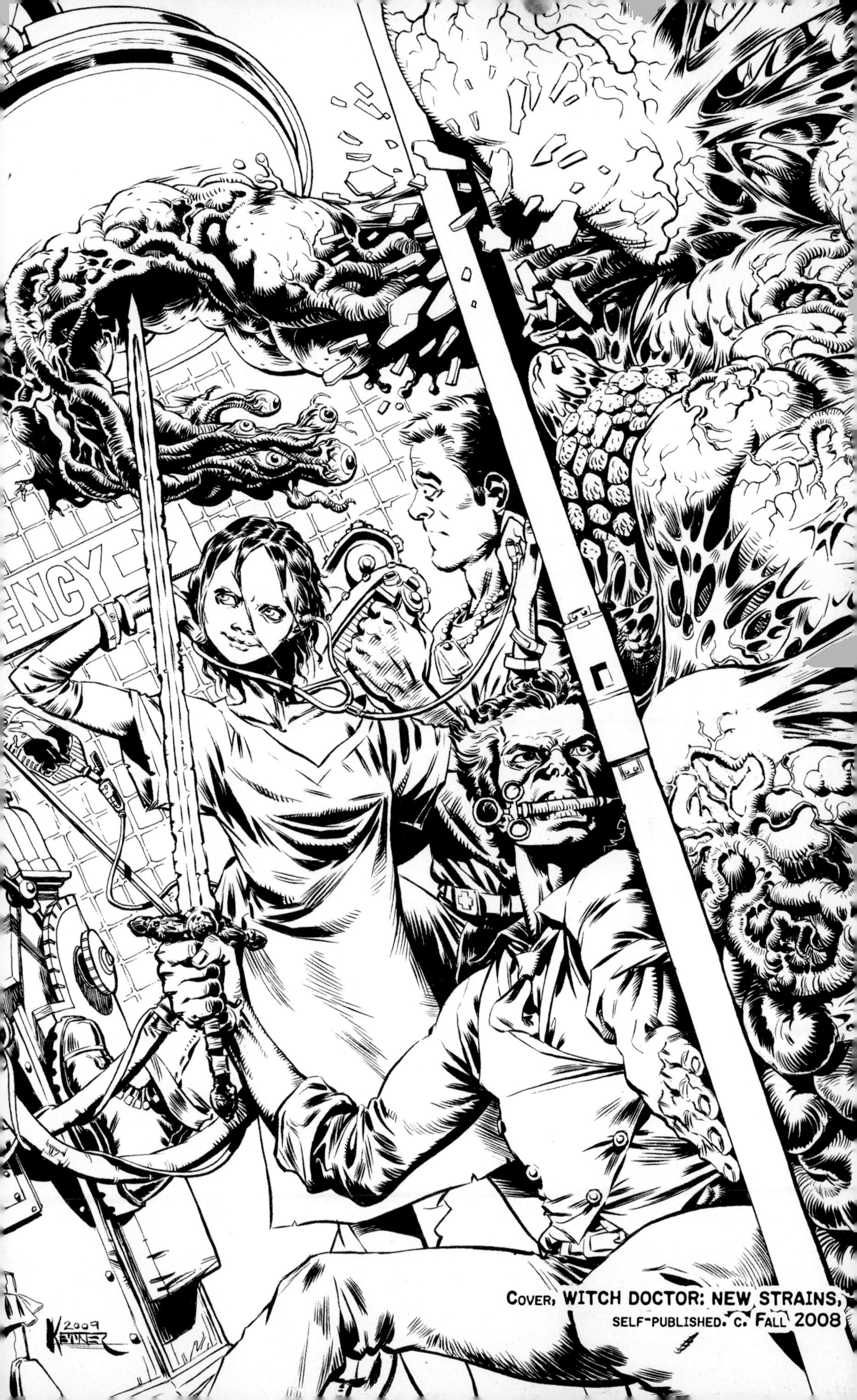
ENCY

COVER, WITCH DOCTOR: NEW STRAINS,
SELF-PUBLISHED. C. FALL 2008

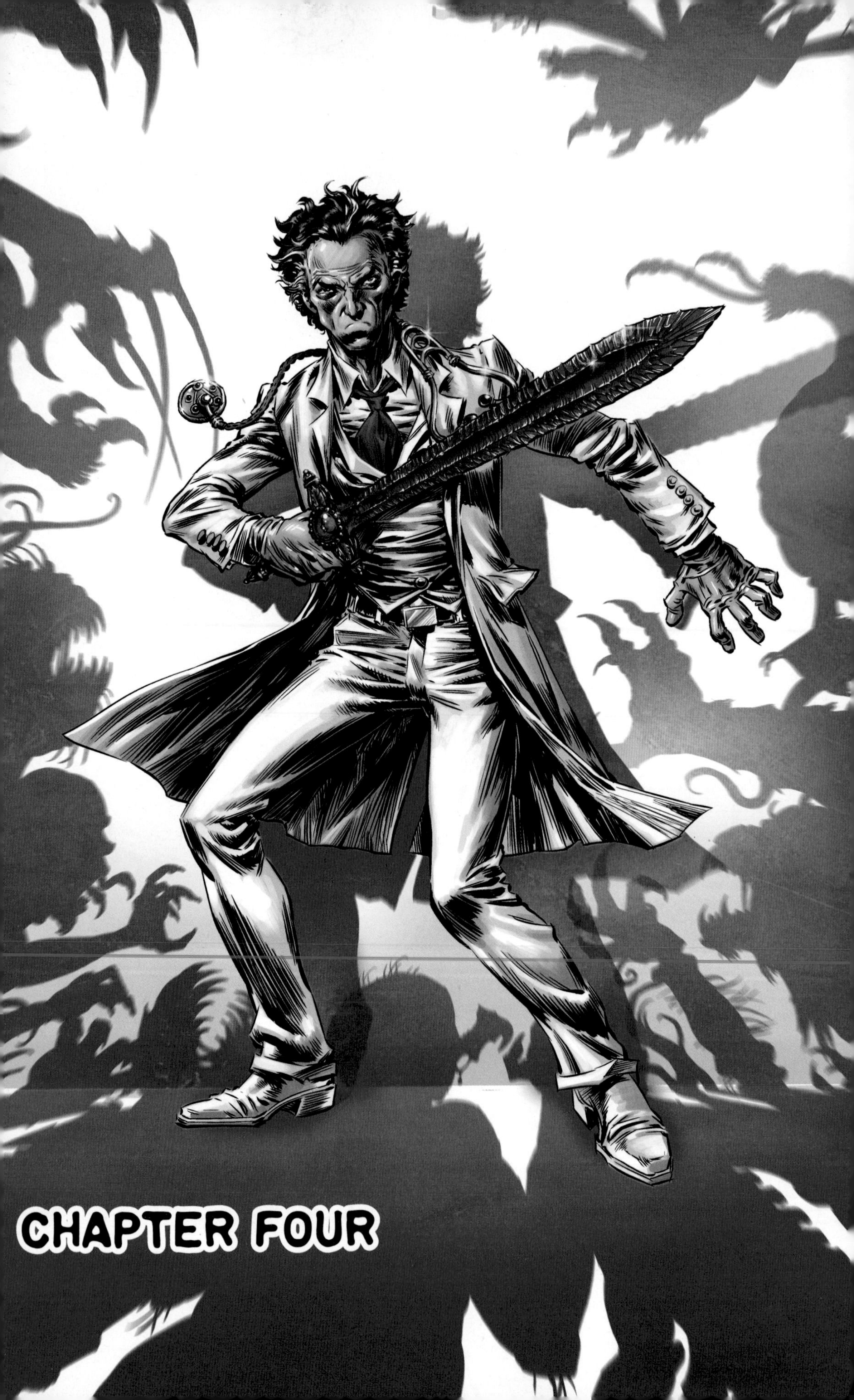
CHAPTER FOUR

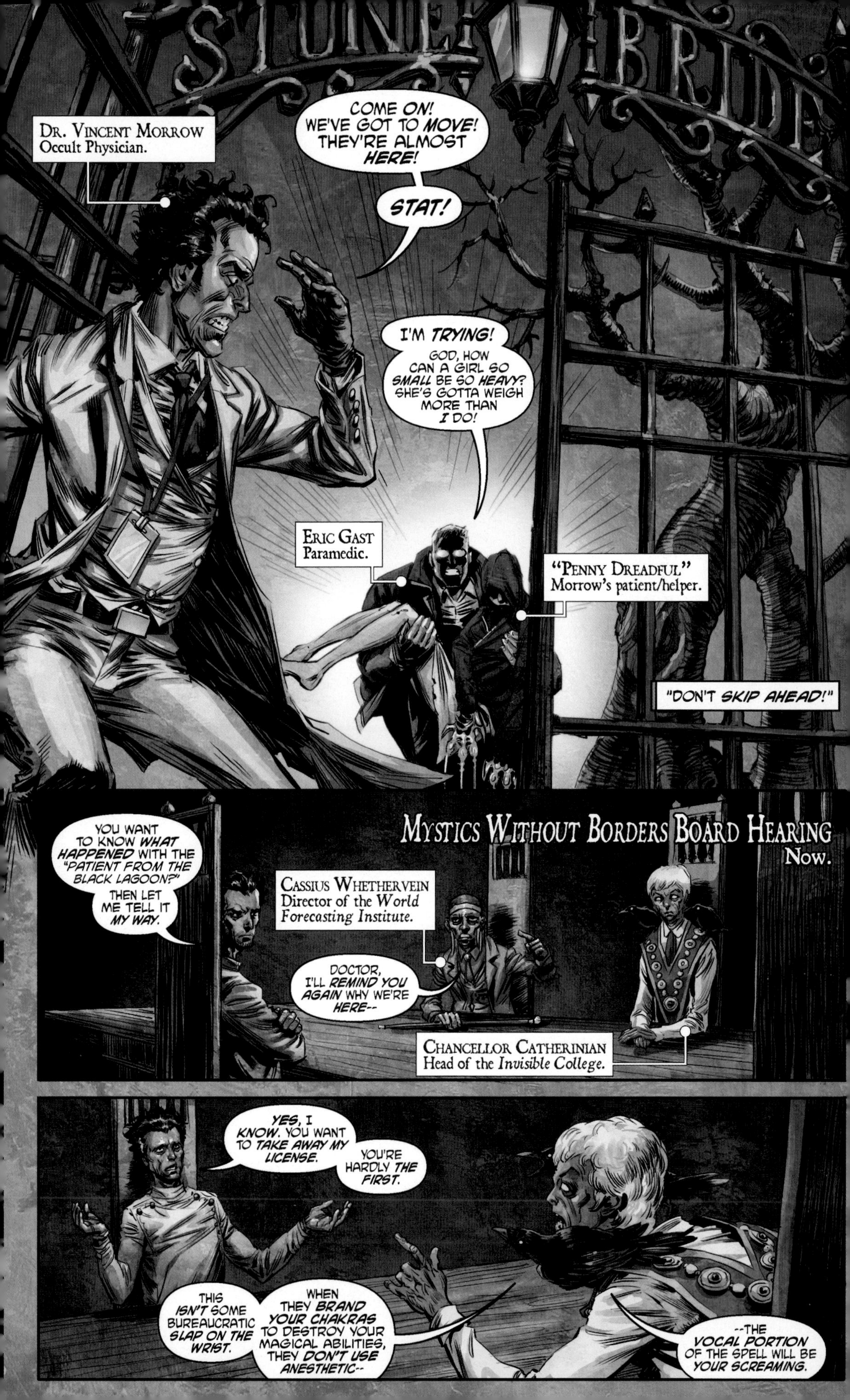
STONE BRIDGE
Dr. Vincent Morrow
Occult Physician.
COME ON! WE'VE GOT TO MOVE! THEY'RE ALMOST HERE!
STAT!
I'M TRYING!
GOD, HOW CAN A GIRL SO SMALL BE SO HEAVY? SHE'S GOTTA WEIGH MORE THAN I DO!
Eric Gast
Paramedic.
"Penny Dreadful"
Morrow's patient/helper.
"DON'T SKIP AHEAD!"
Mystics Without Borders Board Hearing
Now.
YOU WANT TO KNOW WHAT HAPPENED WITH THE "PATIENT FROM THE BLACK LAGOON?" THEN LET ME TELL IT MY WAY.
Cassius Whethervein
Director of the World Forecasting Institute.
DOCTOR, I'LL REMIND YOU AGAIN WHY WE'RE HERE--
Chancellor Catherinian
Head of the Invisible College.
YES, I KNOW. YOU WANT TO TAKE AWAY MY LICENSE.
YOU'RE HARDLY THE FIRST.
THIS ISN'T SOME BUREAUCRATIC SLAP ON THE WRIST.
WHEN THEY BRAND YOUR CHAKRAS TO DESTROY YOUR MAGICAL ABILITIES, THEY DON'T USE ANESTHETIC--
--THE VOCAL PORTION OF THE SPELL WILL BE YOUR SCREAMING.

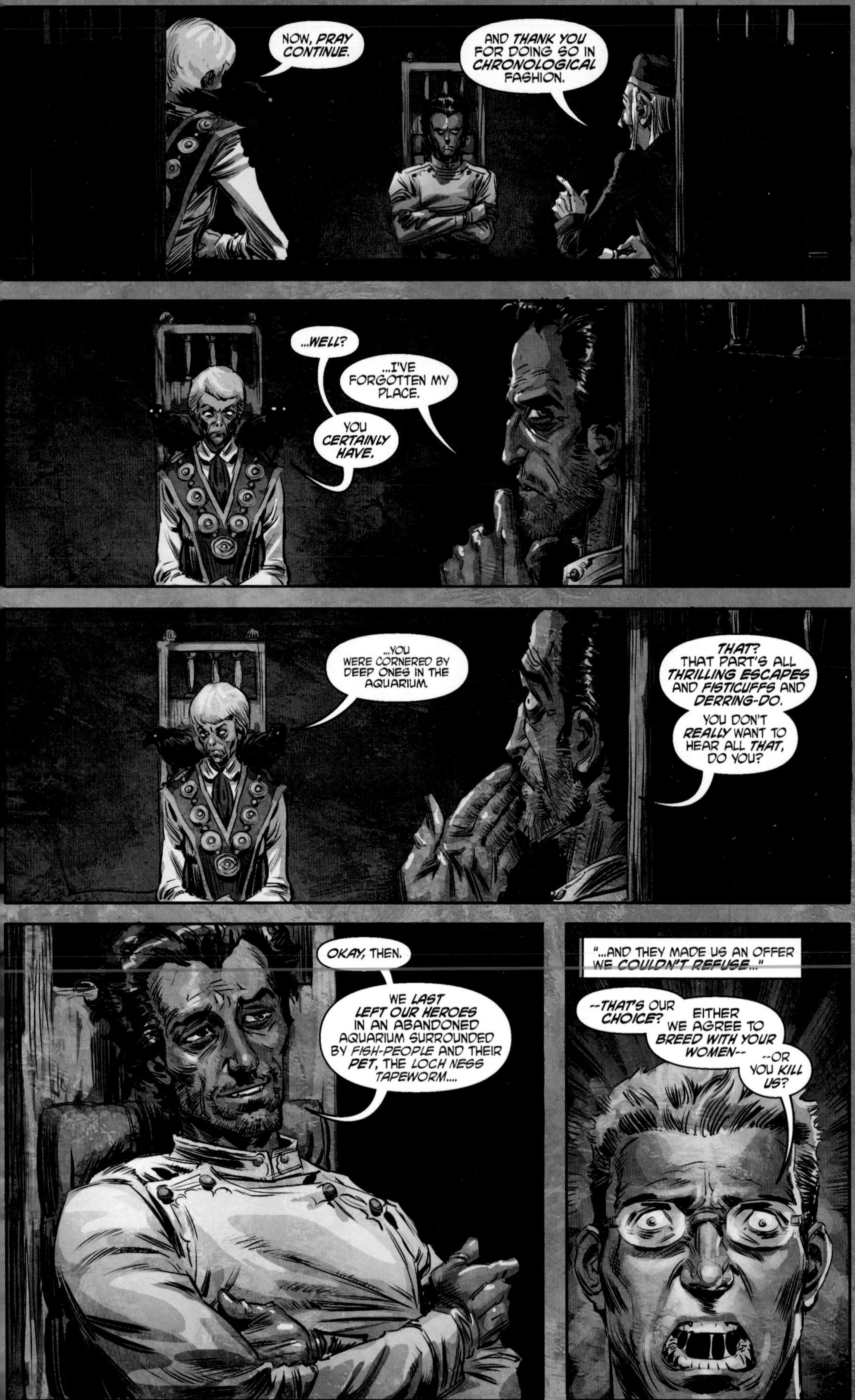
NOW, PRAY CONTINUE.
AND THANK YOU FOR DOING SO IN CHRONOLOGICAL FASHION.
...WELL?
...I'VE FORGOTTEN MY PLACE.
YOU CERTAINLY HAVE.
...YOU WERE CORNERED BY DEEP ONES IN THE AQUARIUM.
THAT? THAT PART'S ALL THRILLING ESCAPES AND FISTICUFFS AND DERRING-DO.
YOU DON'T REALLY WANT TO HEAR ALL THAT, DO YOU?
OKAY, THEN.
WE LAST LEFT OUR HEROES IN AN ABANDONED AQUARIUM SURROUNDED BY FISH-PEOPLE AND THEIR PET, THE LOCH NESS TAPEWORM....
"...AND THEY MADE US AN OFFER WE COULDN'T REFUSE..."
--THAT'S OUR CHOICE?
EITHER WE AGREE TO BREED WITH YOUR WOMEN--
--OR YOU KILL US?

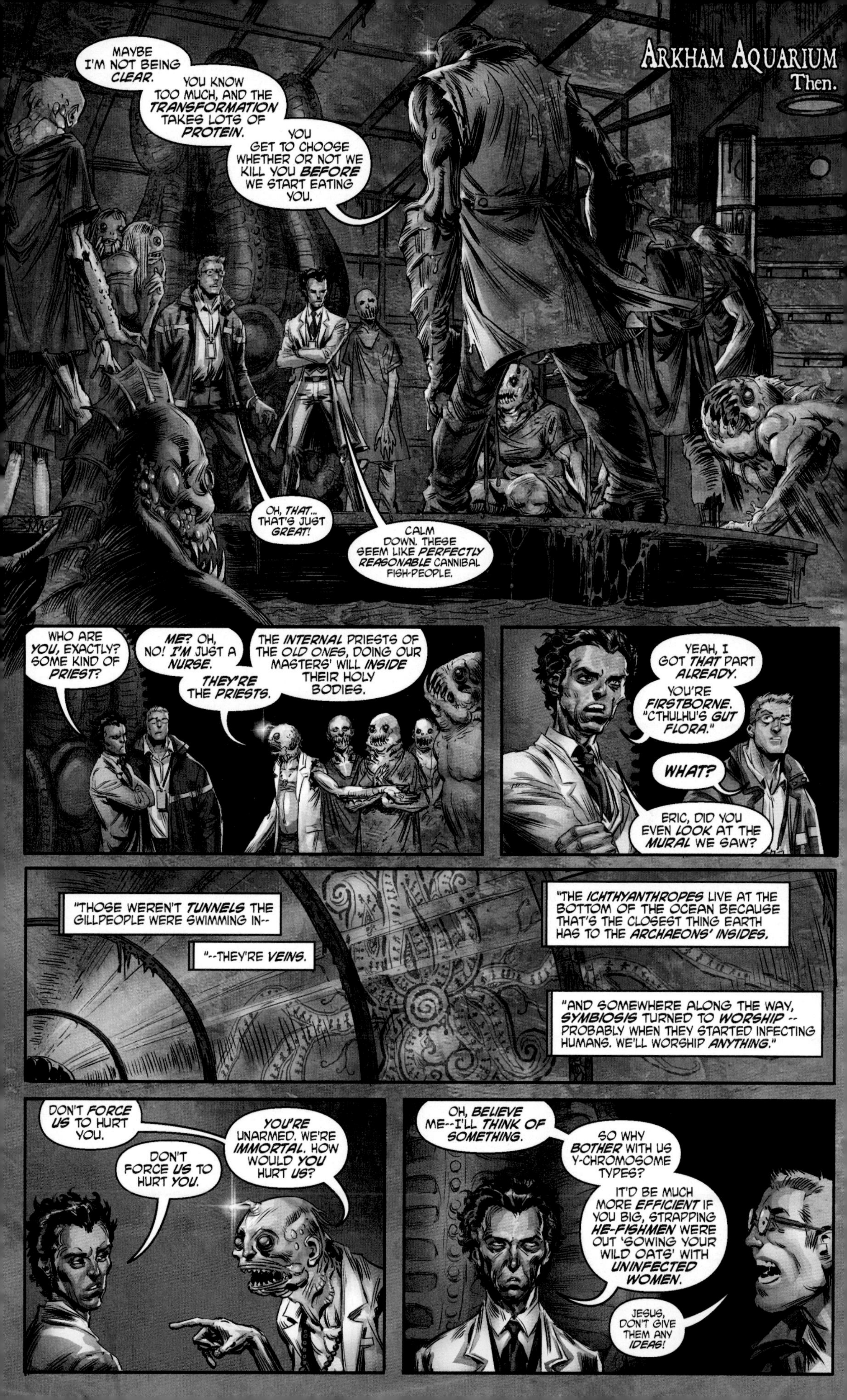
ARKHAM AQUARIUM
Then.
MAYBE I'M NOT BEING CLEAR.
YOU KNOW TOO MUCH, AND THE TRANSFORMATION TAKES LOTS OF PROTEIN.
YOU GET TO CHOOSE WHETHER OR NOT WE KILL YOU BEFORE WE START EATING YOU.
OH, THAT... THAT'S JUST GREAT!
CALM DOWN. THESE SEEM LIKE PERFECTLY REASONABLE CANNIBAL FISH-PEOPLE.
WHO ARE YOU, EXACTLY? SOME KIND OF PRIEST?
ME? OH, NO! I'M JUST A NURSE.
THEY'RE THE PRIESTS.
THE INTERNAL PRIESTS OF THE OLD ONES, DOING OUR MASTERS' WILL INSIDE THEIR HOLY BODIES.
YEAH, I GOT THAT PART ALREADY.
YOU'RE FIRSTBORNE. "CTHULHU'S GUT FLORA."
WHAT?
ERIC, DID YOU EVEN LOOK AT THE MURAL WE SAW?
"THOSE WEREN'T TUNNELS THE GILLPEOPLE WERE SWIMMING IN--
"--THEY'RE VEINS.
"THE ICHTHYANTHROPES LIVE AT THE BOTTOM OF THE OCEAN BECAUSE THAT'S THE CLOSEST THING EARTH HAS TO THE ARCHAEONS' INSIDES.
"AND SOMEWHERE ALONG THE WAY, SYMBIOSIS TURNED TO WORSHIP -- PROBABLY WHEN THEY STARTED INFECTING HUMANS. WE'LL WORSHIP ANYTHING."
DON'T FORCE US TO HURT YOU.
DON'T FORCE US TO HURT YOU.
YOU'RE UNARMED. WE'RE IMMORTAL. HOW WOULD YOU HURT US?
OH, BELIEVE ME--I'LL THINK OF SOMETHING.
SO WHY BOTHER WITH US Y-CHROMOSOME TYPES?
IT'D BE MUCH MORE EFFICIENT IF YOU BIG, STRAPPING HE-FISHMEN WERE OUT 'SOWING YOUR WILD OATS' WITH UNINFECTED WOMEN.
JESUS, DON'T GIVE THEM ANY IDEAS!

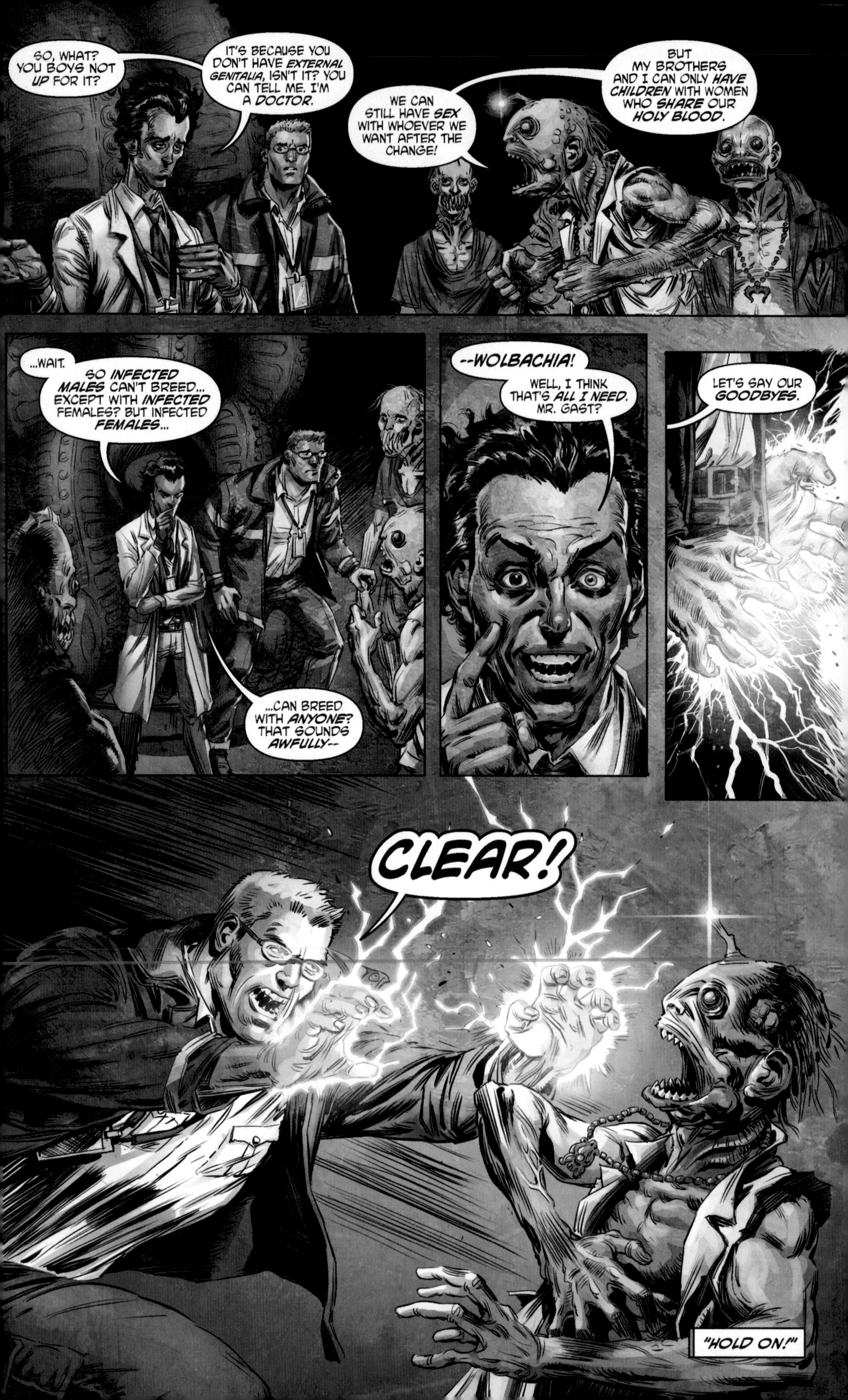
SO, WHAT? YOU BOYS NOT UP FOR IT?
IT'S BECAUSE YOU DON'T HAVE EXTERNAL GENITALIA, ISN'T IT? YOU CAN TELL ME. I'M A DOCTOR.
WE CAN STILL HAVE SEX WITH WHOEVER WE WANT AFTER THE CHANGE!
BUT MY BROTHERS AND I CAN ONLY HAVE CHILDREN WITH WOMEN WHO SHARE OUR HOLY BLOOD.
...WAIT.
SO INFECTED MALES CAN'T BREED... EXCEPT WITH INFECTED FEMALES? BUT INFECTED FEMALES...
...CAN BREED WITH ANYONE? THAT SOUNDS AWFULLY--
--WOLBACHIA!
WELL, I THINK THAT'S ALL I NEED. MR. GAST?
LET'S SAY OUR GOODBYES.
CLEAR!
"HOLD ON!"

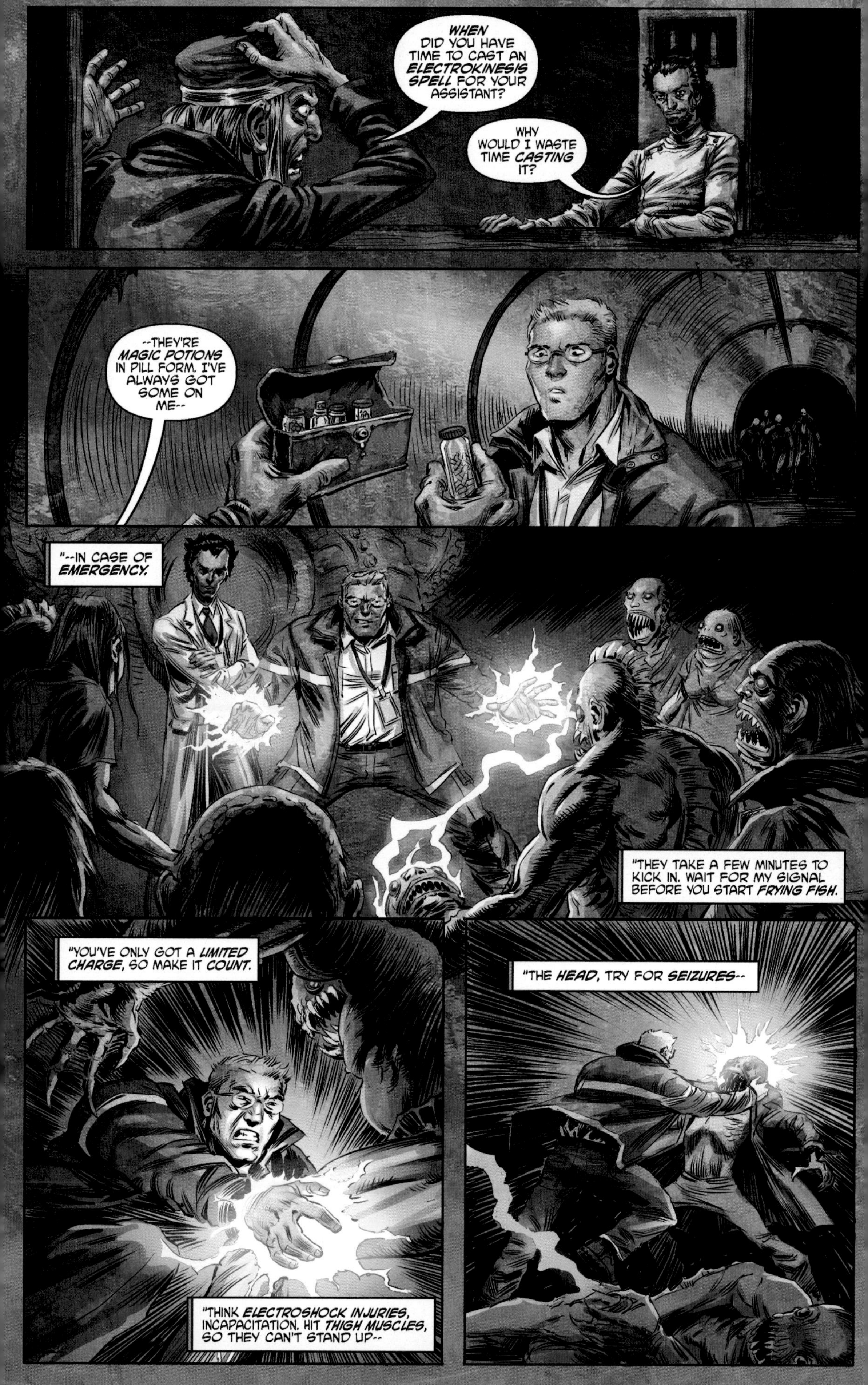
WHEN DID YOU HAVE TIME TO CAST AN ELECTROKINESIS SPELL FOR YOUR ASSISTANT?
WHY WOULD I WASTE TIME CASTING IT?
--THEY'RE MAGIC POTIONS IN PILL FORM. I'VE ALWAYS GOT SOME ON ME--
"--IN CASE OF EMERGENCY.
"THEY TAKE A FEW MINUTES TO KICK IN. WAIT FOR MY SIGNAL BEFORE YOU START FRYING FISH.
"YOU'VE ONLY GOT A LIMITED CHARGE, SO MAKE IT COUNT.
"THINK ELECTROSHOCK INJURIES, INCAPACITATION. HIT THIGH MUSCLES, SO THEY CAN'T STAND UP--
"THE HEAD, TRY FOR SEIZURES--

"AND OF COURSE--

"--THE *HEART*."

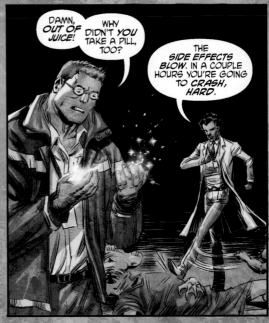

DAMN, *OUT OF JUICE!*

WHY DIDN'T *YOU* TAKE A PILL, TOO?

THE *SIDE EFFECTS BLOW*. IN A COUPLE HOURS YOU'RE GOING TO *CRASH, HARD.*

WELL, *THAT'S* AWESO-- UM-- THE ONES I *SHOCKED?* THEY'RE GETTING BACK UP AGAIN!

THEY *HEAL!* WE NEED THEIR *KRYPTONITE*-- --BUT I DON'T KNOW WHAT IT *IS*, YET!

OH, *NOW YOU TELL*-- --HUH?

≑URRG≑

≑HRRRRCK≑

WHEN I RUN, YOU SHOULD RUN TOO.

...OH.

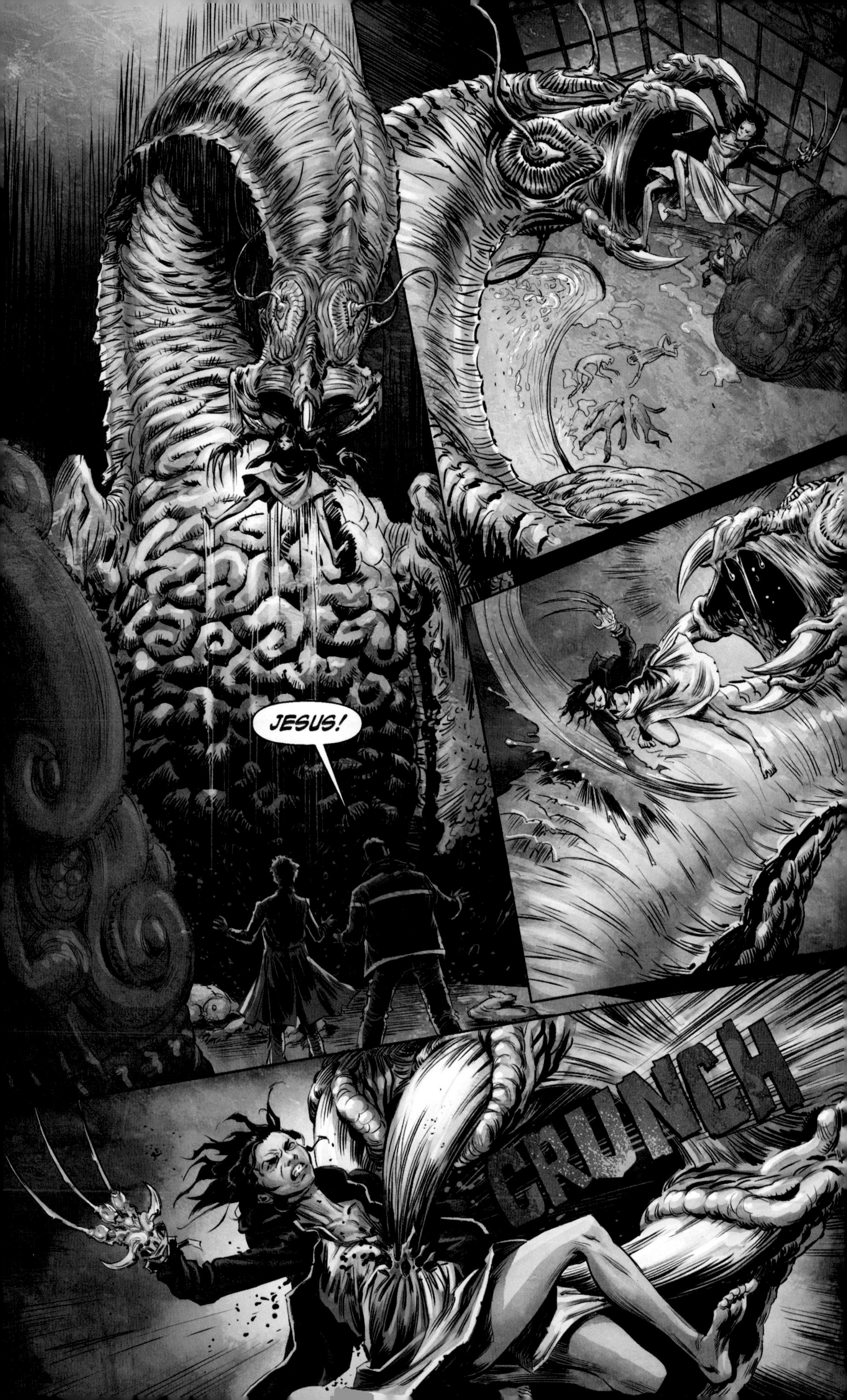
JESUS!
CRUNCH

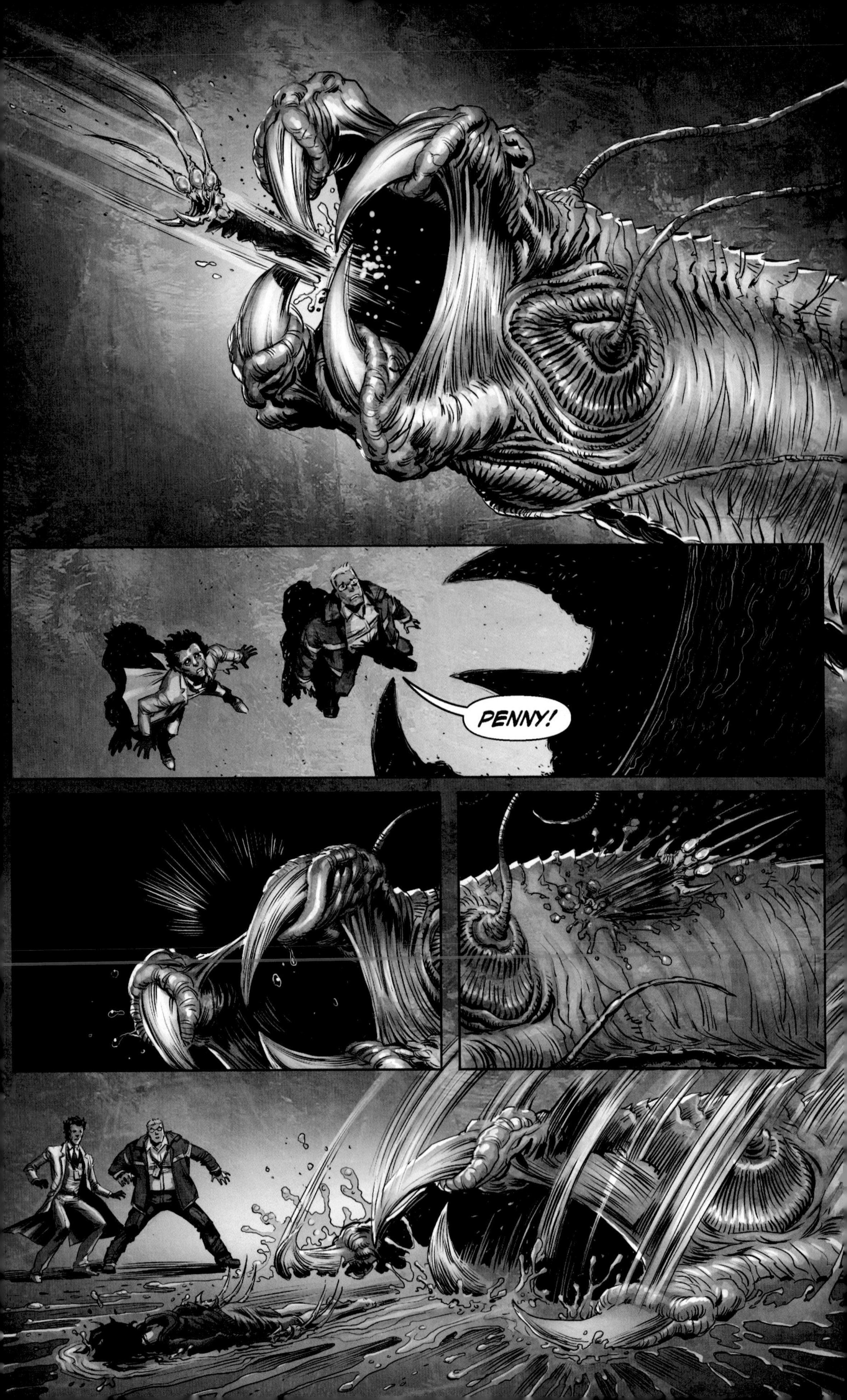
PENNY!

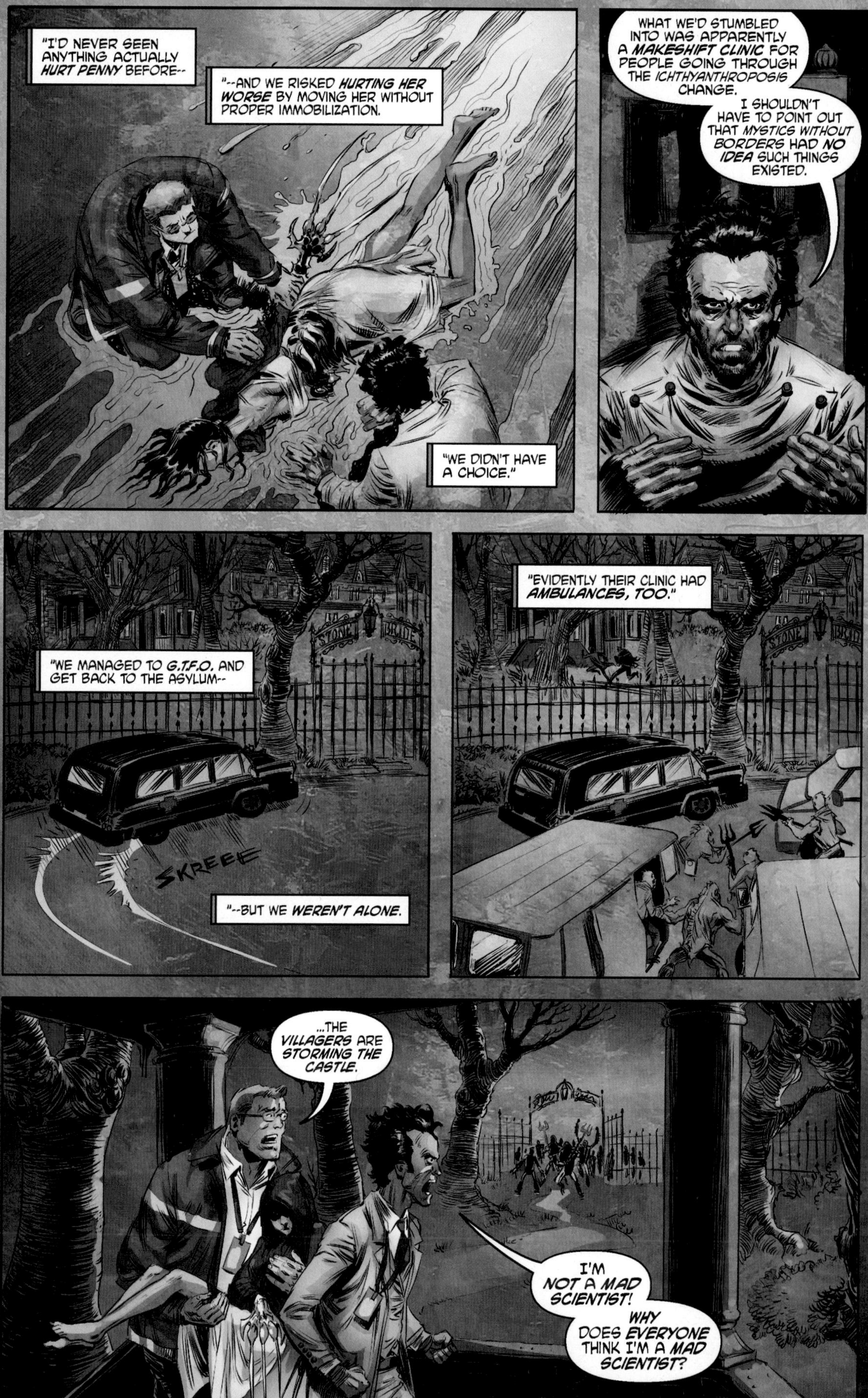
"I'D NEVER SEEN ANYTHING ACTUALLY HURT PENNY BEFORE--
"--AND WE RISKED HURTING HER WORSE BY MOVING HER WITHOUT PROPER IMMOBILIZATION.
"WE DIDN'T HAVE A CHOICE."
WHAT WE'D STUMBLED INTO WAS APPARENTLY A MAKESHIFT CLINIC FOR PEOPLE GOING THROUGH THE ICHTHYANTHROPOSIS CHANGE.
I SHOULDN'T HAVE TO POINT OUT THAT MYSTICS WITHOUT BORDERS HAD NO IDEA SUCH THINGS EXISTED.
STONE BRIDE
"WE MANAGED TO G.T.F.O. AND GET BACK TO THE ASYLUM--
SKREEE
"--BUT WE WEREN'T ALONE.
"EVIDENTLY THEIR CLINIC HAD AMBULANCES, TOO."
STONE BRIDE
...THE VILLAGERS ARE STORMING THE CASTLE.
I'M NOT A MAD SCIENTIST!
WHY DOES EVERYONE THINK I'M A MAD SCIENTIST?

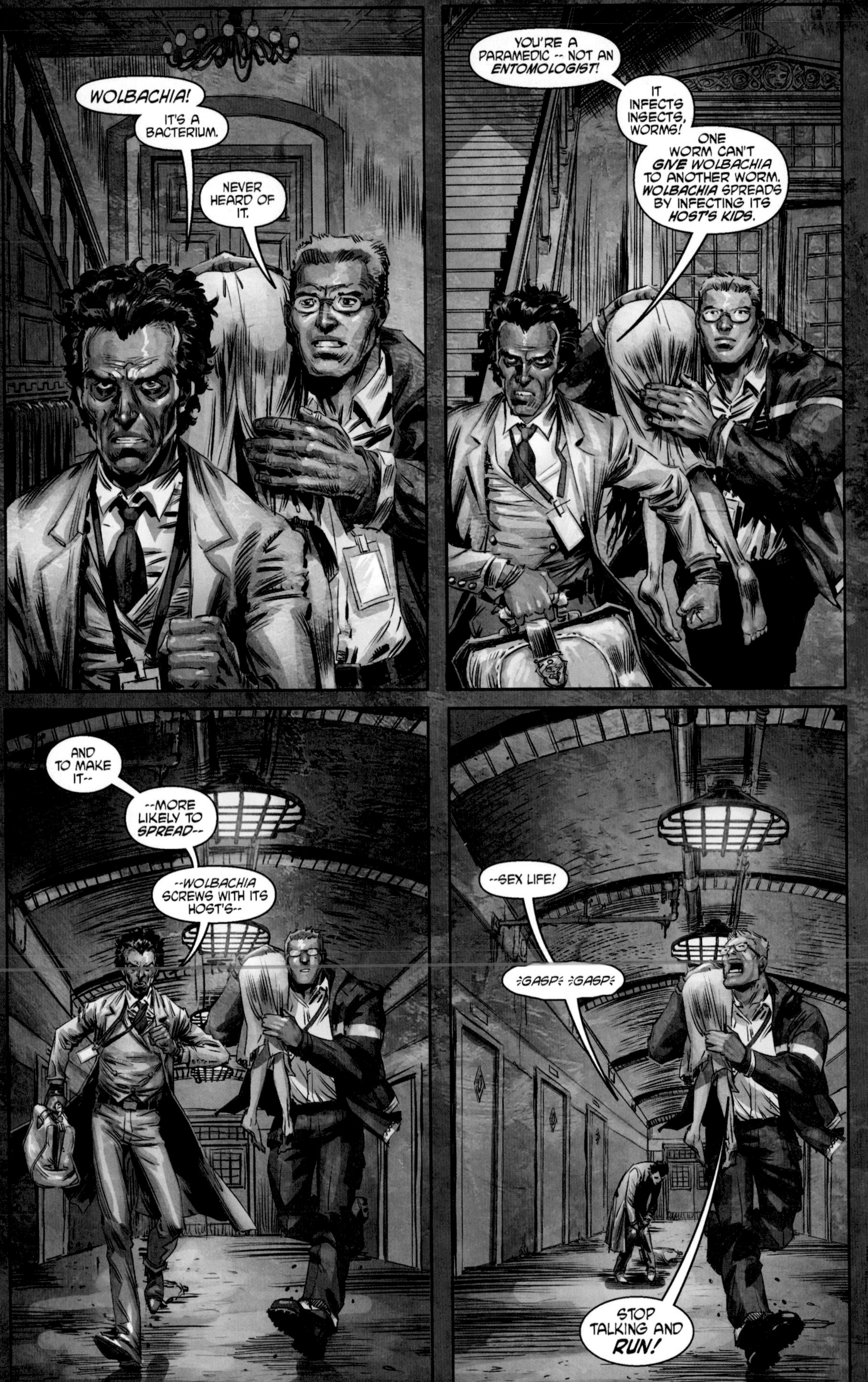
WOLBACHIA!
IT'S A BACTERIUM.
NEVER HEARD OF IT.
YOU'RE A PARAMEDIC -- NOT AN ENTOMOLOGIST!
IT INFECTS INSECTS, WORMS!
ONE WORM CAN'T GIVE WOLBACHIA TO ANOTHER WORM. WOLBACHIA SPREADS BY INFECTING ITS HOST'S KIDS.
AND TO MAKE IT--
--MORE LIKELY TO SPREAD--
--WOLBACHIA SCREWS WITH ITS HOST'S--
--SEX LIFE!
GASP GASP
STOP TALKING AND RUN!

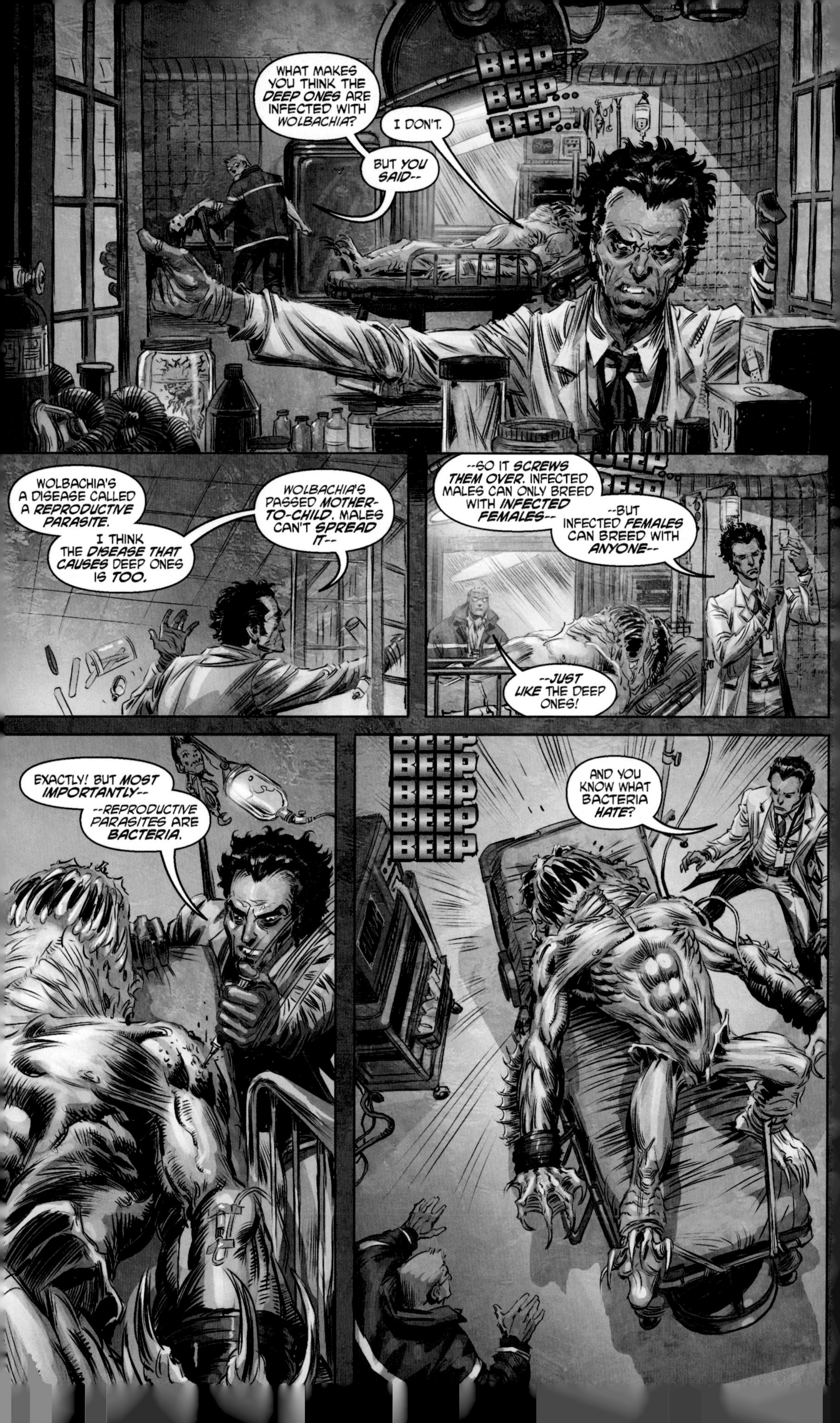
WHAT MAKES YOU THINK THE DEEP ONES ARE INFECTED WITH WOLBACHIA?
BEEP... BEEP... BEEP...
I DON'T.
BUT YOU SAID--
WOLBACHIA'S A DISEASE CALLED A REPRODUCTIVE PARASITE.
I THINK THE DISEASE THAT CAUSES DEEP ONES IS TOO.
WOLBACHIA'S PASSED MOTHER-TO-CHILD. MALES CAN'T SPREAD IT--
--SO IT SCREWS THEM OVER. INFECTED MALES CAN ONLY BREED WITH INFECTED FEMALES--
--BUT INFECTED FEMALES CAN BREED WITH ANYONE--
--JUST LIKE THE DEEP ONES!
EXACTLY! BUT MOST IMPORTANTLY--
--REPRODUCTIVE PARASITES ARE BACTERIA.
BEEP BEEP BEEP BEEP
AND YOU KNOW WHAT BACTERIA HATE?

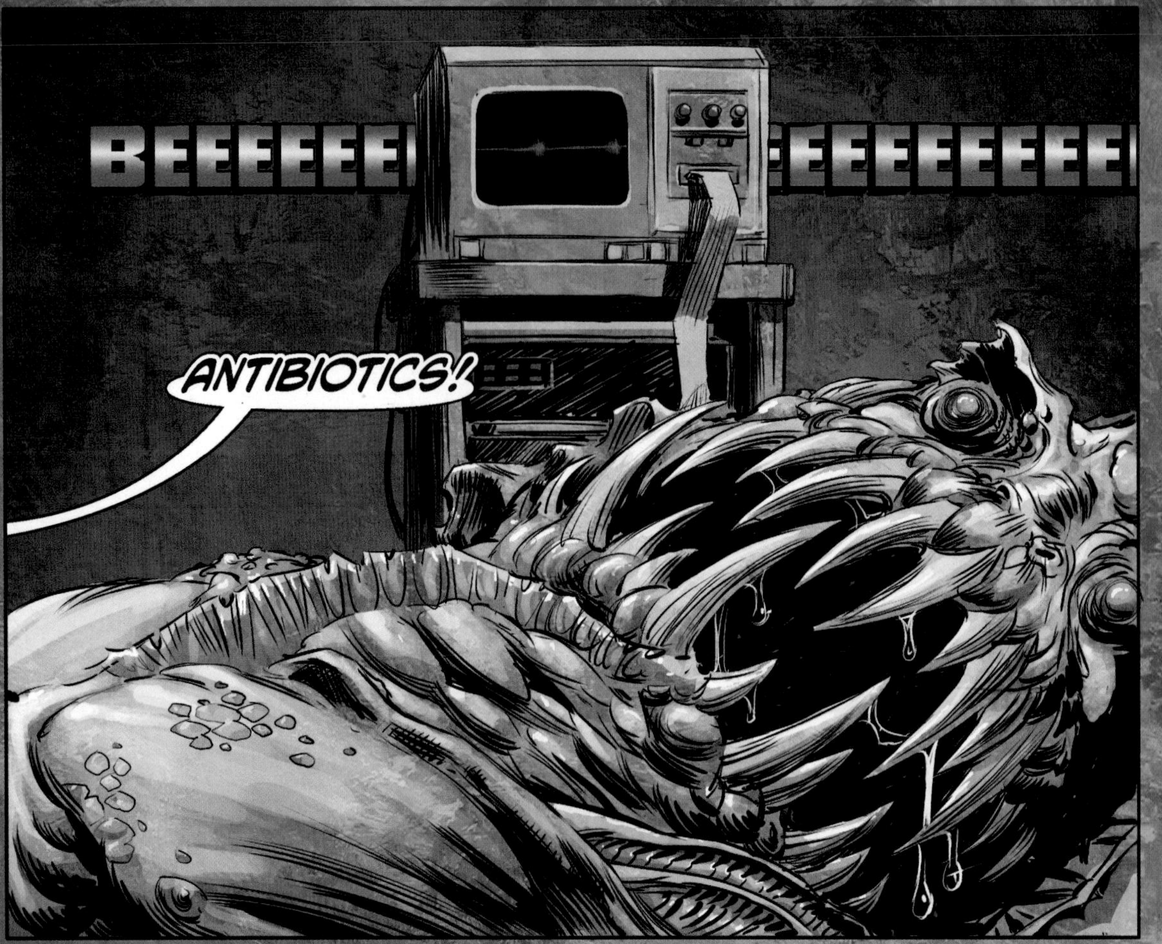

BEEEEEEEEEEEEEEEEEEEE
ANTIBIOTICS!

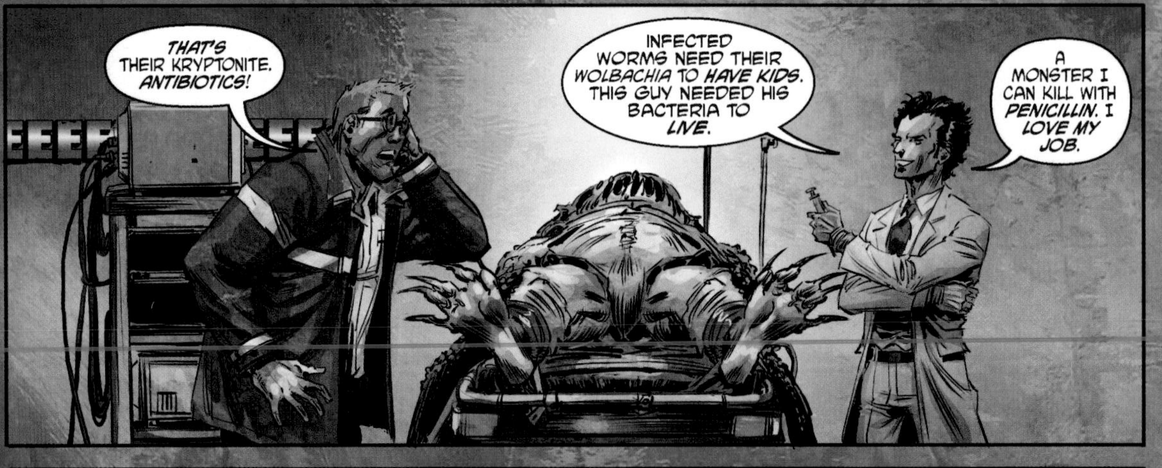

EEEE
THAT'S THEIR KRYPTONITE. ANTIBIOTICS!
INFECTED WORMS NEED THEIR WOLBACHIA TO HAVE KIDS. THIS GUY NEEDED HIS BACTERIA TO LIVE.
A MONSTER I CAN KILL WITH PENICILLIN. I LOVE MY JOB.

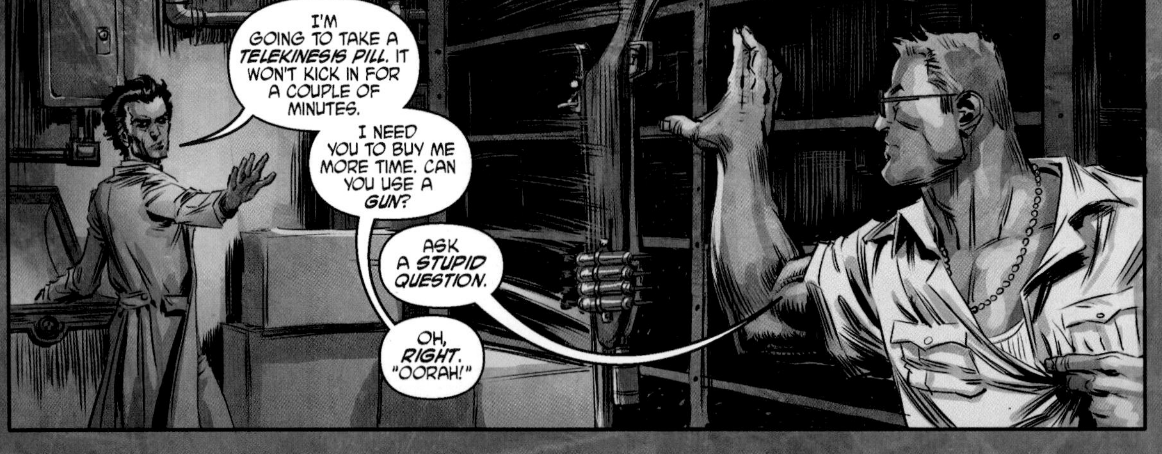

I'M GOING TO TAKE A TELEKINESIS PILL. IT WON'T KICK IN FOR A COUPLE OF MINUTES.
I NEED YOU TO BUY ME MORE TIME. CAN YOU USE A GUN?
ASK A STUPID QUESTION.
OH, RIGHT. "OORAH!"

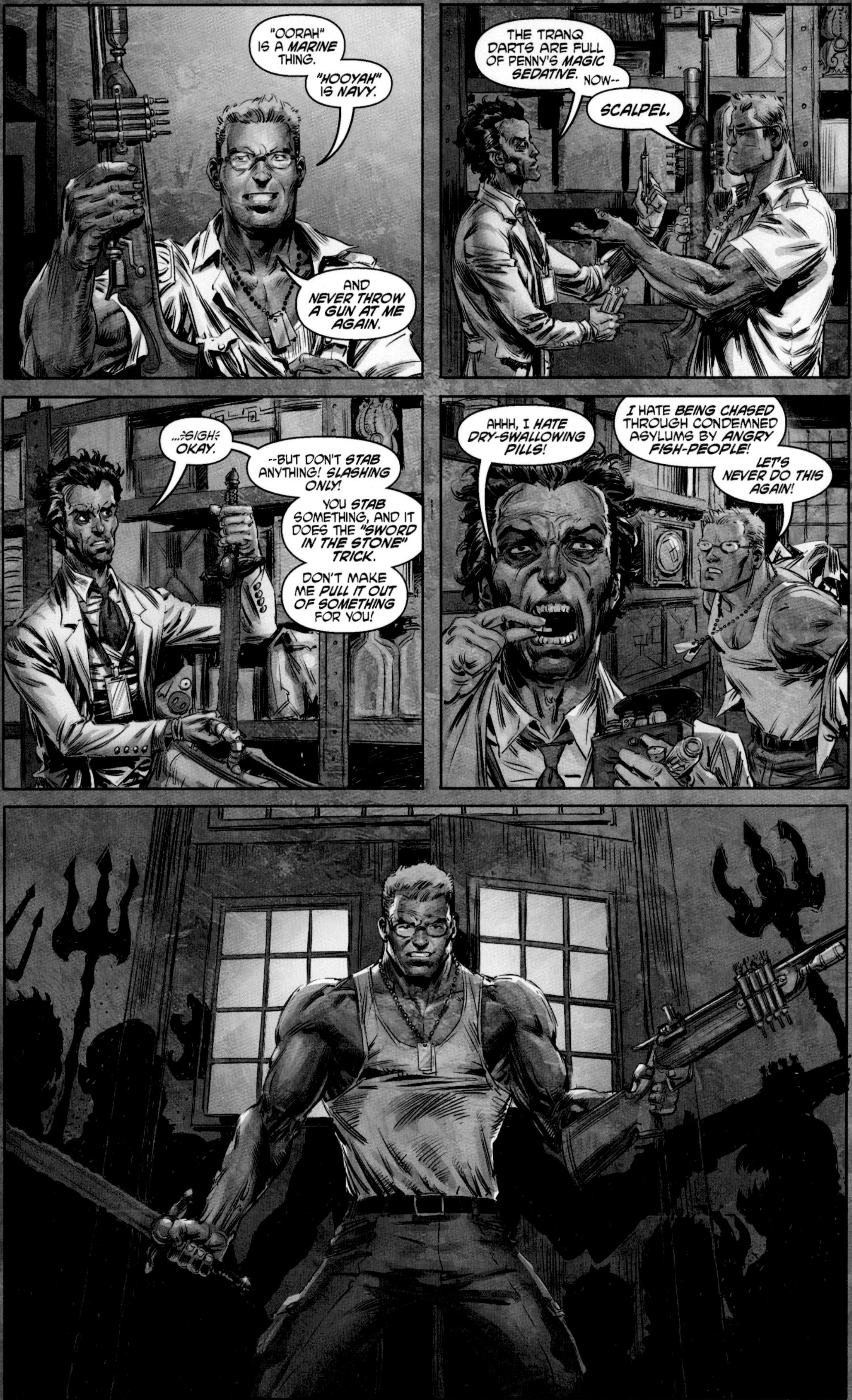
"OORAH" IS A MARINE THING.
"HOOYAH" IS NAVY.
AND NEVER THROW A GUN AT ME AGAIN.
THE TRANQ DARTS ARE FULL OF PENNY'S MAGIC SEDATIVE. NOW--
SCALPEL.
...SIGH... OKAY.
--BUT DON'T STAB ANYTHING! SLASHING ONLY!
YOU STAB SOMETHING, AND IT DOES THE "SWORD IN THE STONE" TRICK.
DON'T MAKE ME PULL IT OUT OF SOMETHING FOR YOU!
AHHH, I HATE DRY-SWALLOWING PILLS!
I HATE BEING CHASED THROUGH CONDEMNED ASYLUMS BY ANGRY FISH-PEOPLE!
LET'S NEVER DO THIS AGAIN!

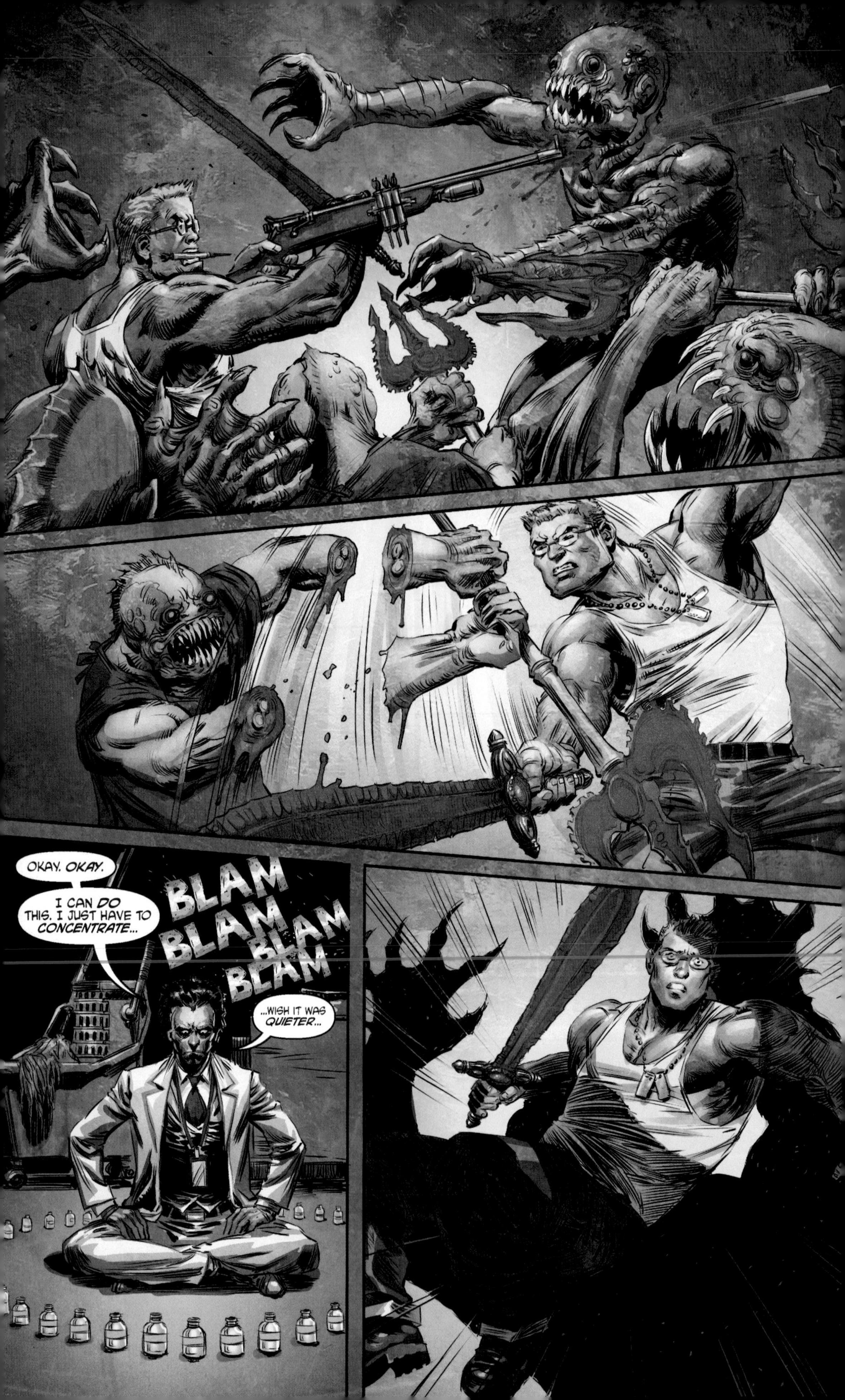
OKAY. OKAY.
I CAN DO THIS. I JUST HAVE TO CONCENTRATE...
BLAM BLAM BLAM BLAM
...WISH IT WAS QUIETER...

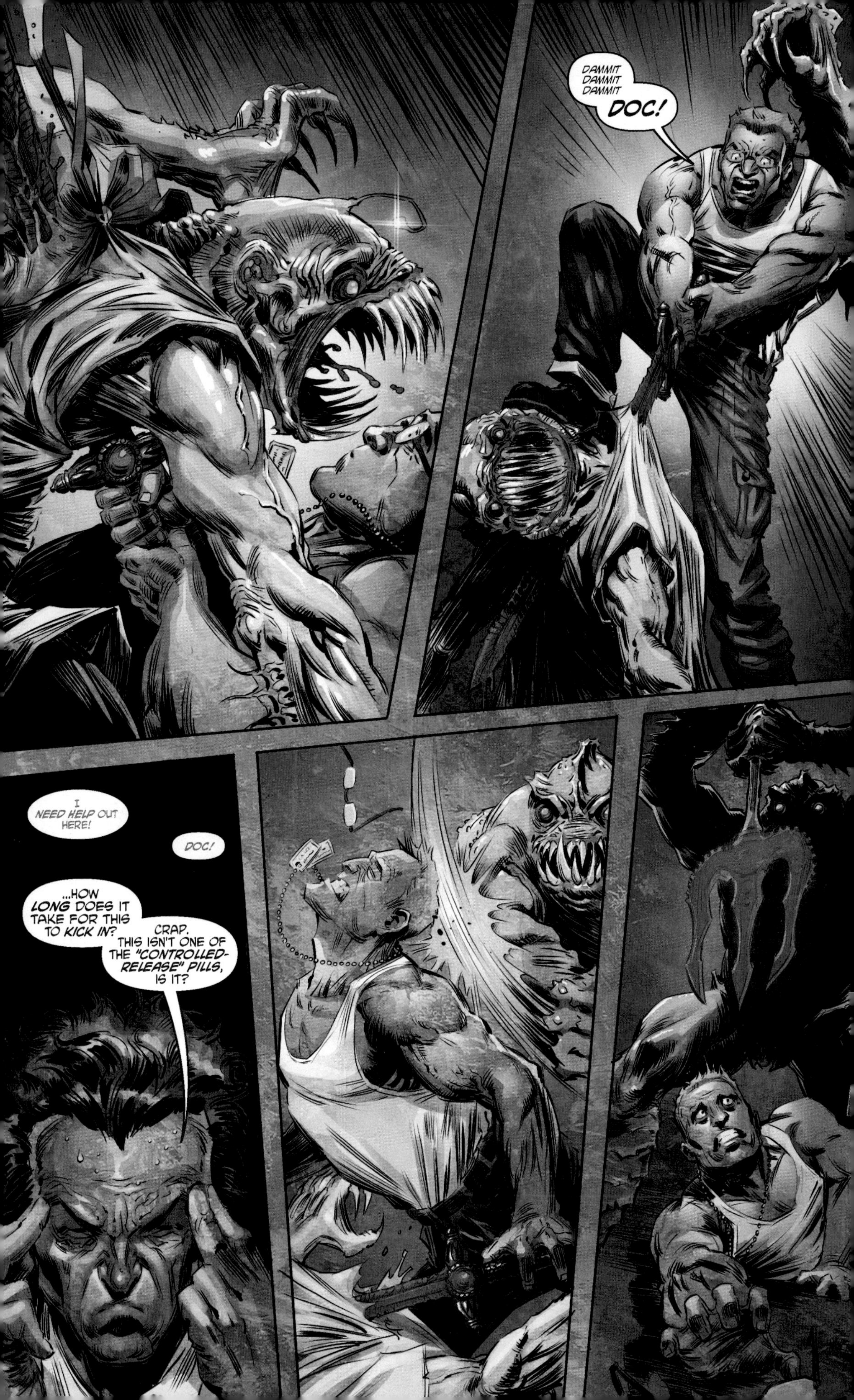
DAMMIT DAMMIT DAMMIT
DOC!
I NEED HELP OUT HERE!
DOC!
...HOW LONG DOES IT TAKE FOR THIS TO KICK IN?
CRAP. THIS ISN'T ONE OF THE "CONTROLLED-RELEASE" PILLS, IS IT?

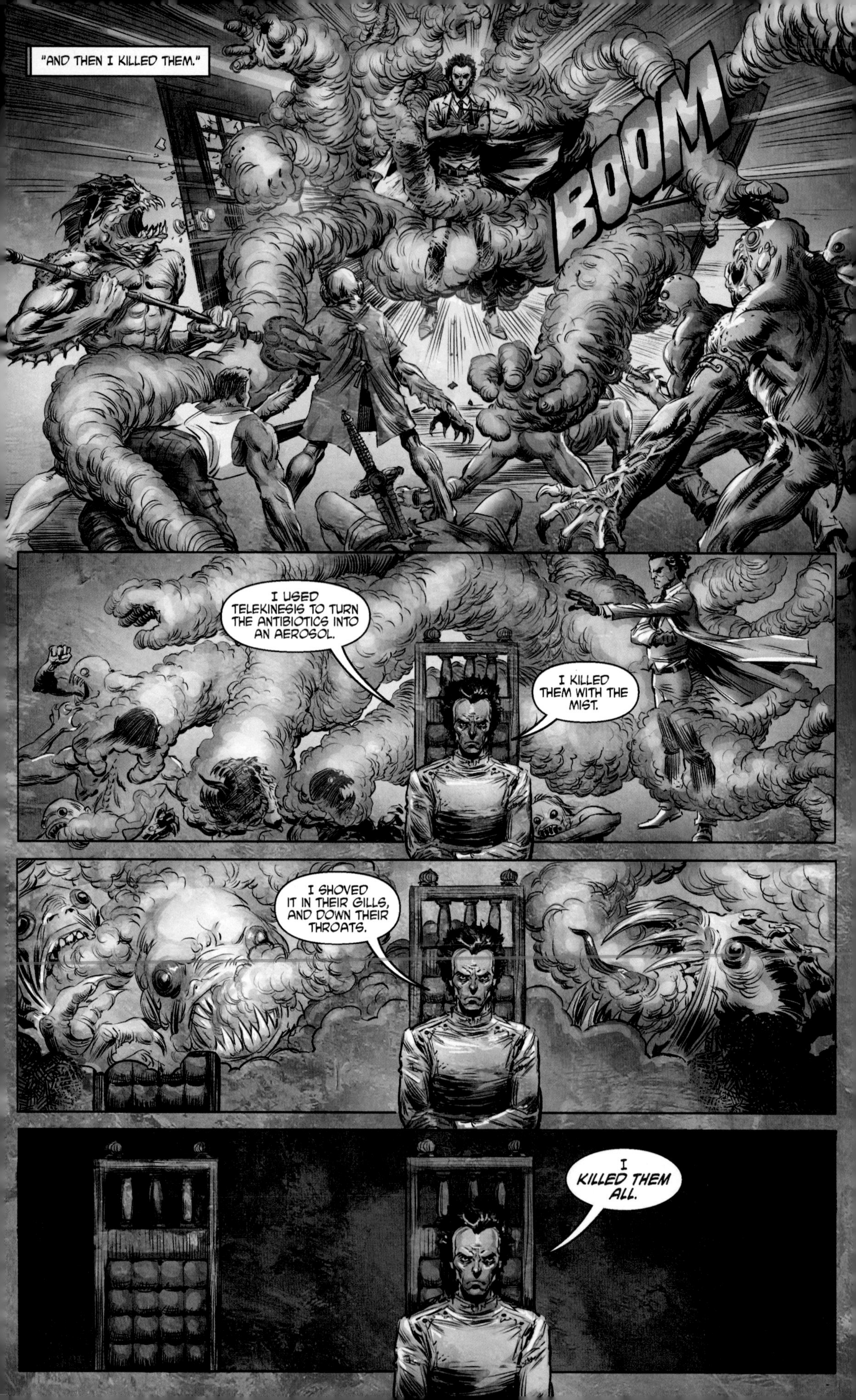
"AND THEN I KILLED THEM."
BOOM
I USED TELEKINESIS TO TURN THE ANTIBIOTICS INTO AN AEROSOL.
I KILLED THEM WITH THE MIST.
I SHOVED IT IN THEIR GILLS, AND DOWN THEIR THROATS.
I KILLED THEM ALL.

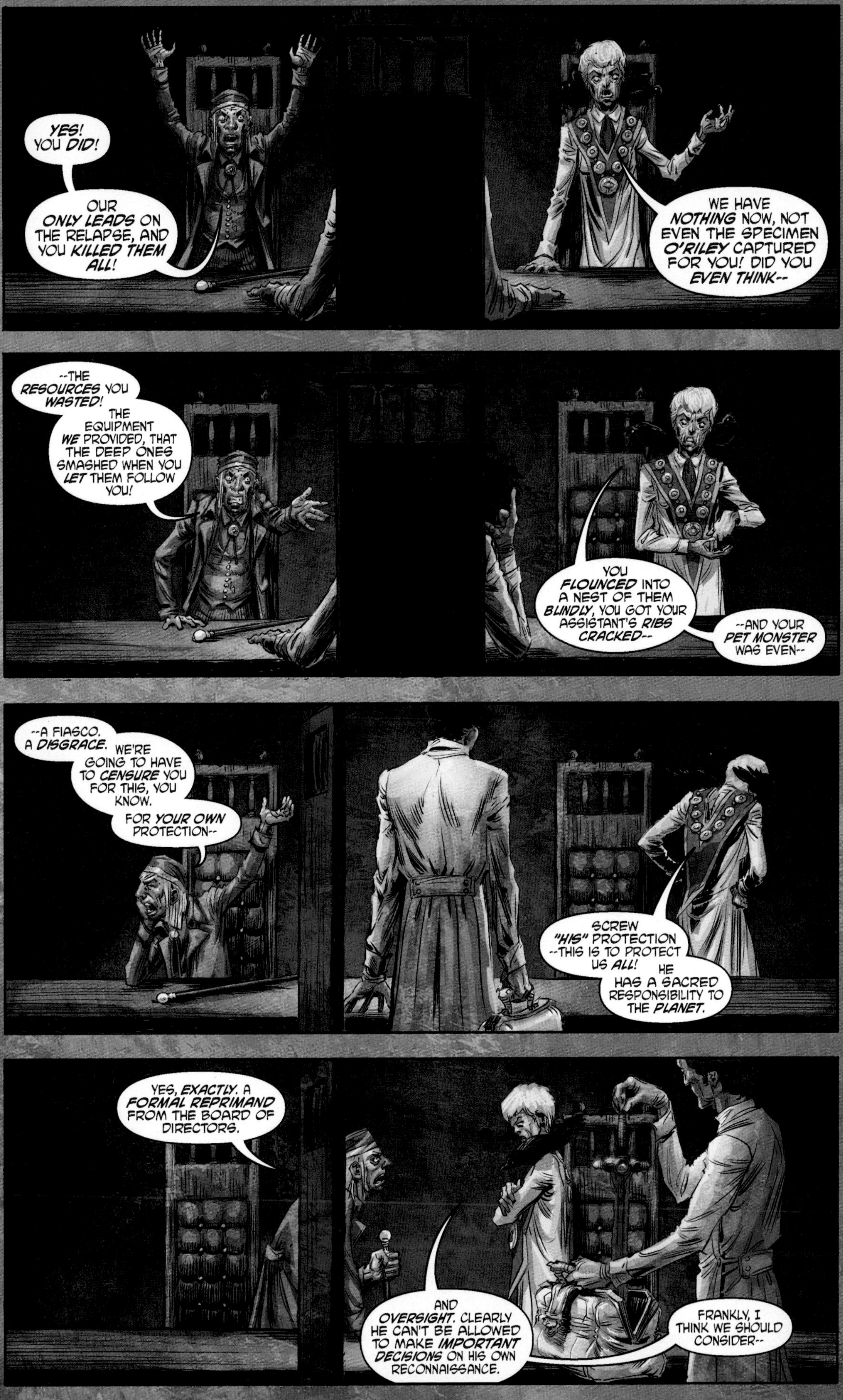
YES! YOU DID!
OUR ONLY LEADS ON THE RELAPSE, AND YOU KILLED THEM ALL!
WE HAVE NOTHING NOW, NOT EVEN THE SPECIMEN O'RILEY CAPTURED FOR YOU! DID YOU EVEN THINK--
--THE RESOURCES YOU WASTED!
THE EQUIPMENT WE PROVIDED, THAT THE DEEP ONES SMASHED WHEN YOU LET THEM FOLLOW YOU!
YOU FLOUNCED INTO A NEST OF THEM BLINDLY, YOU GOT YOUR ASSISTANT'S RIBS CRACKED--
--AND YOUR PET MONSTER WAS EVEN--
--A FIASCO. A DISGRACE.
WE'RE GOING TO HAVE TO CENSURE YOU FOR THIS, YOU KNOW.
FOR YOUR OWN PROTECTION--
SCREW "HIS" PROTECTION --THIS IS TO PROTECT US ALL!
HE HAS A SACRED RESPONSIBILITY TO THE PLANET.
YES, EXACTLY. A FORMAL REPRIMAND FROM THE BOARD OF DIRECTORS.
AND OVERSIGHT. CLEARLY HE CAN'T BE ALLOWED TO MAKE IMPORTANT DECISIONS ON HIS OWN RECONNAISSANCE.
FRANKLY, I THINK WE SHOULD CONSIDER--

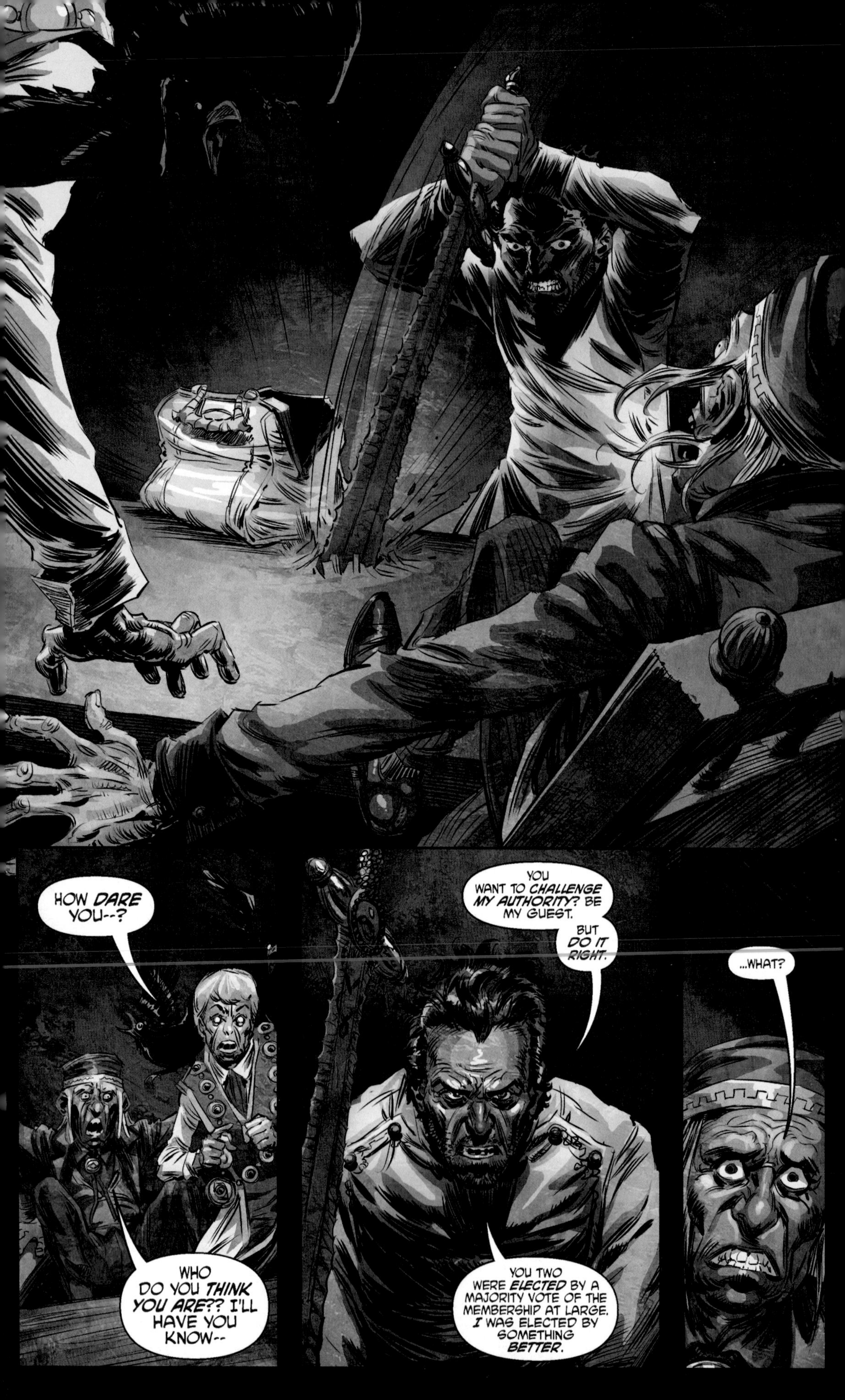
HOW DARE YOU--?
WHO DO YOU THINK YOU ARE?? I'LL HAVE YOU KNOW--
YOU WANT TO CHALLENGE MY AUTHORITY? BE MY GUEST.
BUT DO IT RIGHT.
YOU TWO WERE ELECTED BY A MAJORITY VOTE OF THE MEMBERSHIP AT LARGE. I WAS ELECTED BY SOMETHING BETTER.
...WHAT?

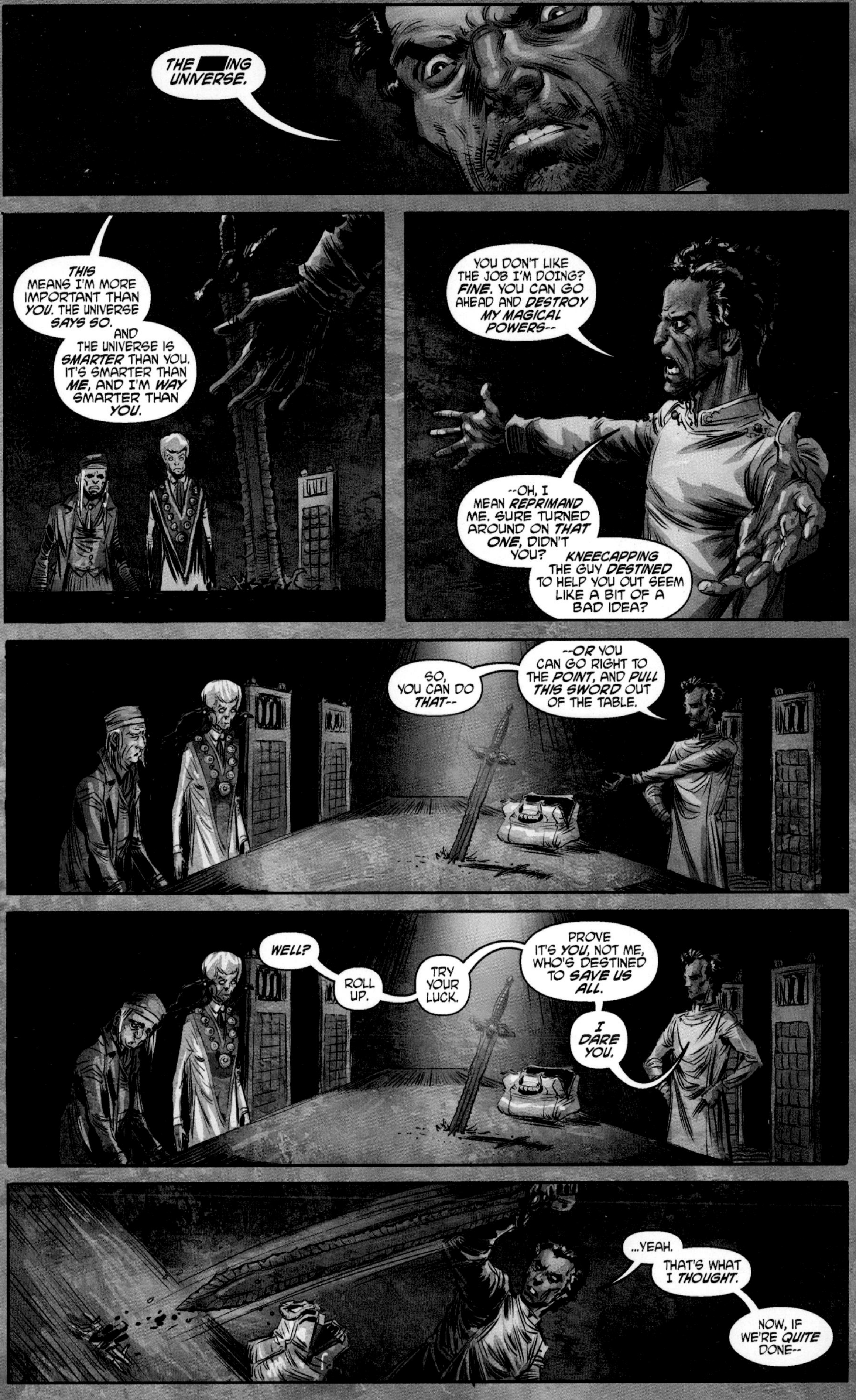
THE [redacted]ING UNIVERSE.
THIS MEANS I'M MORE IMPORTANT THAN YOU. THE UNIVERSE SAYS SO.
AND THE UNIVERSE IS SMARTER THAN YOU. IT'S SMARTER THAN ME, AND I'M WAY SMARTER THAN YOU.
YOU DON'T LIKE THE JOB I'M DOING? FINE. YOU CAN GO AHEAD AND DESTROY MY MAGICAL POWERS--
--OH, I MEAN REPRIMAND ME. SURE TURNED AROUND ON THAT ONE, DIDN'T YOU?
KNEECAPPING THE GUY DESTINED TO HELP YOU OUT SEEM LIKE A BIT OF A BAD IDEA?
SO, YOU CAN DO THAT--
--OR YOU CAN GO RIGHT TO THE POINT, AND PULL THIS SWORD OUT OF THE TABLE.
WELL?
ROLL UP.
TRY YOUR LUCK.
PROVE IT'S YOU, NOT ME, WHO'S DESTINED TO SAVE US ALL.
I DARE YOU.
...YEAH.
THAT'S WHAT I THOUGHT.
NOW, IF WE'RE QUITE DONE--

--I'VE GOT *APOCALYPSES* TO PREVENT.

"SO HOW'D *THAT* WORK OUT FOR YOU?"

WELL, I'M NOT GETTING MY MAGIC POWERS *BURNED OUT OF ME* WITH RED-HOT BRANDING IRONS.

SO *THAT'S* NICE.

WHETHERVEIN OPENLY HATES ME NOW. I'M SURE THAT'LL MAKE THINGS *INTERESTING* SOMEDAY -- HE'S GOT A LOT OF PULL WITH THE *BOARD OF DIRECTORS.*

AND CATHERINIAN... SEEMS TO HAVE A *CRUSH* ON ME. FRANKLY, I DON'T KNOW WHAT COLUMN TO PUT *THAT* IN. HOW ARE WE FEELING TODAY, PENNY?

I'M *HUNGRY.*

THAT'S MY GIRL.

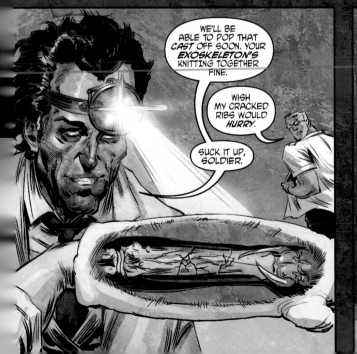

WE'LL BE ABLE TO POP THAT *CAST OFF* SOON. YOUR *EXOSKELETON'S* KNITTING TOGETHER FINE.

WISH MY CRACKED RIBS WOULD *HURRY.*

SUCK IT UP, SOLDIER.

IT'LL BE GOOD TO HAVE HER BACK TO *NORMAL*-- --*RUNNING AWAY* IN EMERGENCIES AND TRYING TO *EAT THE PATIENTS.*

HEY, SHE *DID* COME BACK!

PENNY'S... A *LONG-TERM* CASE. LOTS OF QUESTIONS THERE -- AND LOTS TO *LEARN,* I THINK.

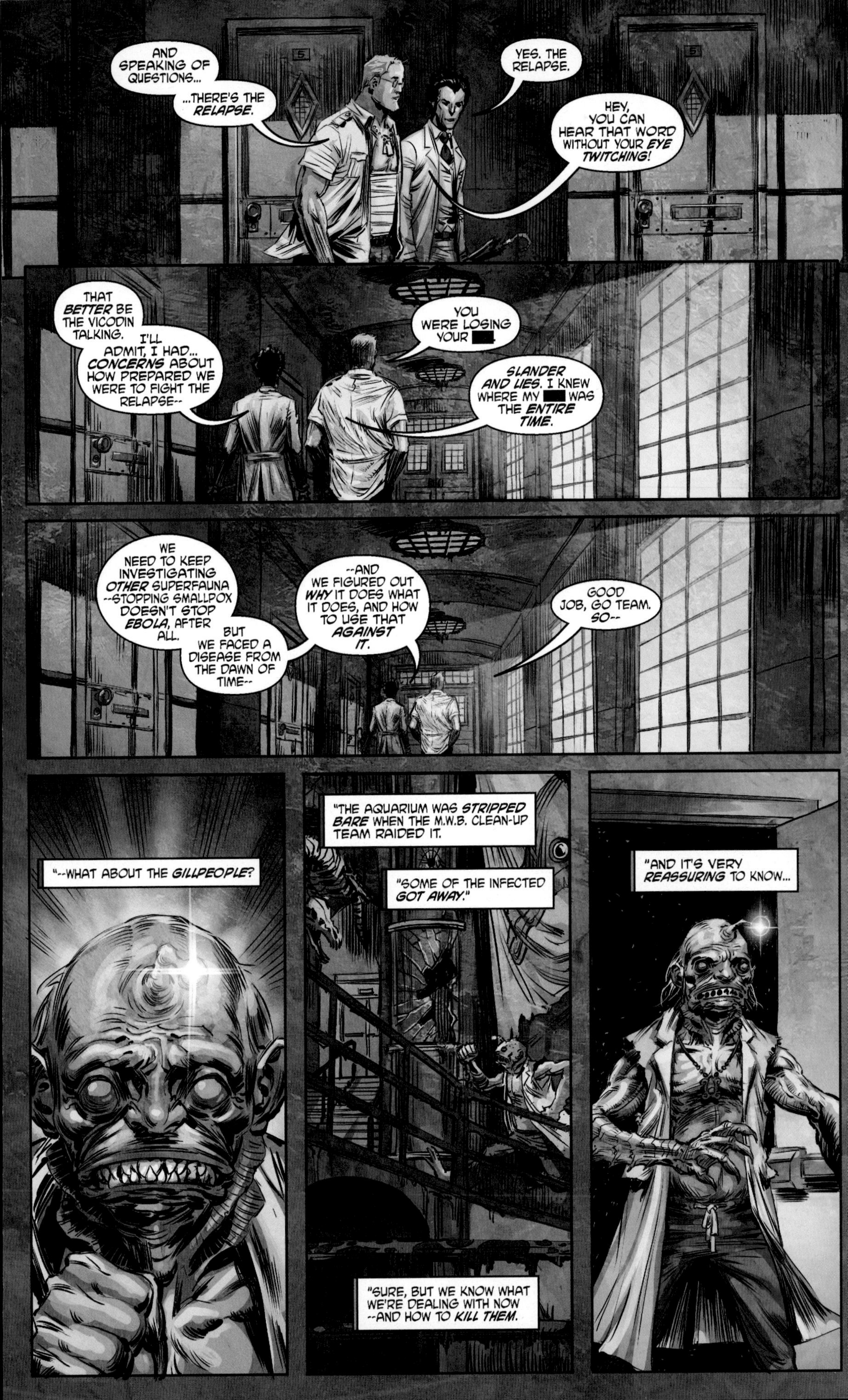

AND SPEAKING OF QUESTIONS...
...THERE'S THE *RELAPSE*.
YES. THE RELAPSE.
HEY, YOU CAN HEAR THAT WORD WITHOUT YOUR *EYE TWITCHING*!
THAT *BETTER* BE THE VICODIN TALKING.
YOU WERE LOSING YOUR [redacted].
I'LL ADMIT, I HAD... *CONCERNS* ABOUT HOW PREPARED WE WERE TO FIGHT THE RELAPSE--
SLANDER AND LIES. I KNEW WHERE MY [redacted] WAS THE *ENTIRE TIME*.
WE NEED TO KEEP INVESTIGATING *OTHER* SUPERFAUNA --STOPPING SMALLPOX DOESN'T STOP *EBOLA*, AFTER ALL.
BUT WE FACED A DISEASE FROM THE DAWN OF TIME--
--AND WE FIGURED OUT *WHY* IT DOES WHAT IT DOES, AND HOW TO USE THAT *AGAINST IT*.
GOOD JOB, GO TEAM. *SO*--
"--WHAT ABOUT THE *GILLPEOPLE*?
"THE AQUARIUM WAS *STRIPPED BARE* WHEN THE M.W.B. CLEAN-UP TEAM RAIDED IT.
"SOME OF THE INFECTED *GOT AWAY*."
"SURE, BUT WE KNOW WHAT WE'RE DEALING WITH NOW --AND HOW TO *KILL THEM*.
"AND IT'S VERY *REASSURING* TO KNOW...

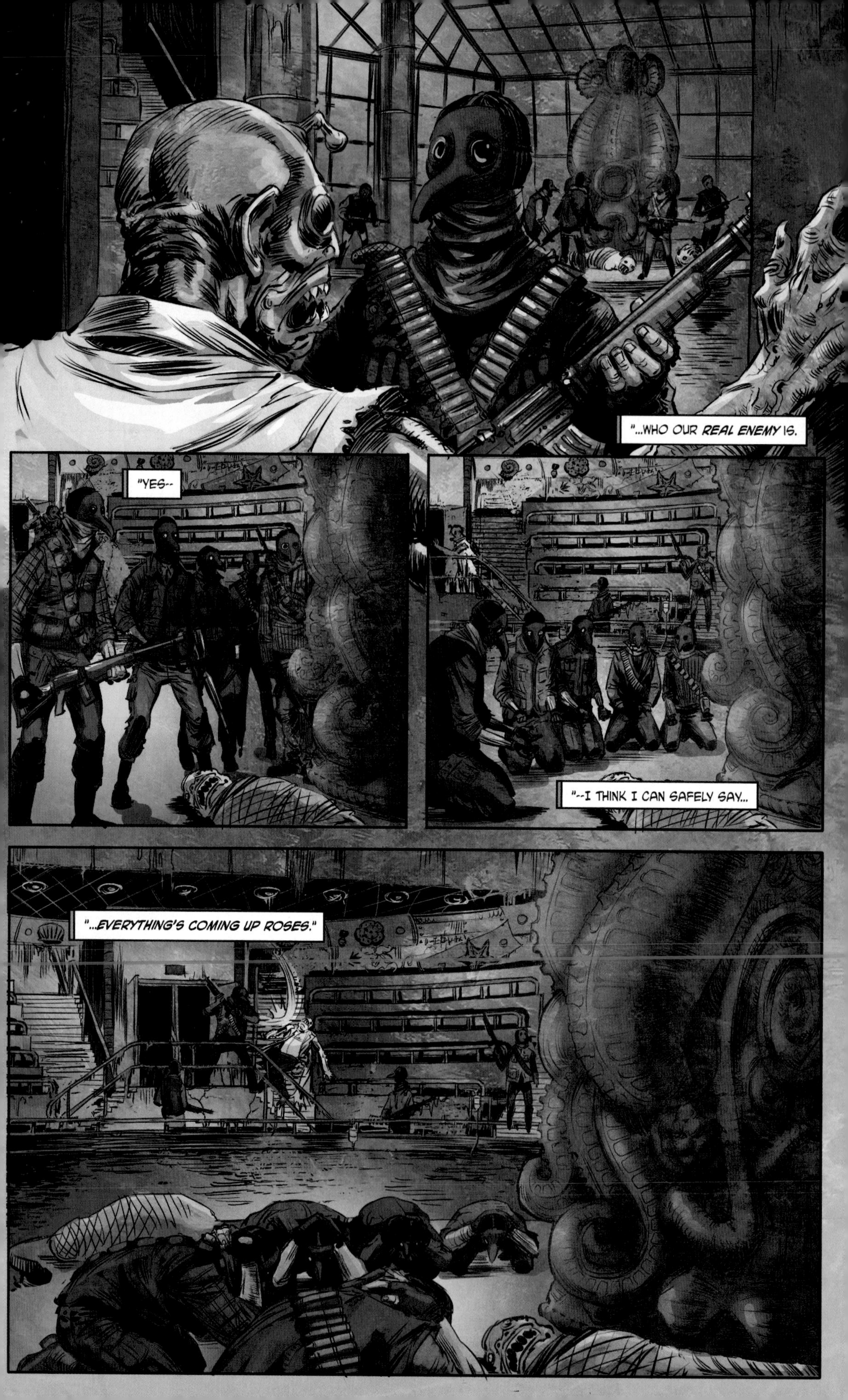
"...WHO OUR REAL ENEMY IS.
"YES--
"--I THINK I CAN SAFELY SAY...
"...EVERYTHING'S COMING UP ROSES."

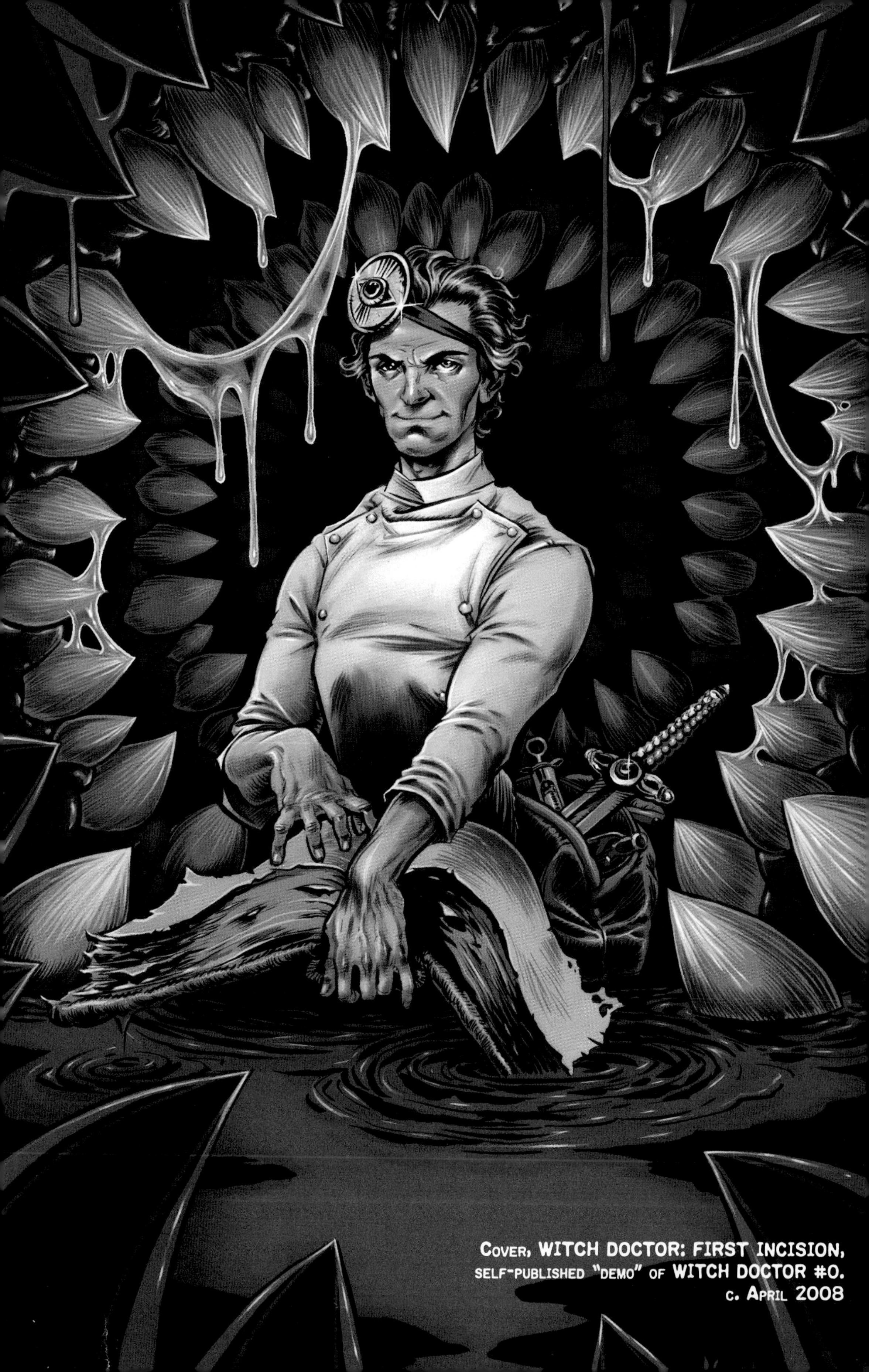

Cover, WITCH DOCTOR: FIRST INCISION,
self-published "demo" of WITCH DOCTOR #0.
c. April 2008

CHAPTER ZERO

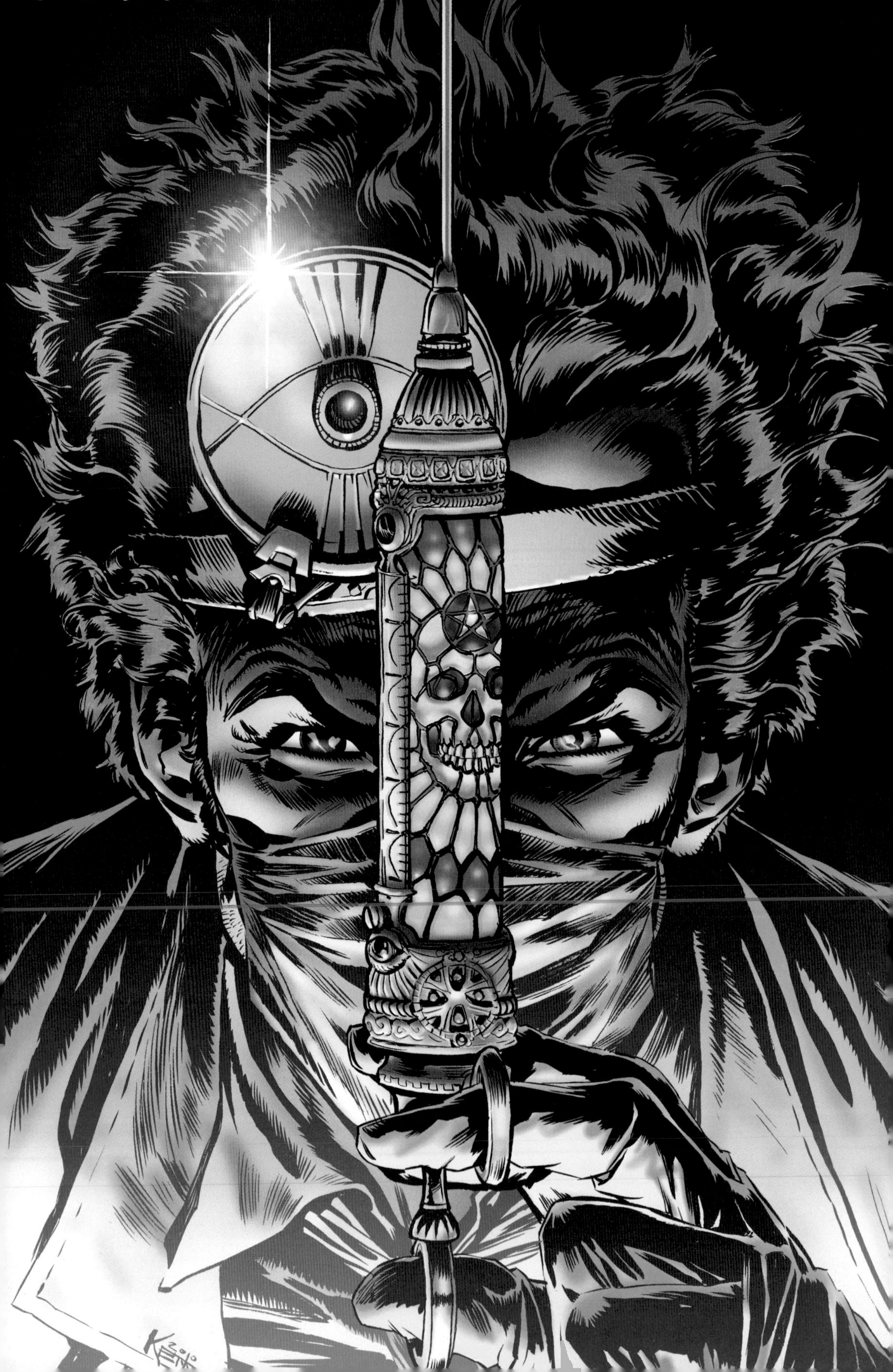

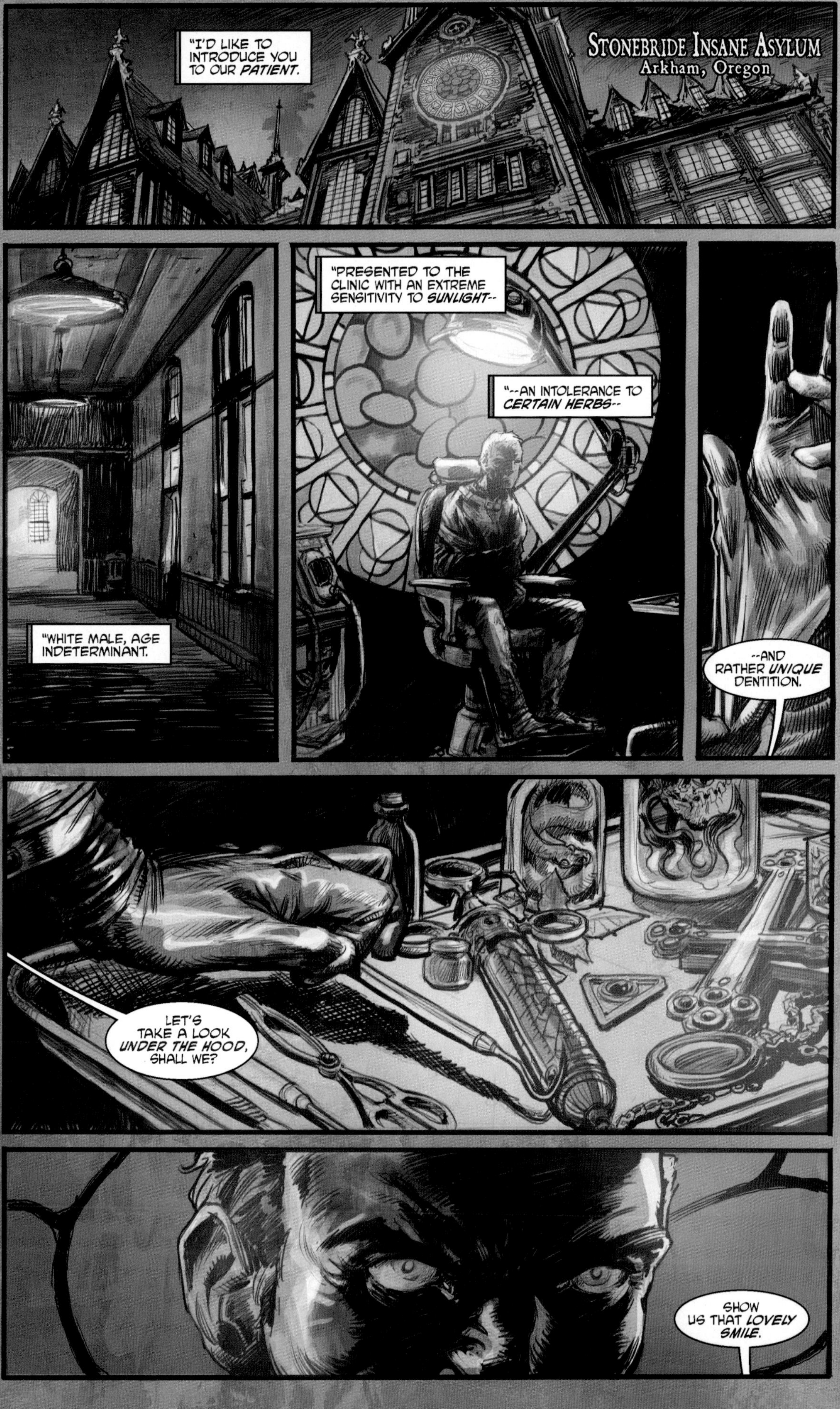

"I'D LIKE TO INTRODUCE YOU TO OUR *PATIENT*.
STONEBRIDE INSANE ASYLUM
Arkham, Oregon
"WHITE MALE, AGE INDETERMINANT.
"PRESENTED TO THE CLINIC WITH AN EXTREME SENSITIVITY TO *SUNLIGHT*--
"--AN INTOLERANCE TO *CERTAIN HERBS*--
--AND RATHER *UNIQUE* DENTITION.
LET'S TAKE A LOOK *UNDER THE HOOD*, SHALL WE?
SHOW US THAT *LOVELY SMILE*.

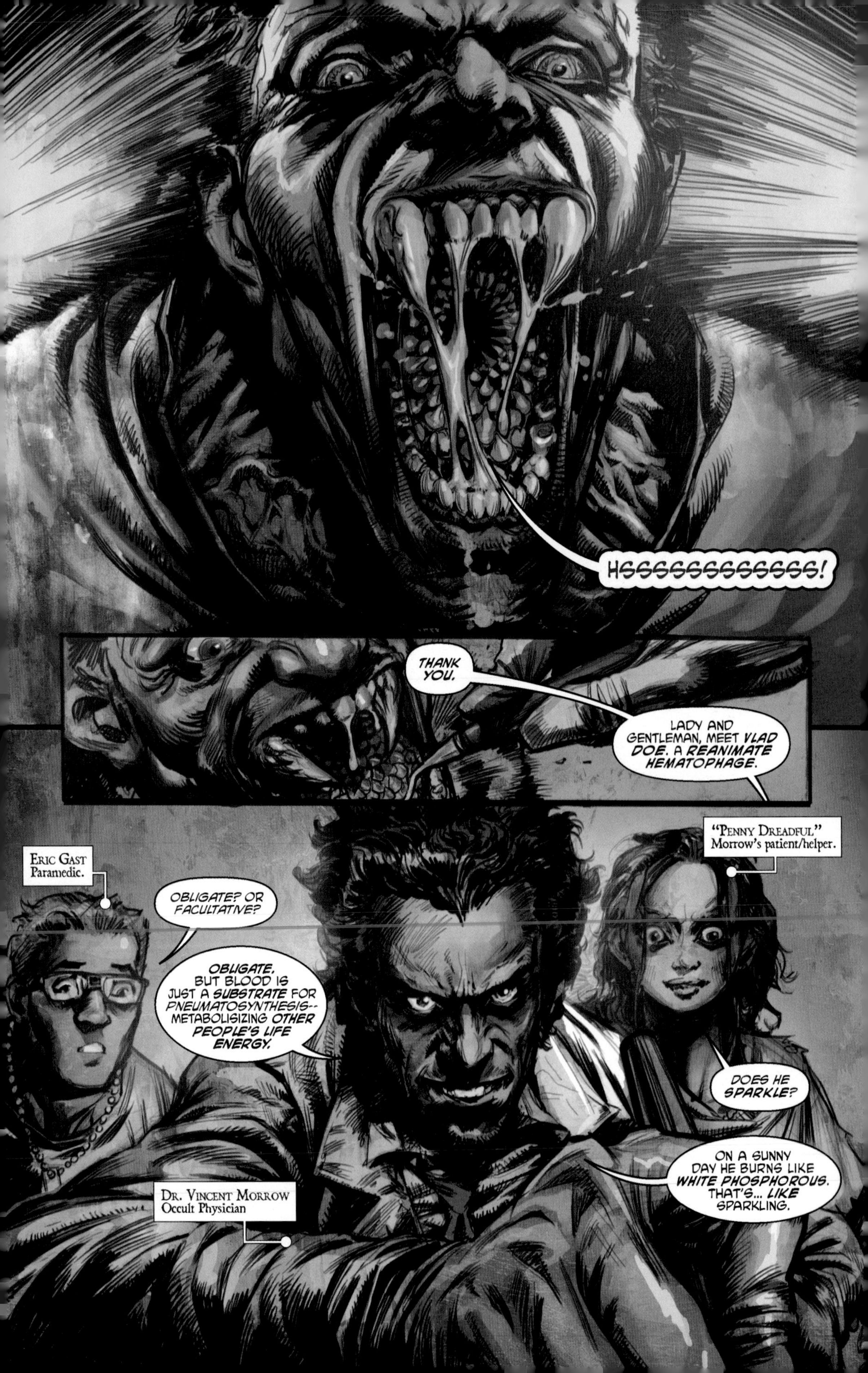
HSSSSSSSSSSSS!
THANK YOU.
LADY AND GENTLEMAN, MEET VLAD DOE. A REANIMATE HEMATOPHAGE.
ERIC GAST Paramedic.
"PENNY DREADFUL" Morrow's patient/helper.
OBLIGATE? OR FACULTATIVE?
OBLIGATE. BUT BLOOD IS JUST A SUBSTRATE FOR PNEUMATOSYNTHESIS-- METABOLISIZING OTHER PEOPLE'S LIFE ENERGY.
DOES HE SPARKLE?
ON A SUNNY DAY HE BURNS LIKE WHITE PHOSPHOROUS. THAT'S... LIKE SPARKLING.
DR. VINCENT MORROW Occult Physician

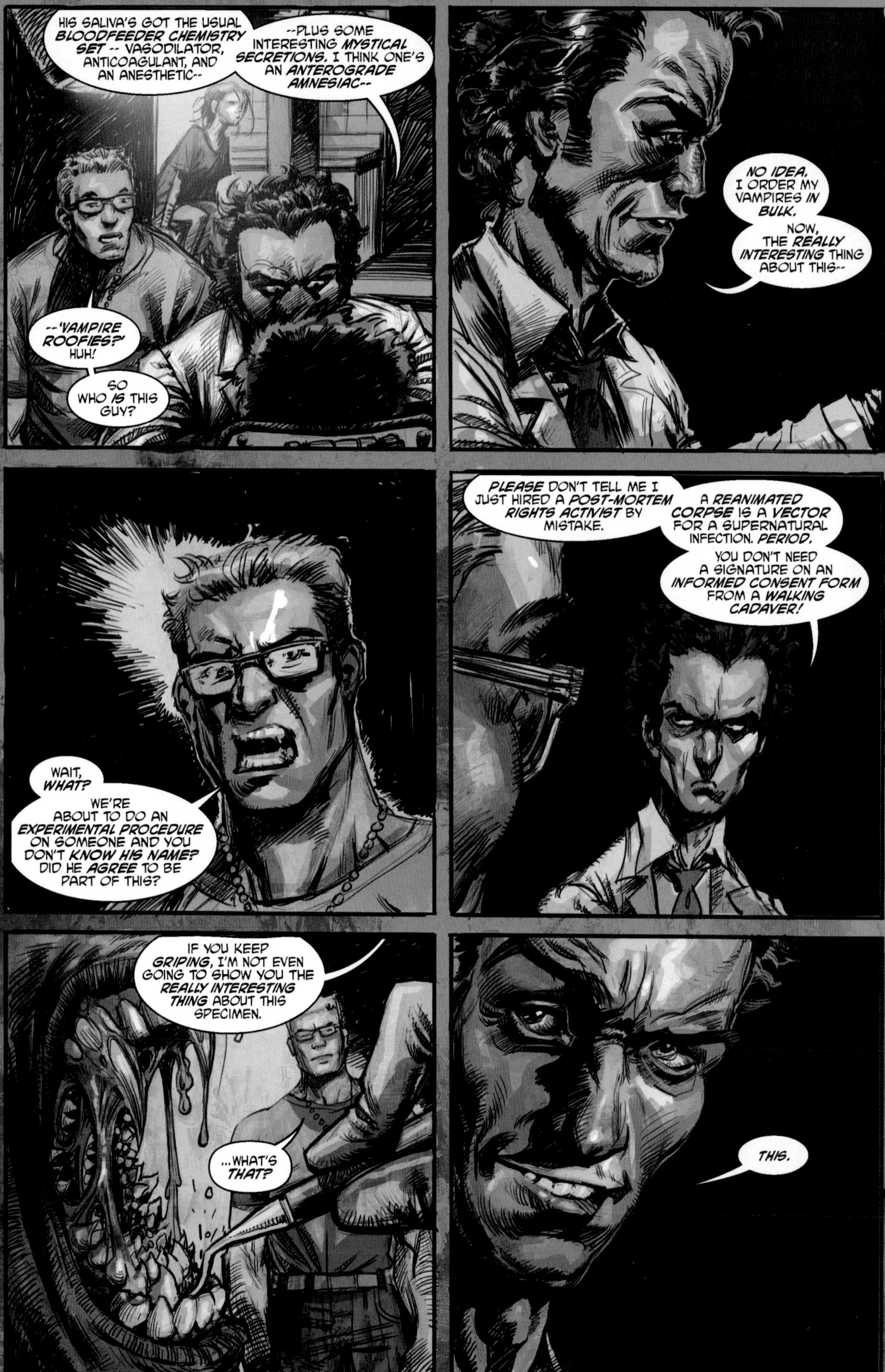
HIS SALIVA'S GOT THE USUAL BLOODFEEDER CHEMISTRY SET -- VASODILATOR, ANTICOAGULANT, AND AN ANESTHETIC--
--PLUS SOME INTERESTING MYSTICAL SECRETIONS. I THINK ONE'S AN ANTEROGRADE AMNESIAC--
--'VAMPIRE ROOFIES?' HUH!
SO WHO IS THIS GUY?
NO IDEA. I ORDER MY VAMPIRES IN BULK.
NOW, THE REALLY INTERESTING THING ABOUT THIS--
WAIT, WHAT?
WE'RE ABOUT TO DO AN EXPERIMENTAL PROCEDURE ON SOMEONE AND YOU DON'T KNOW HIS NAME? DID HE AGREE TO BE PART OF THIS?
PLEASE DON'T TELL ME I JUST HIRED A POST-MORTEM RIGHTS ACTIVIST BY MISTAKE.
A REANIMATED CORPSE IS A VECTOR FOR A SUPERNATURAL INFECTION. PERIOD.
YOU DON'T NEED A SIGNATURE ON AN INFORMED CONSENT FORM FROM A WALKING CADAVER!
IF YOU KEEP GRIPING, I'M NOT EVEN GOING TO SHOW YOU THE REALLY INTERESTING THING ABOUT THIS SPECIMEN.
...WHAT'S THAT?
THIS.

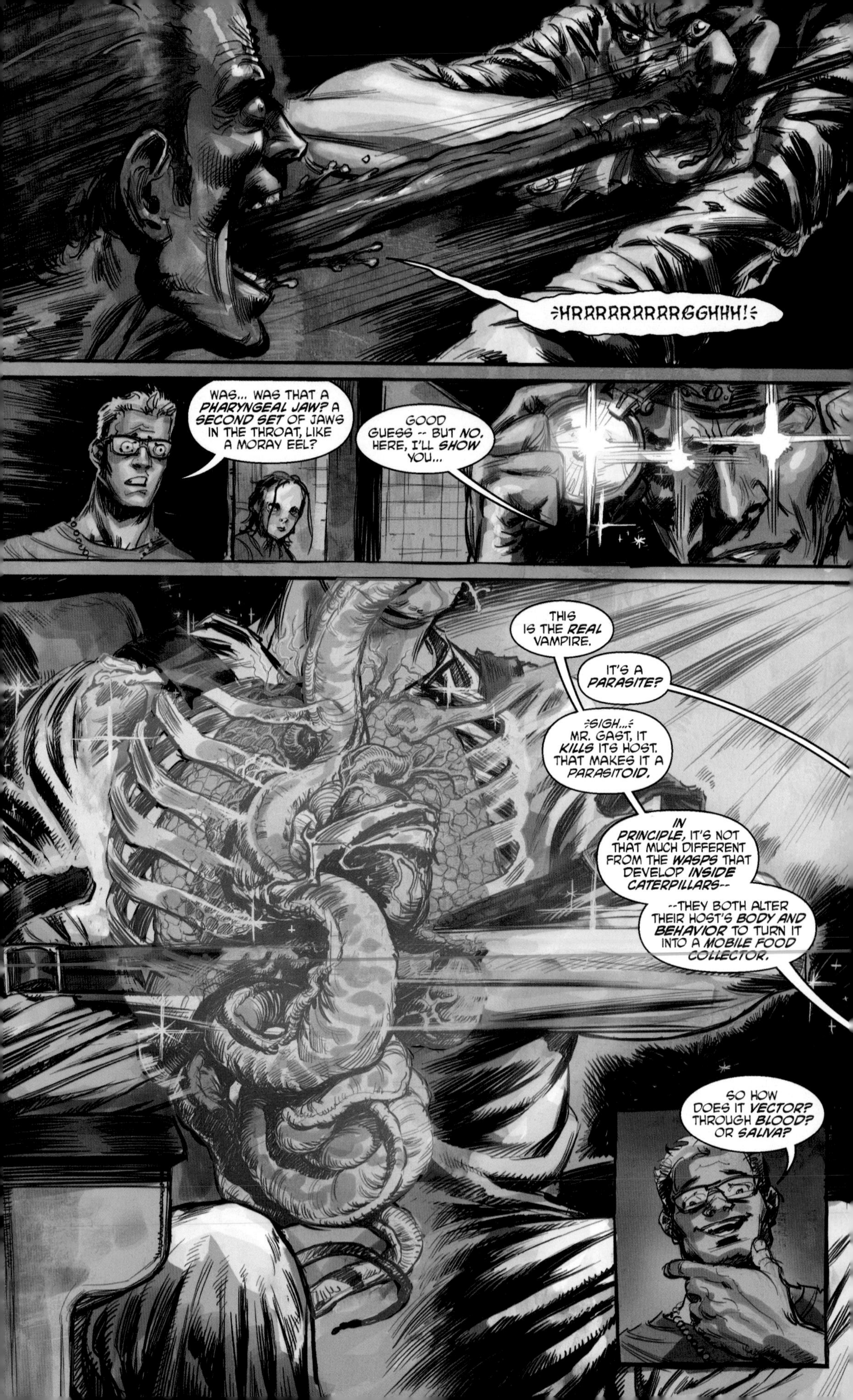

HRRRRRRRRRGGHHH!
WAS... WAS THAT A PHARYNGEAL JAW? A SECOND SET OF JAWS IN THE THROAT, LIKE A MORAY EEL?
GOOD GUESS -- BUT NO. HERE, I'LL SHOW YOU...
THIS IS THE REAL VAMPIRE.
IT'S A PARASITE?
SIGH... MR. GAST, IT KILLS ITS HOST. THAT MAKES IT A PARASITOID.
IN PRINCIPLE, IT'S NOT THAT MUCH DIFFERENT FROM THE WASPS THAT DEVELOP INSIDE CATERPILLARS--
--THEY BOTH ALTER THEIR HOST'S BODY AND BEHAVIOR TO TURN IT INTO A MOBILE FOOD COLLECTOR.
SO HOW DOES IT VECTOR? THROUGH BLOOD? OR SALIVA?

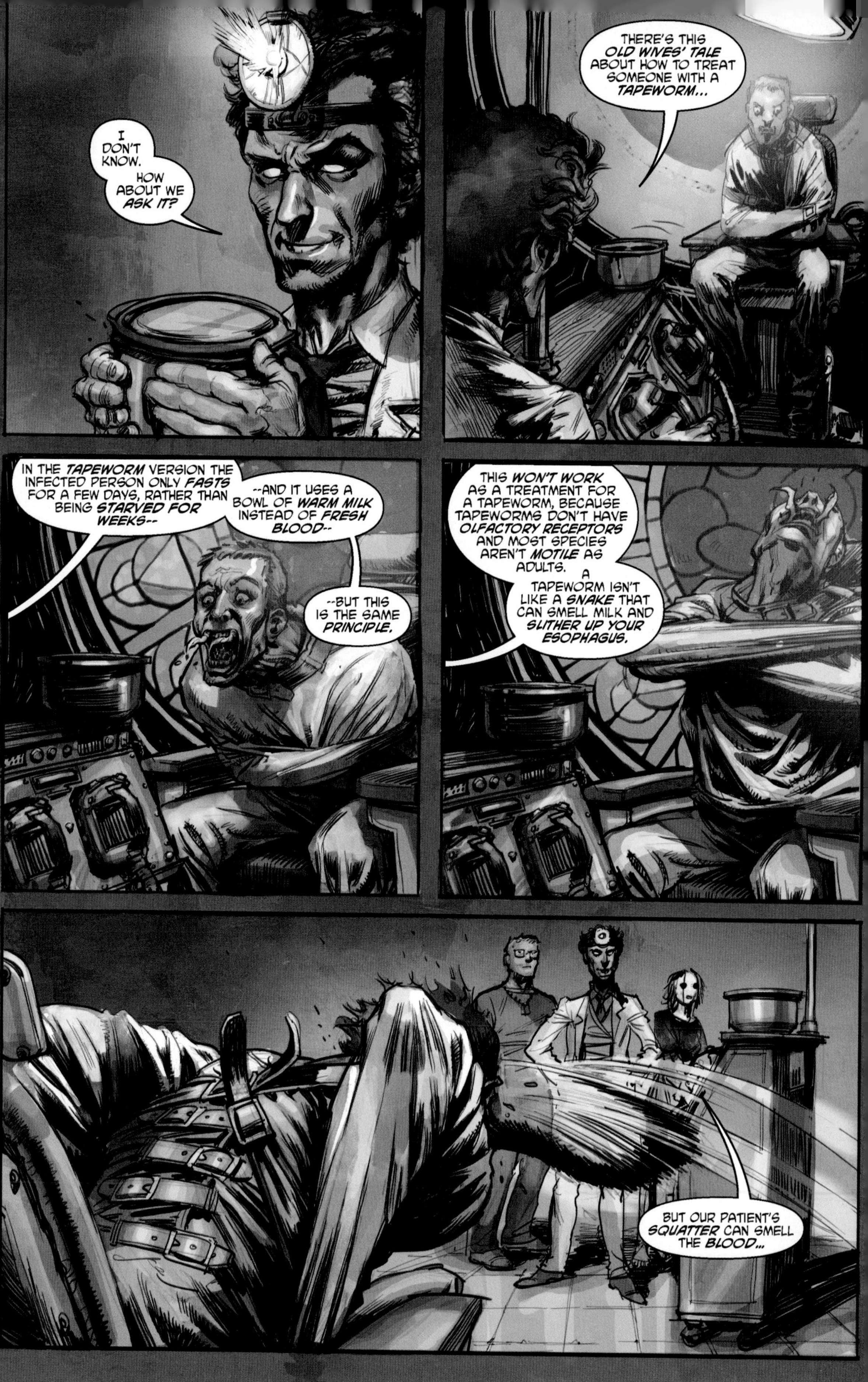
I DON'T KNOW. HOW ABOUT WE ASK IT?
THERE'S THIS OLD WIVES' TALE ABOUT HOW TO TREAT SOMEONE WITH A TAPEWORM...
IN THE TAPEWORM VERSION THE INFECTED PERSON ONLY FASTS FOR A FEW DAYS, RATHER THAN BEING STARVED FOR WEEKS--
--AND IT USES A BOWL OF WARM MILK INSTEAD OF FRESH BLOOD--
--BUT THIS IS THE SAME PRINCIPLE.
THIS WON'T WORK AS A TREATMENT FOR A TAPEWORM, BECAUSE TAPEWORMS DON'T HAVE OLFACTORY RECEPTORS AND MOST SPECIES AREN'T MOTILE AS ADULTS.
A TAPEWORM ISN'T LIKE A SNAKE THAT CAN SMELL MILK AND SLITHER UP YOUR ESOPHAGUS.
BUT OUR PATIENT'S SQUATTER CAN SMELL THE BLOOD...

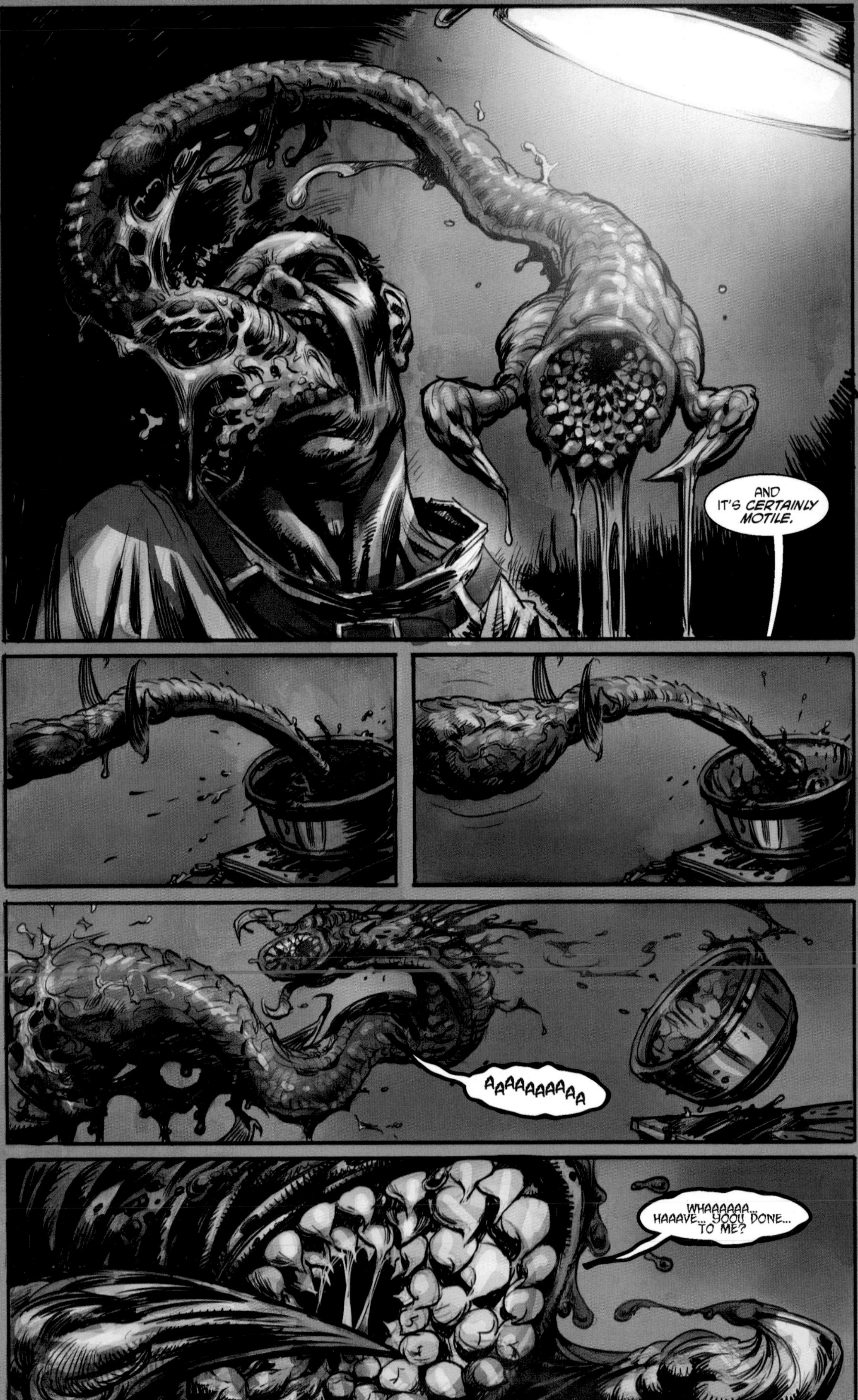
AND IT'S CERTAINLY MOTILE.
AAAAAAAAAA
WHAAAAAA... HAAAVE... YOOU DONE... TO ME?

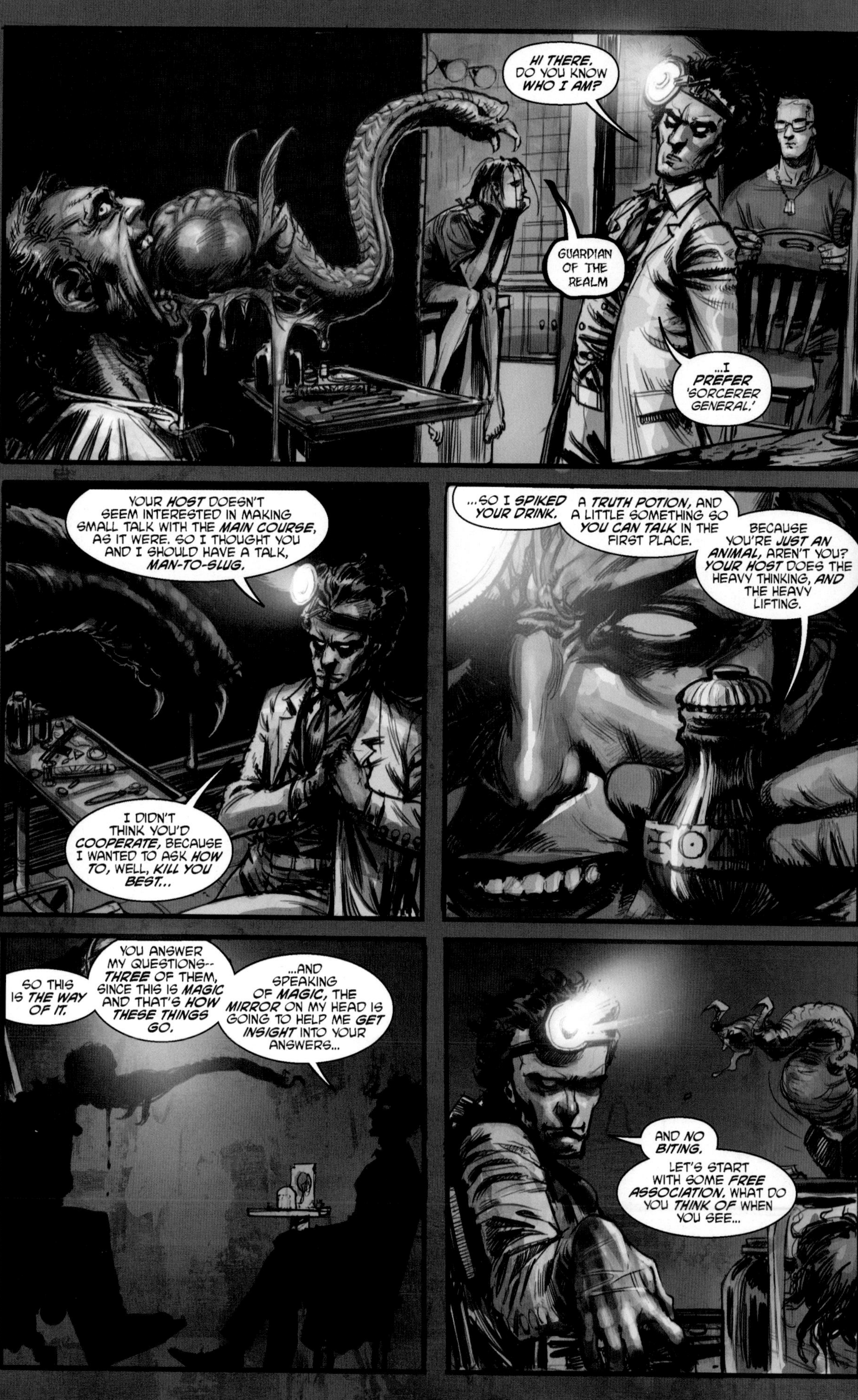
HI THERE. DO YOU KNOW WHO I AM?
GUARDIAN OF THE REALM
...I PREFER 'SORCERER GENERAL.'
YOUR HOST DOESN'T SEEM INTERESTED IN MAKING SMALL TALK WITH THE MAIN COURSE, AS IT WERE. SO I THOUGHT YOU AND I SHOULD HAVE A TALK, MAN-TO-SLUG.
I DIDN'T THINK YOU'D COOPERATE, BECAUSE I WANTED TO ASK HOW TO, WELL, KILL YOU BEST...
...SO I SPIKED YOUR DRINK.
A TRUTH POTION, AND A LITTLE SOMETHING SO YOU CAN TALK IN THE FIRST PLACE.
BECAUSE YOU'RE JUST AN ANIMAL, AREN'T YOU? YOUR HOST DOES THE HEAVY THINKING, AND THE HEAVY LIFTING.
SO THIS IS THE WAY OF IT.
YOU ANSWER MY QUESTIONS-- THREE OF THEM, SINCE THIS IS MAGIC AND THAT'S HOW THESE THINGS GO.
...AND SPEAKING OF MAGIC, THE MIRROR ON MY HEAD IS GOING TO HELP ME GET INSIGHT INTO YOUR ANSWERS...
AND NO BITING.
LET'S START WITH SOME FREE ASSOCIATION. WHAT DO YOU THINK OF WHEN YOU SEE...

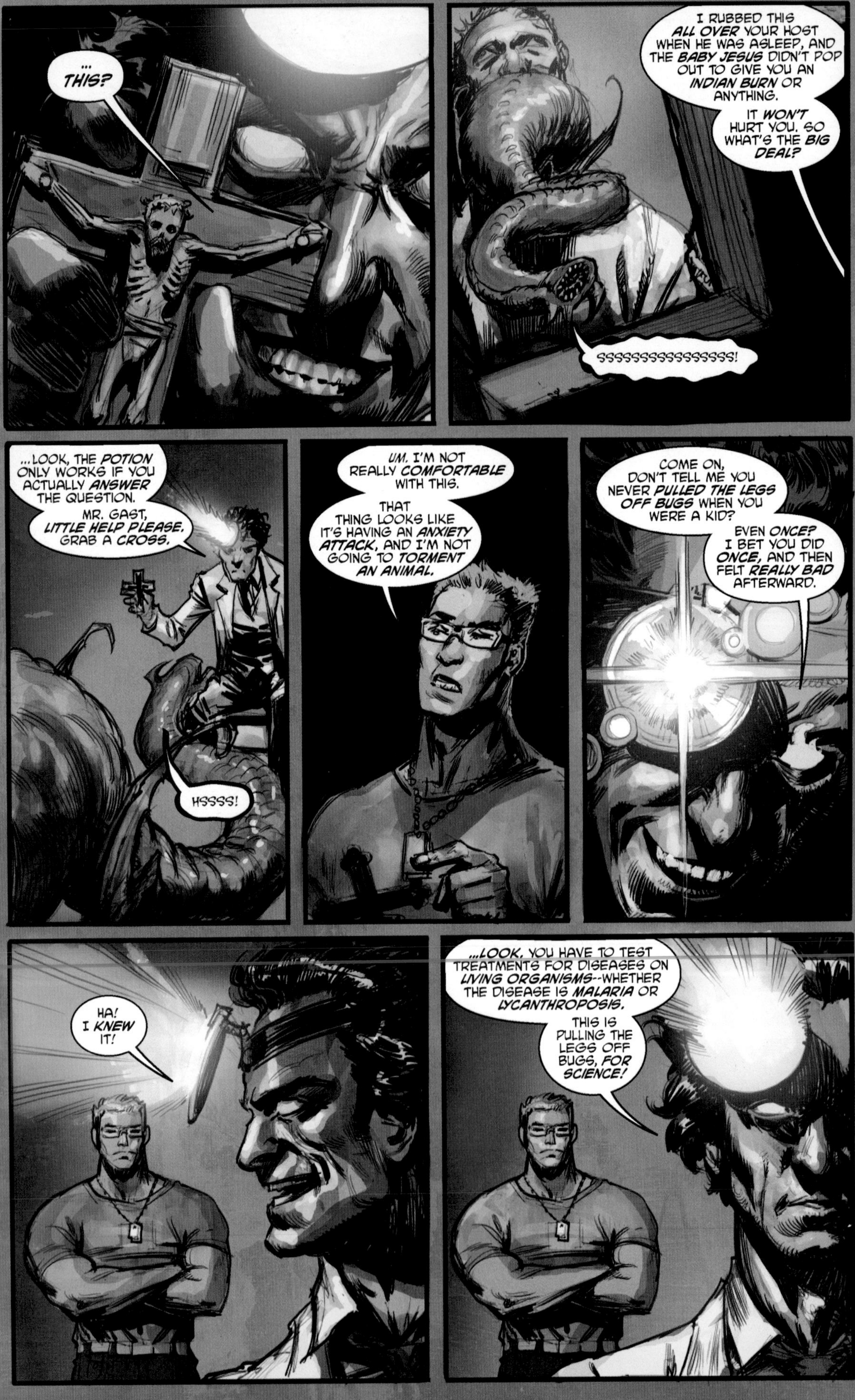
...THIS?
I RUBBED THIS ALL OVER YOUR HOST WHEN HE WAS ASLEEP, AND THE BABY JESUS DIDN'T POP OUT TO GIVE YOU AN INDIAN BURN OR ANYTHING.
IT WON'T HURT YOU. SO WHAT'S THE BIG DEAL?
SSSSSSSSSSSSSSSS!
...LOOK, THE POTION ONLY WORKS IF YOU ACTUALLY ANSWER THE QUESTION.
MR. GAST, LITTLE HELP PLEASE. GRAB A CROSS.
HSSSS!
UM. I'M NOT REALLY COMFORTABLE WITH THIS.
THAT THING LOOKS LIKE IT'S HAVING AN ANXIETY ATTACK, AND I'M NOT GOING TO TORMENT AN ANIMAL.
COME ON, DON'T TELL ME YOU NEVER PULLED THE LEGS OFF BUGS WHEN YOU WERE A KID?
EVEN ONCE? I BET YOU DID ONCE, AND THEN FELT REALLY BAD AFTERWARD.
HA! I KNEW IT!
...LOOK. YOU HAVE TO TEST TREATMENTS FOR DISEASES ON LIVING ORGANISMS--WHETHER THE DISEASE IS MALARIA OR LYCANTHROPOSIS.
THIS IS PULLING THE LEGS OFF BUGS, FOR SCIENCE!

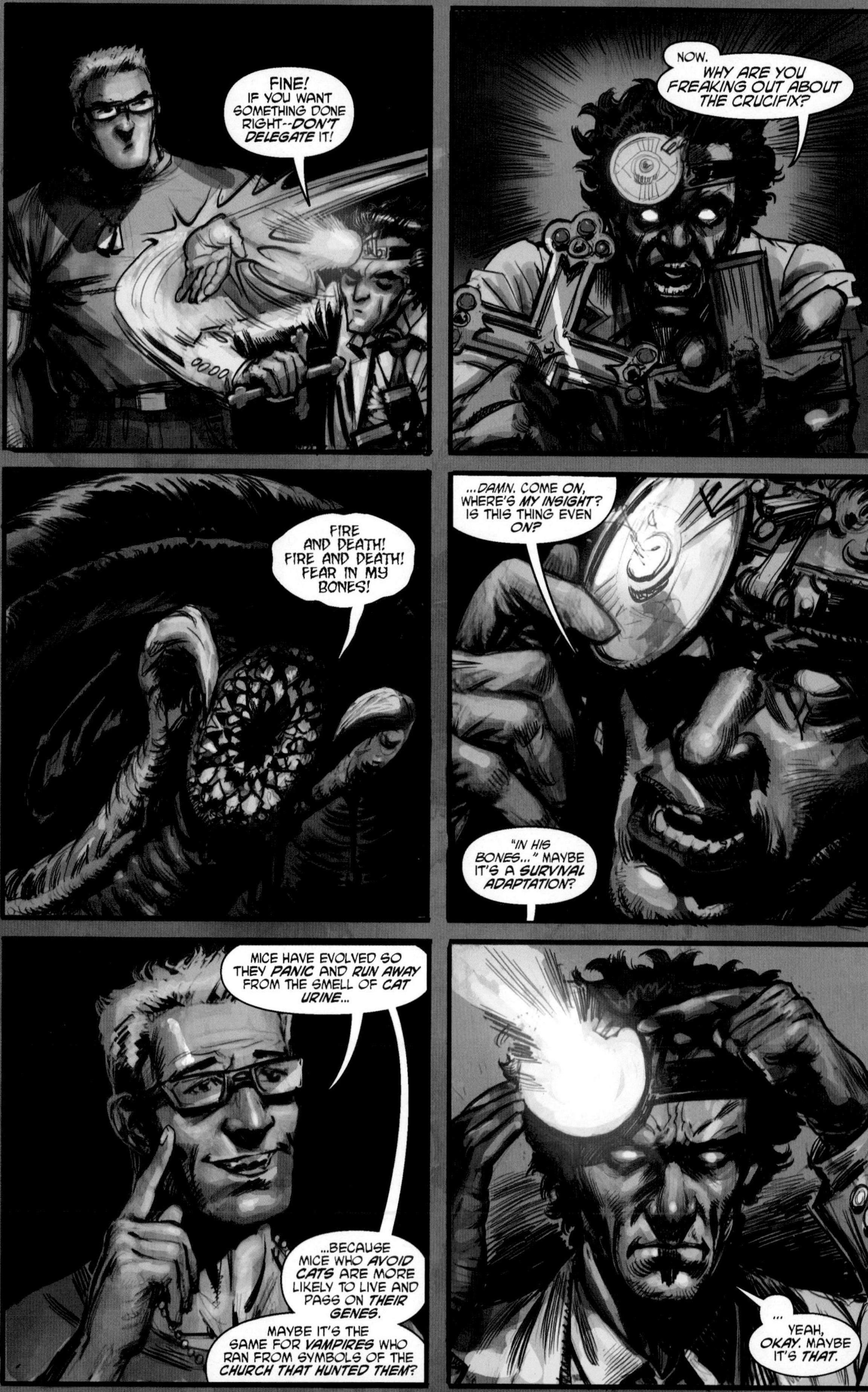
FINE! IF YOU WANT SOMETHING DONE RIGHT--DON'T DELEGATE IT!
NOW. WHY ARE YOU FREAKING OUT ABOUT THE CRUCIFIX?
FIRE AND DEATH! FIRE AND DEATH! FEAR IN MY BONES!
...DAMN. COME ON, WHERE'S MY INSIGHT? IS THIS THING EVEN ON?
"IN HIS BONES..." MAYBE IT'S A SURVIVAL ADAPTATION?
MICE HAVE EVOLVED SO THEY PANIC AND RUN AWAY FROM THE SMELL OF CAT URINE...
...BECAUSE MICE WHO AVOID CATS ARE MORE LIKELY TO LIVE AND PASS ON THEIR GENES.
MAYBE IT'S THE SAME FOR VAMPIRES WHO RAN FROM SYMBOLS OF THE CHURCH THAT HUNTED THEM?
... YEAH, OKAY. MAYBE IT'S THAT.

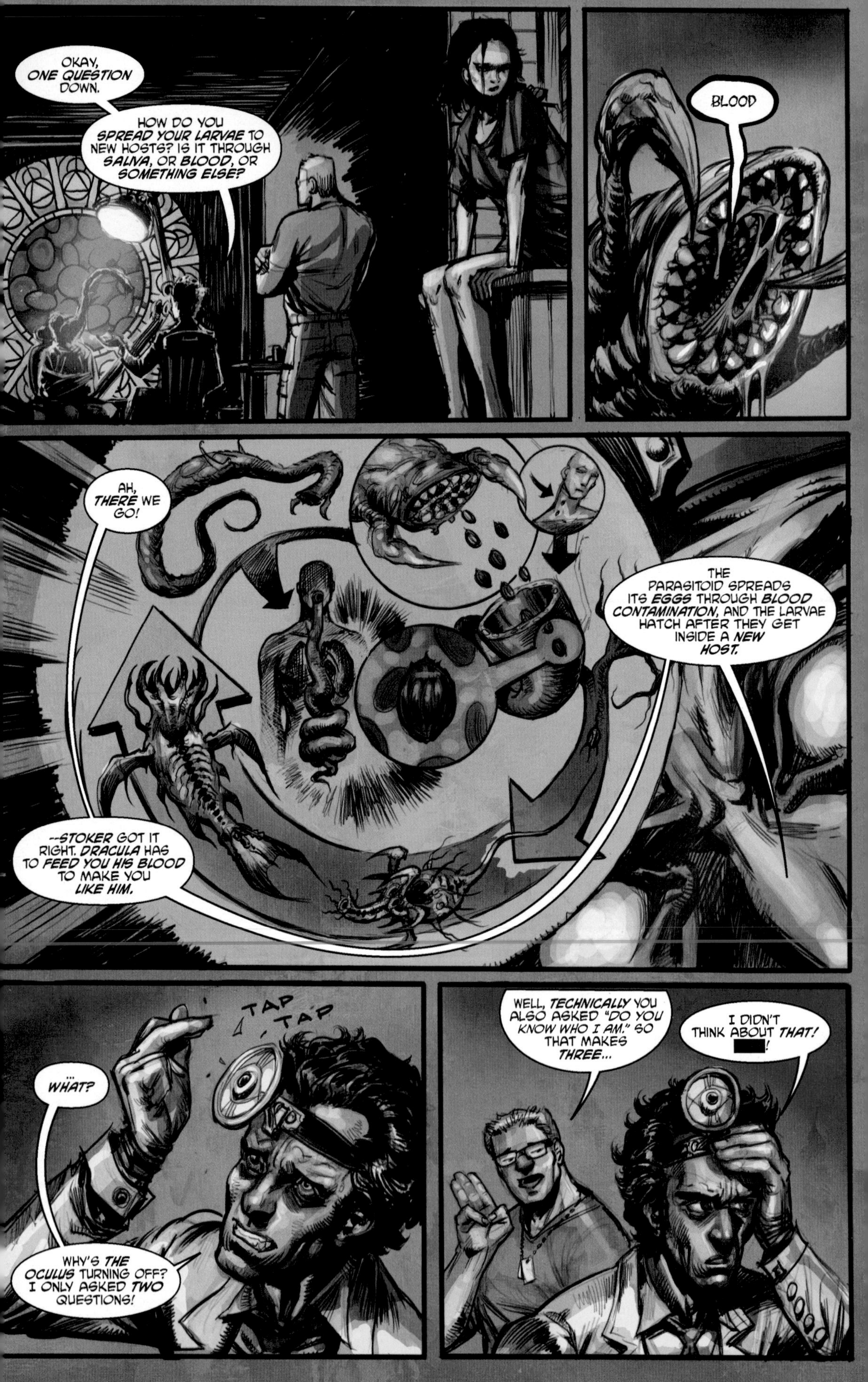
OKAY, ONE QUESTION DOWN.
HOW DO YOU SPREAD YOUR LARVAE TO NEW HOSTS? IS IT THROUGH SALIVA, OR BLOOD, OR SOMETHING ELSE?
BLOOD
AH, THERE WE GO!
THE PARASITOID SPREADS ITS EGGS THROUGH BLOOD CONTAMINATION, AND THE LARVAE HATCH AFTER THEY GET INSIDE A NEW HOST.
--STOKER GOT IT RIGHT. DRACULA HAS TO FEED YOU HIS BLOOD TO MAKE YOU LIKE HIM.
TAP TAP
... WHAT?
WHY'S THE OCULUS TURNING OFF? I ONLY ASKED TWO QUESTIONS!
WELL, TECHNICALLY YOU ALSO ASKED "DO YOU KNOW WHO I AM." SO THAT MAKES THREE...
I DIDN'T THINK ABOUT THAT! [redacted]!

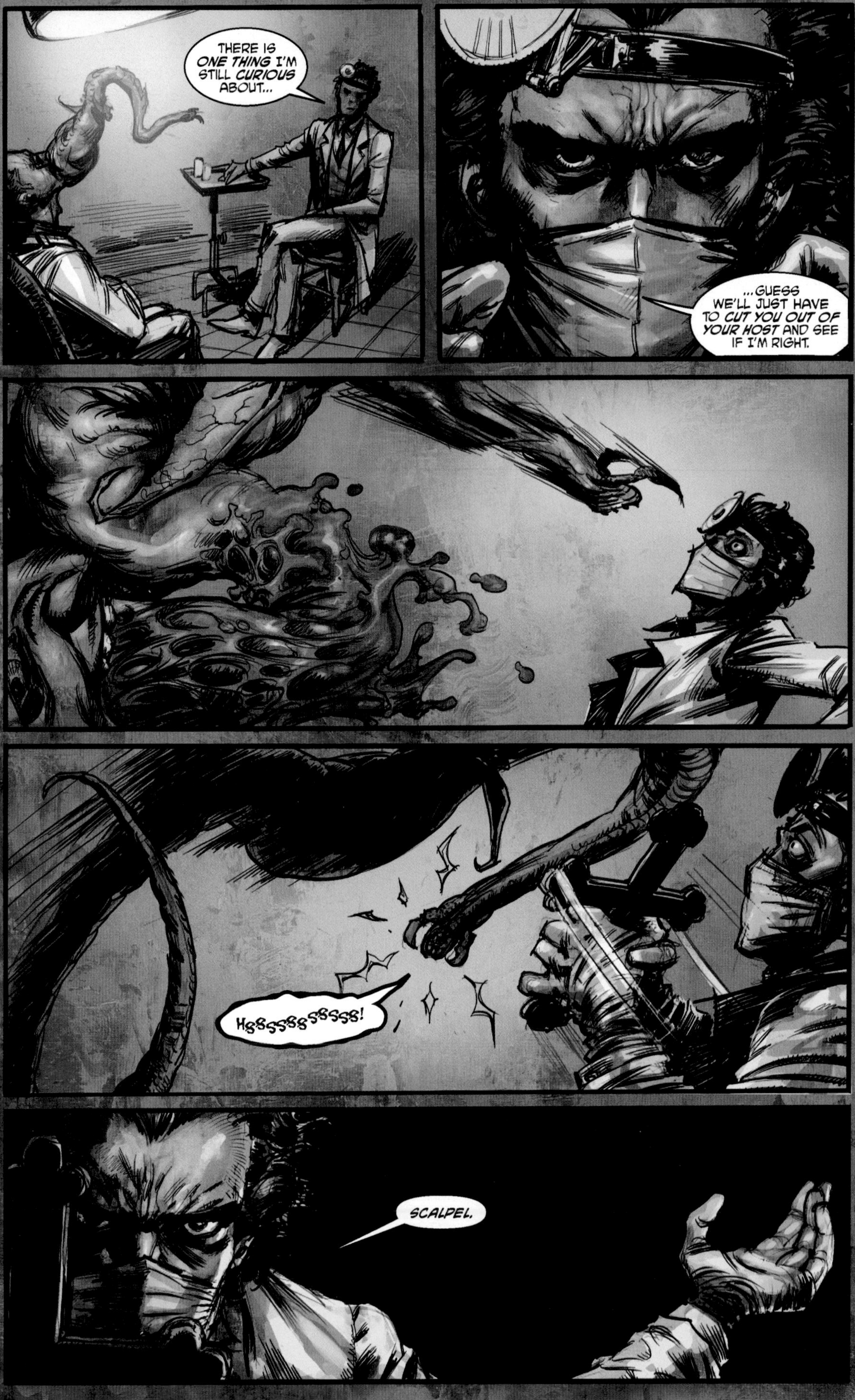
THERE IS ONE THING I'M STILL CURIOUS ABOUT...
...GUESS WE'LL JUST HAVE TO CUT YOU OUT OF YOUR HOST AND SEE IF I'M RIGHT.
HSSSSSSSSSSS!
SCALPEL.

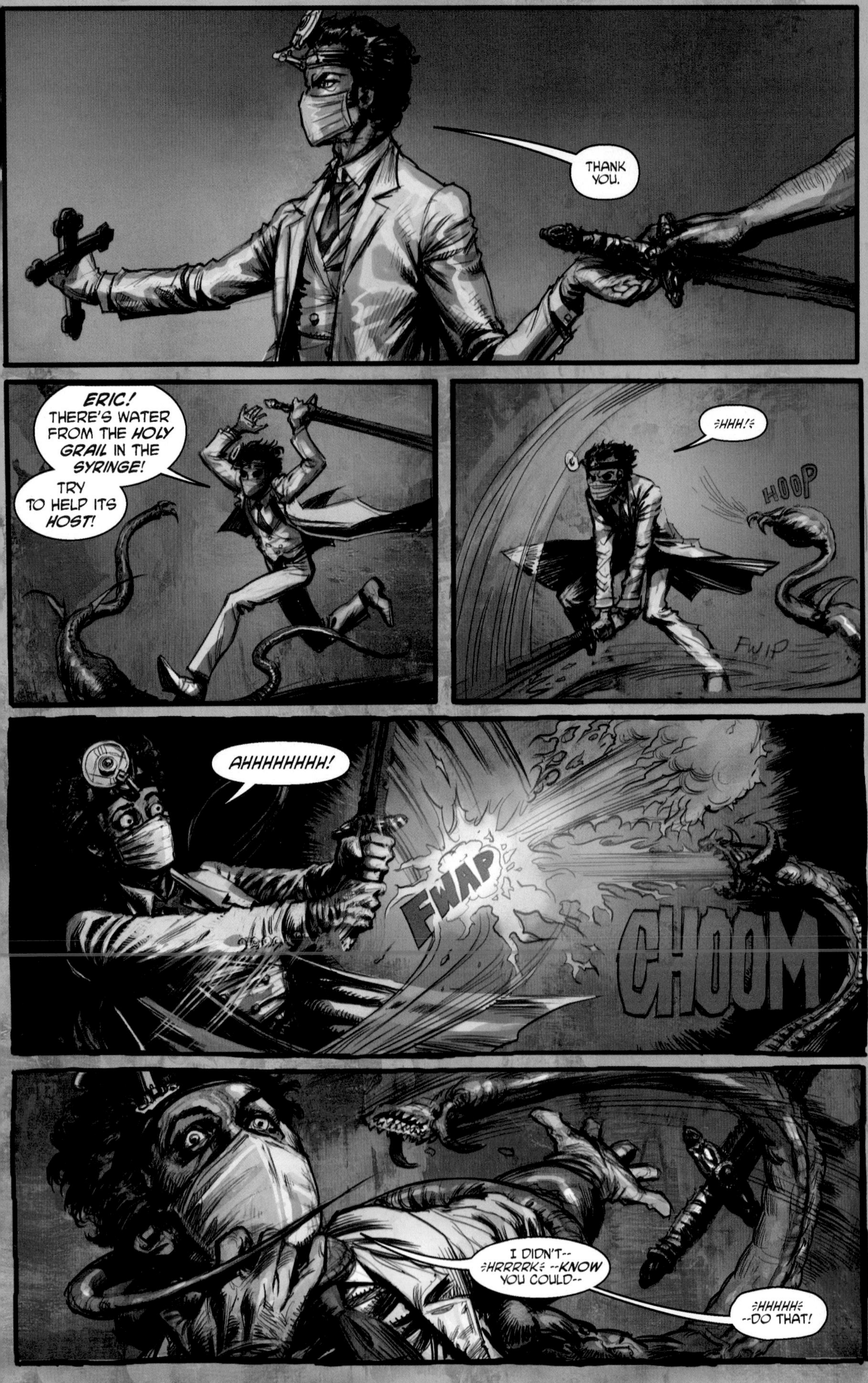
THANK YOU.
ERIC! THERE'S WATER FROM THE HOLY GRAIL IN THE SYRINGE!
TRY TO HELP ITS HOST!
HHH!
HOOP
FWIP
AHHHHHHHH!
FWAP
CHOOM
I DIDN'T-- HRRRRK --KNOW YOU COULD--
HHHHH --DO THAT!

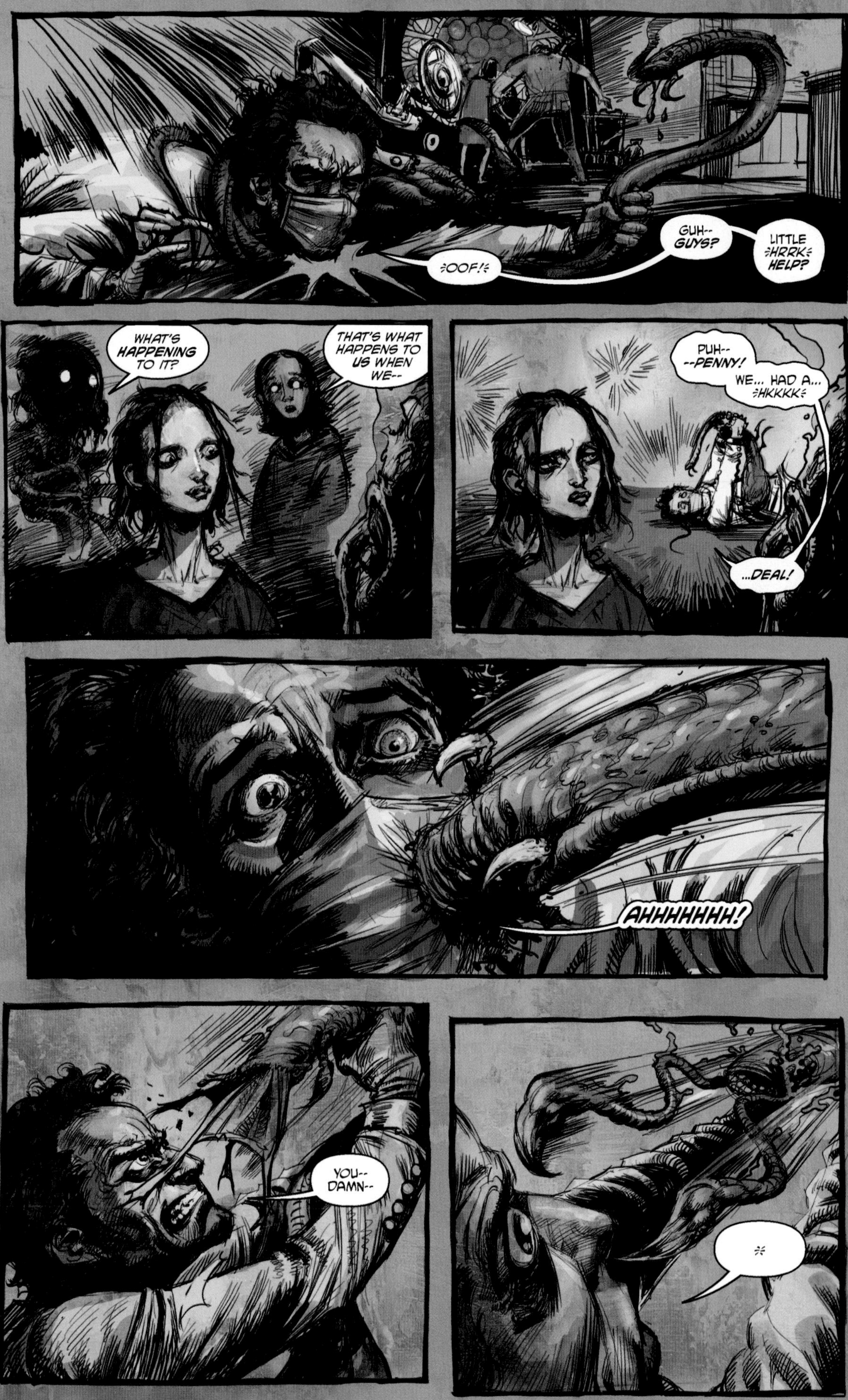
OOF!
GUH-- GUYS?
LITTLE HRRK HELP?
WHAT'S HAPPENING TO IT?
THAT'S WHAT HAPPENS TO US WHEN WE--
PUH-- --PENNY!
WE... HAD A... HKKKK
...DEAL!
AHHHHHHH!
YOU-- DAMN--

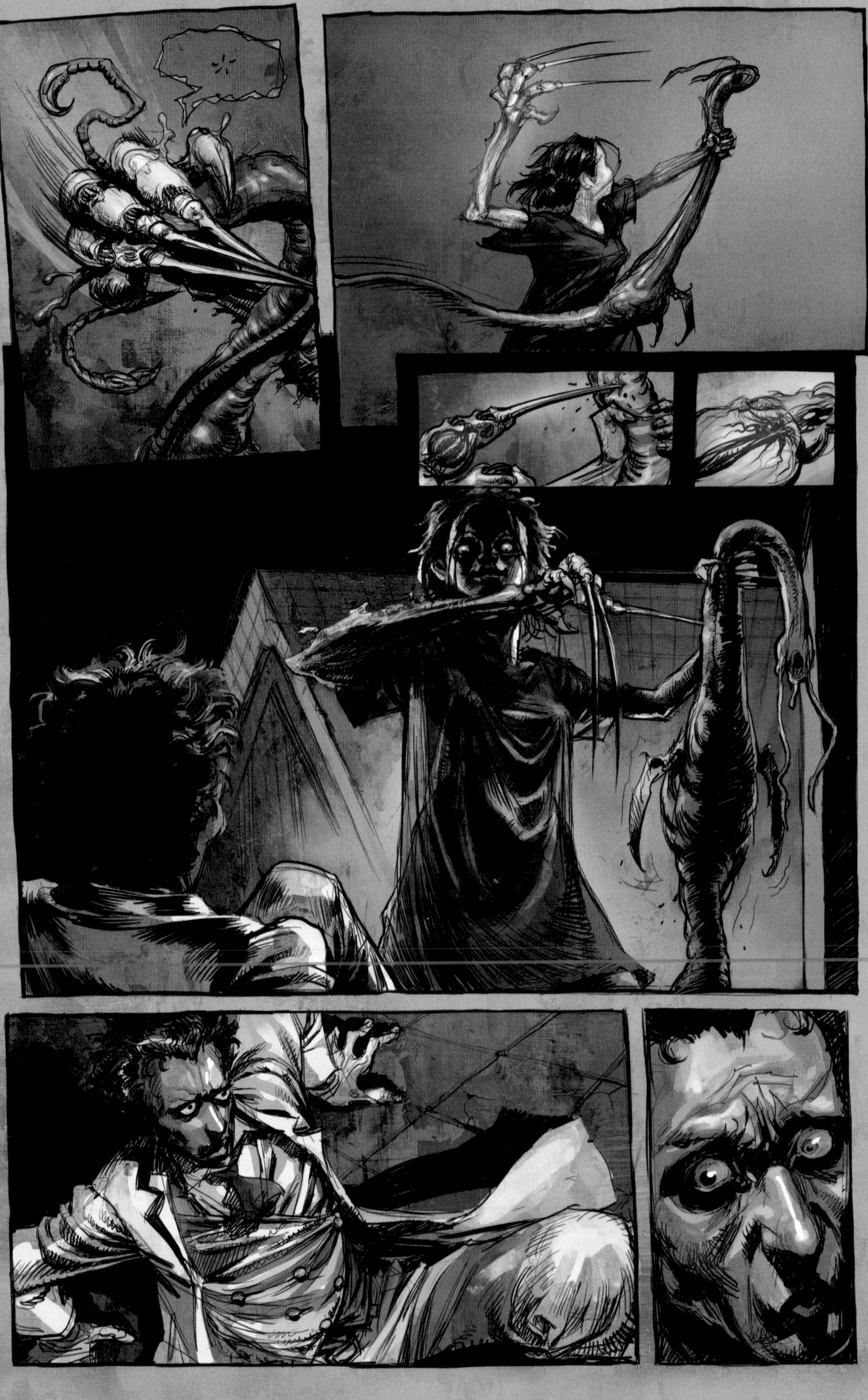

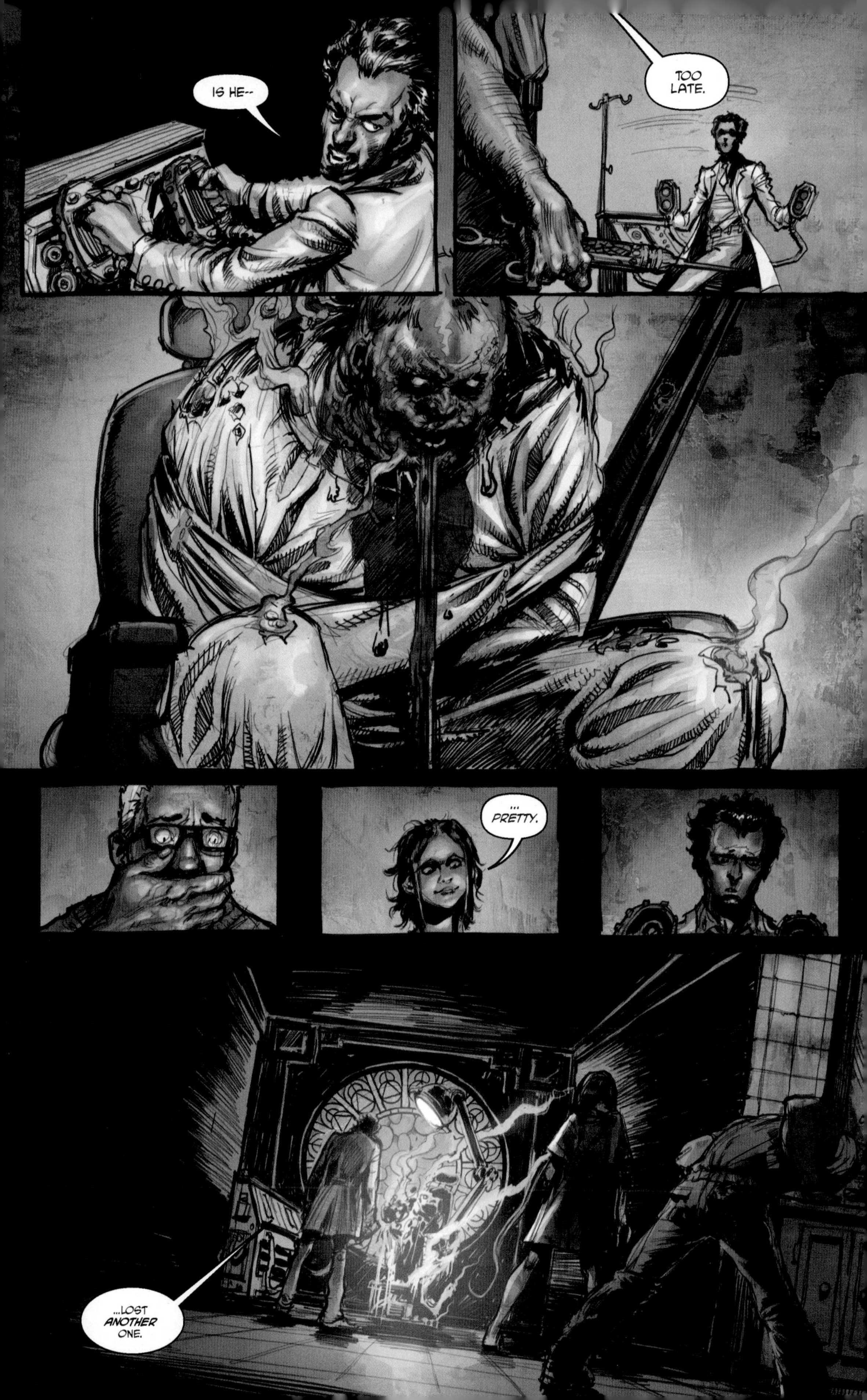
IS HE--
TOO LATE.
...PRETTY.
...LOST ANOTHER ONE.

I THOUGHT THE PARASITOID MIGHT BE *PRESERVING* ITS HOST'S BODY, AND MAYBE WE COULD MAGICALLY *RESUSCITATE* HIM.

SOME WATER FROM THE *HOLY GRAIL* TO REPAIR THE DAMAGED TISSUE, MY SPECIAL *DEFIBRILLATOR* TO SHOCK HIS 'SOUL' BACK IN...

BUT NO. I DIDN'T BRING OUR PATIENT *BACK*. I THREW HIM AWAY ON A *ST. JUDE'S* CHANCE.

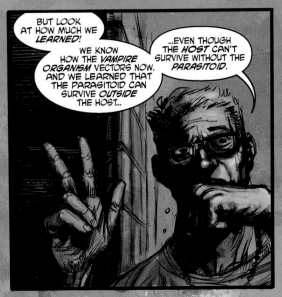

BUT LOOK AT HOW MUCH WE *LEARNED!*

WE KNOW HOW THE *VAMPIRE ORGANISM* VECTORS NOW. AND WE LEARNED THAT THE PARASITOID CAN SURVIVE *OUTSIDE* THE HOST...

...EVEN THOUGH THE *HOST* CAN'T SURVIVE WITHOUT THE *PARASITOID.*

..AND MAYBE IF YOU ADMINISTERED THE WATER FROM THE GRAIL *SOONER--*

--PERHAPS THROUGH AN *I.V. DRIP*, WE COULD PREVENT THE IMMEDIATE *DECOMPOSITION?* HMM.

YEAH! AND YOU'VE GOT AN INTACT *PARASITOID* TO STUDY--

--THAT'S *TRUE!* PENNY, THERE'S A FISH TANK IN MY OFFICE FOR OUR *PLECOSTOMUS FROM HELL.* I WANT EASIER ACCESS TO THOSE COMPOUNDS IN ITS *SALIVA* -- THEY MIGHT HAVE *BIOTHERAPY* APPLICATIONS.

NOW LET'S GO *THAW* ANOTHER "VLAD DOE." I'M IN A *DISSECTING* MOOD...

YOU *KNOW* DOC, I WAS KINDA WORRIED YOU WERE GOING TO *CUT YOURSELF* WITH THAT SWORD...

ME *TOO.* MAYBE I SHOULD TAKE *LESSONS...*

End.

It's all about the monsters, right?

Count Dracula wasn't the protagonist in Bram Stoker's novel; he was the enemy. And yet, he's the part of the story that stuck with us for 100 years. Mary Shelley's most famous creation wasn't Victor Frankenstein, the lead and narrator of her novel — it was the nameless thing Victor built out of corpses. Shelley's monster was so memorable that the reading public stole her hero's name and gave it to her monster, effectively overruling the writer.

Most fiction is defined by its heroes and heroines, but not horror. Horror is defined by its villains. And supernatural horror is defined by its monsters. And the best monsters are diseases.

When I get interviewed about WITCH DOCTOR, one of the things I always end up rambling on about is how the really classic, lasting monsters — vampires, zombies and werewolves — are all disease metaphors. The horror of a zombie isn't just that they're going to eat you — it's that they're going to infect you, to turn you into one of them. Same with vampires, and werewolves. The Horror of Infection is something you see all over the horror field, from demonic possession to the xenomorphs in *Aliens*.

That wasn't always the case. Look at folklore, the stuff people actually believed, about vampires, zombies and werewolves. None of those monsters started out communicable. You turned into a vampire because you were a naughty person in life, or because you didn't properly protect yourself from evil. Vampires were suicides, the unbaptized, witches, murderers, children born out of wedlock. Werewolves willingly sold their souls to the devil for their powers. And zombies were made by evil sorcerers killing and reanimating people as undead servants.

Culture changed over time, and a lot of the things that used to scare people don't anymore. But the Horror of Infection never goes out of fashion. Disease doesn't go away, and it's always got a new face to scare us with. We may not have to worry about smallpox and polio anymore, but now we've got HIV and Ebola.

The diseases we fear have changed; it's time for the disease-monsters we fear to change, too. That's basically the principle behind WITCH DOCTOR. On the writing end, that means injecting a whole lot of real-world science into our monsters — that's my job, and in a lot of ways it's the easy job. But when it comes to really selling these monsters to you, the reader — that's up to Lukas. And I think you'll agree that he rocks it. For my money, Lukas is one of the best creature-designers in comics today.

In the next few pages, we'll show you a bunch of Lukas' design art for WITCH DOCTOR, including stuff from the two years we spent self-publishing the book before Skybound picked us up. You'll see early versions of Morrow and Penny, details of Morrow's occult tools — and lots of monsters.

After all, it's all about the monsters.

Brandon Seifert
Portland, Oregon

SKETCHBOOK

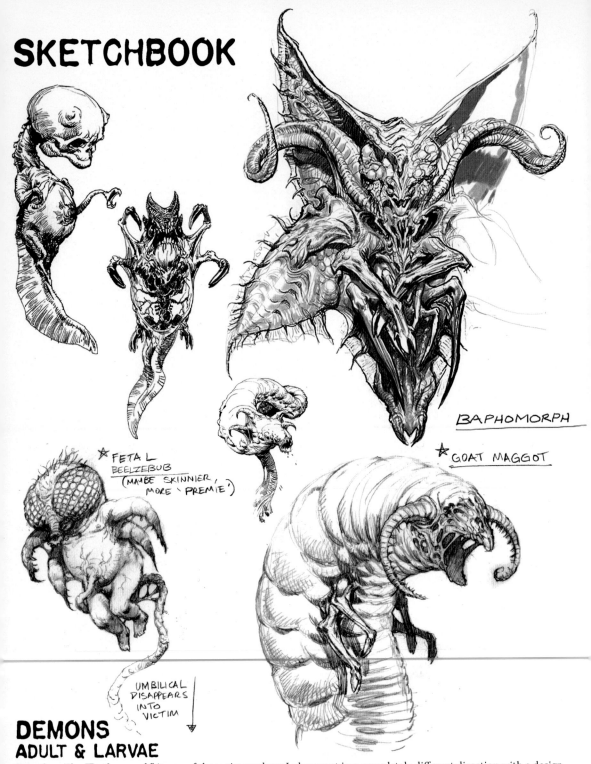

BAPHOMORPH

★ FETAL
BEELZEBUB
(MAYBE SKINNIER,
MORE 'PREMIE')

★ GOAT MAGGOT

UMBILICAL
DISAPPEARS
INTO
VICTIM

DEMONS
ADULT & LARVAE

Brandon: The "Baphomorph" is one of those times where Lukas went in a completely different direction with a design than I was expecting him to, and came up with something a million times awesomer than I could ever imagine.

Lukas did a lot of really awesome "demon larvae" designs in the lead up to #1... but then when he drew the issue, he only used, like, one of them, and just made up the rest. (*Edit: I didn't realize the 'goat maggot' made it into the issue, until Lukas pointed it out!*) I think the demons in the issue turned out really well, but I still really like these guys. I imagine we'll see these designs again in an issue something — we've certainly got a lot more demon-based stories to tell!

Lukas: Only the two strongest designs made it into the final demon larvae attack, the 'goat maggot' and the 'beelzebaby.' The rest are all really organic and cool, but also kind of interchangeable. The one that looks like a tadpole with a fetus skull might have been cool to use.

I'm still pretty proud of the 'Baphomorph' design. The idea for the fear demon, or 'phobophage' was to make something that resembled a goat-head pentagram, but as an organic creature. Wayne Barlowe is a big influence when it comes time to make something supernatural appear biological.

CUCKOO FAERIES
HATCHLING AND MOTHER

Brandon: Sometimes it's hard to get on the same page about a design. Sometimes, I have an idea in my head that's extremely difficult to communicate — or I simply fail at clearly explaining the thing I'm trying to get at. Sometimes there's nothing for it but to meet up at a coffee shop, and for me to explain by ideas and the logic behind them to Lukas while he sketches. The Cuckoo Mother was one of the designs we had to have a sit-down over. I had something very specific in mind, an "uncanny valley" monster that was creepy without being super-blatant about it... but I wasn't really able to articulate what I thought the creature needed, so Lukas was shooting in the dark to try and hit the thing I saw in my head. He came up with some very cool monster visuals (like the one pictured), but they were all more over-the-top than I wanted for the story. So we sat down over coffee, and he sketched the Mother that ended up in the story.

The Cuckoo Hatchling, on the other hand, was pretty easy to agree on.

Lukas: This was totally a design that benefitted from the extra time to get it just right. The faeries' glamour at first seemed like a great opportunity to create something overly monstrous, but this is one creature that needed a softer touch. What we settled on is a much better parallel to biological mimicry. Even though the earlier versions look great and might have worked, it was definitely more effective to create something that just looks creepy and 'off'. We referenced pregnant Barbie dolls (they exist!) to get something that you might walk too close to without noticing the inhumanity of the thing at first glance. In the end, the glamour just fills in gaps in your vision instead of cloaking an entirely different-looking monster.

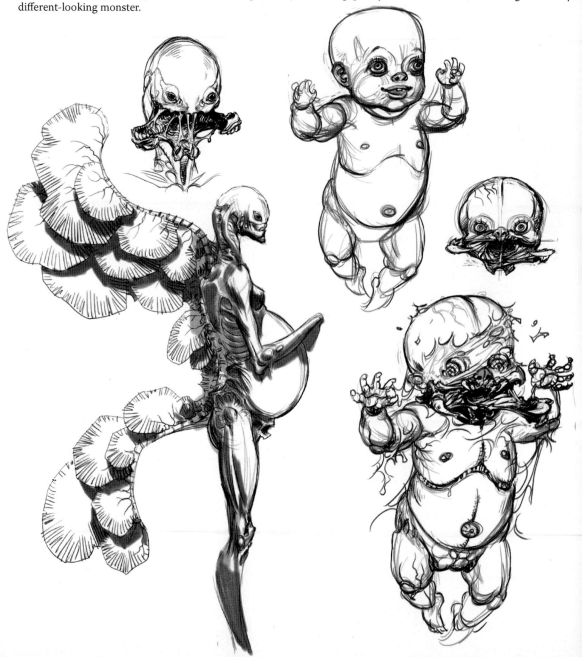

DEEP ONES

Brandon: The Deep Ones were a little tricky, because they're a very important part of Lovecraft's stuff, but Mike Mignola has done a really prominent version of them with the "frogs" in *Hellboy* and *B.P.R.D.* the last few years. To make ours more distinctive, we pulled out the frog-like elements, and added visual allusions to the Creature from the Black Lagoon — who was also an un-aging, amphibious, super-strong fish-person with an interest in humans of the opposite sex, just like the Deep Ones!

My other visual idea for these guys was that they should be based on deep ocean fish, since that's where they live. I had a lupine viperfish thing in mind; Lukas took it in a bloated anglerfish direction.

Lukas: I started out going pretty broad with the fish reference, but these things live in the deep sea, so it was the right call to narrow the influence. I mean, have you *seen* deep sea fish? Like so much of the research for WITCH DOCTOR, looking these things up rendered horrors that I'm not sure I was able to top in the designs, so these are more of a anthropomorphic translation of existing creatures than anything else.

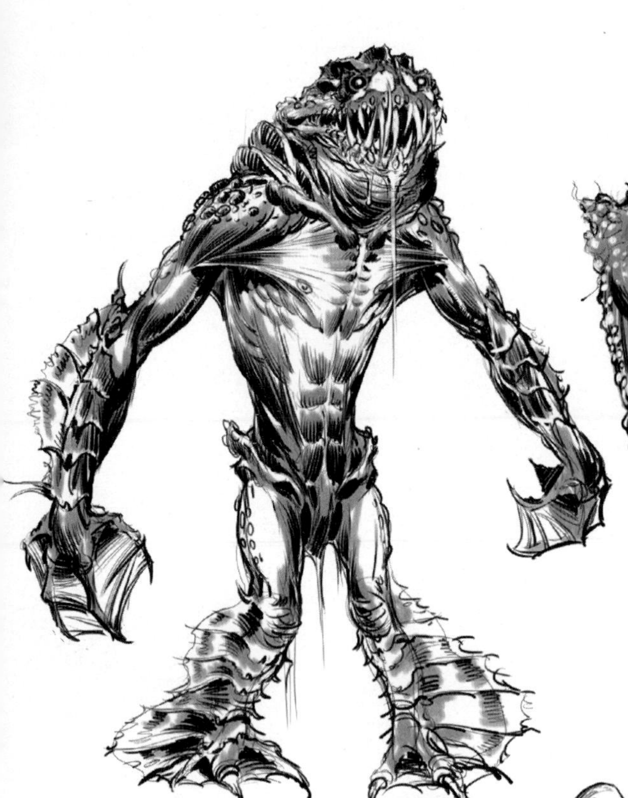

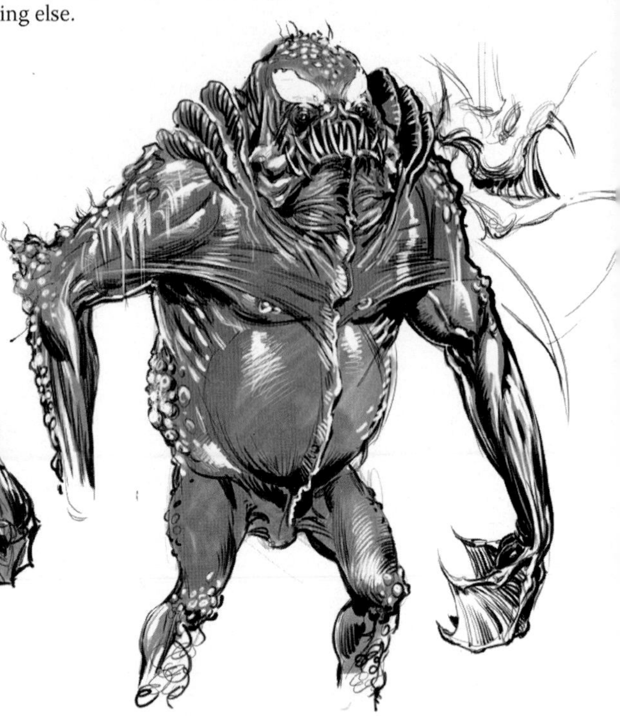

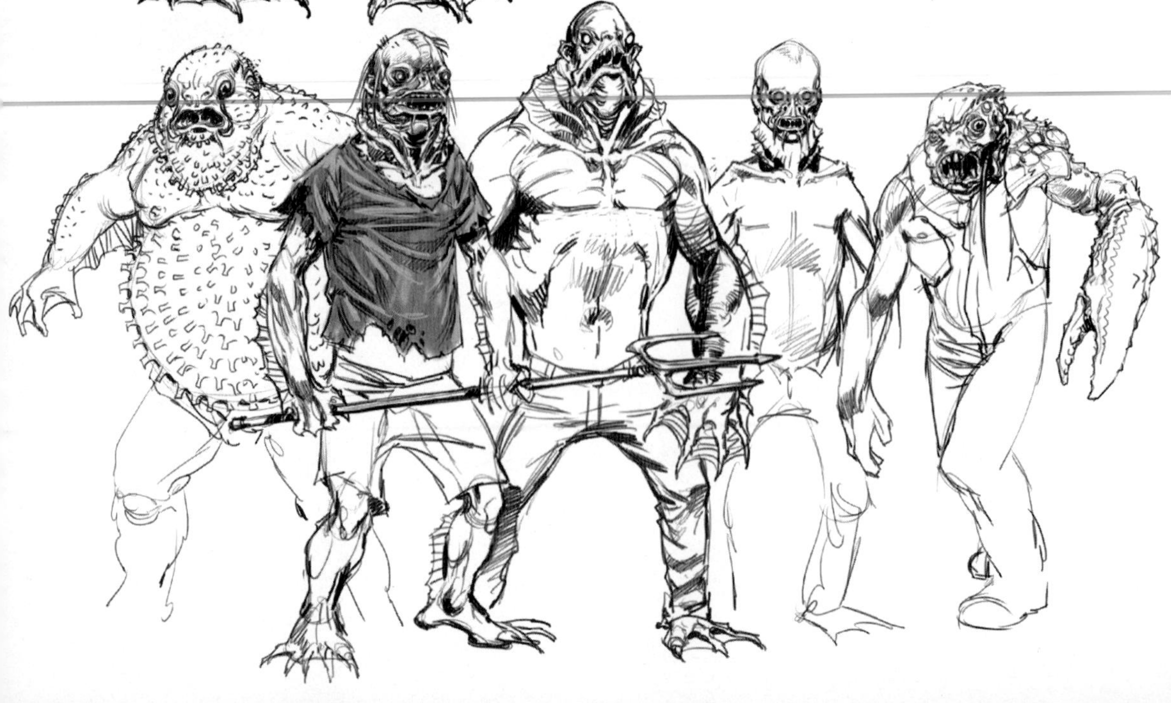

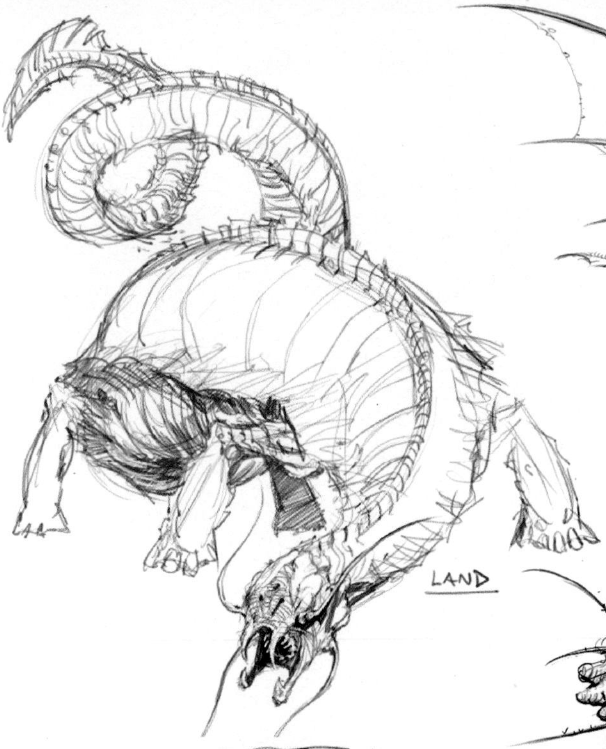
LAND

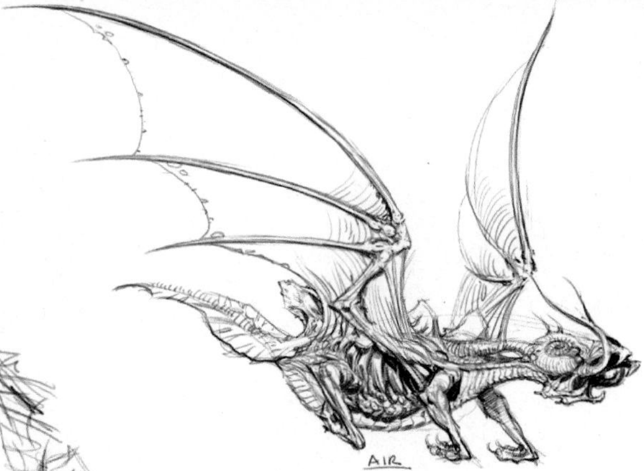
AIR

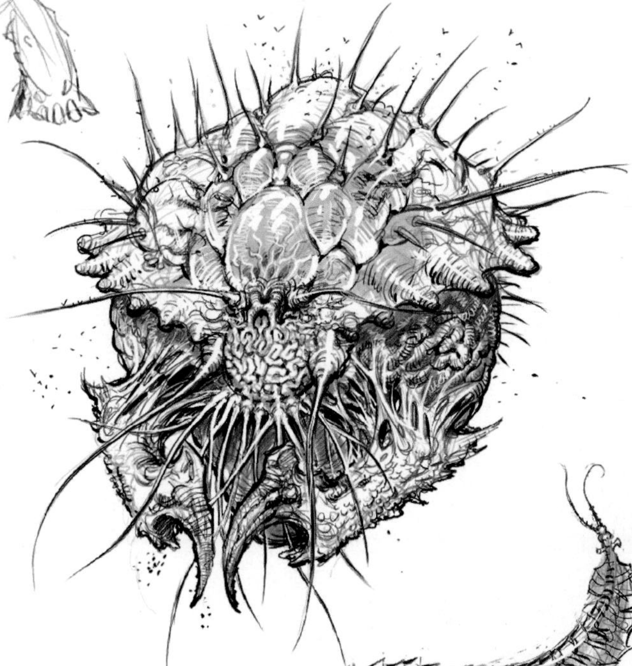

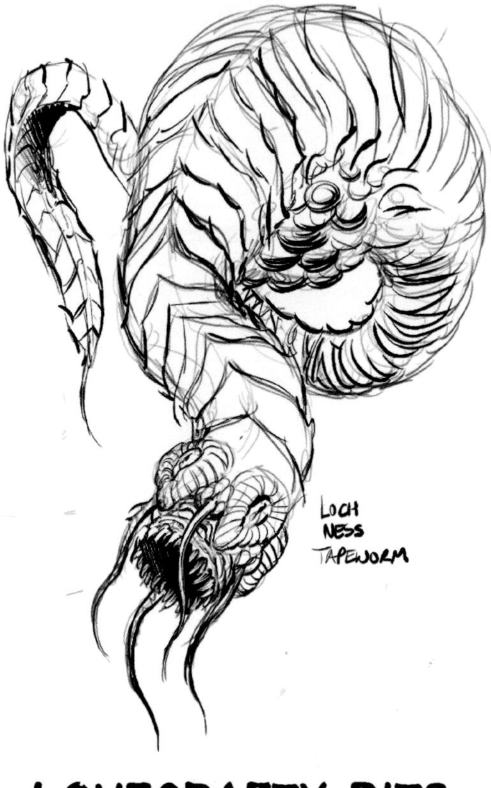
LOCH
NESS
TAPEWORM

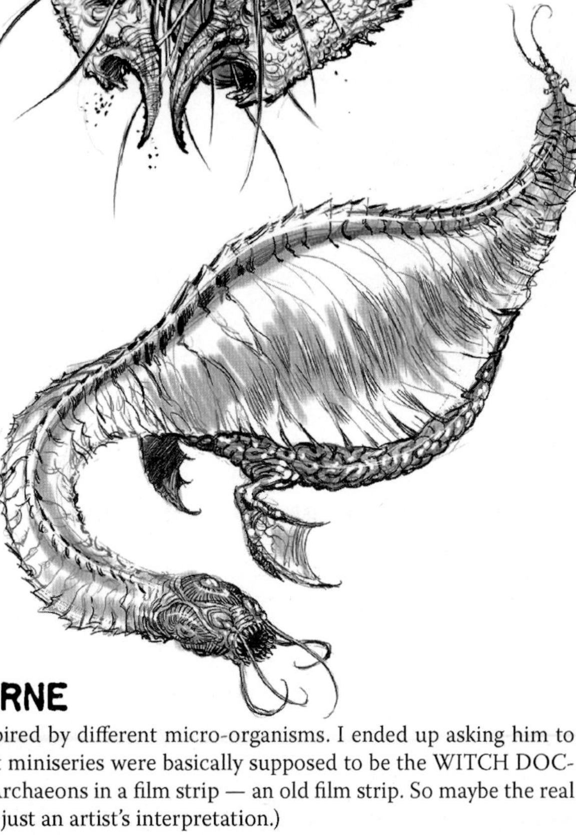

LOVECRAFTY BITS

ARCHAEONS AND THE FIRSTBORNE

Brandon: Lukas' first takes on the Archaeons were inspired by different micro-organisms. I ended up asking him to go more Cthulhu-ish, because the Archaeons in the first miniseries were basically supposed to be the WITCH DOCTOR Cthulhu. (The great thing is, we only showed you Archaeons in a film strip — an old film strip. So maybe the real Archaeons don't look anything like them! Maybe they're just an artist's interpretation.)

Lukas: When asked to create this film strip for Mystics Without Borders back in the fifties, I really didn't have much to go on. The gargantuan cavern we visited beneath Iceland housed the only known visitable creature, and its cocoon is largely impenetrable to all known spectrums of physical (and metaphysical) light. A sonar reading rendered a basic shape that was cross referenced with murals created by a colony of Ichyanthropes, now abandoned.

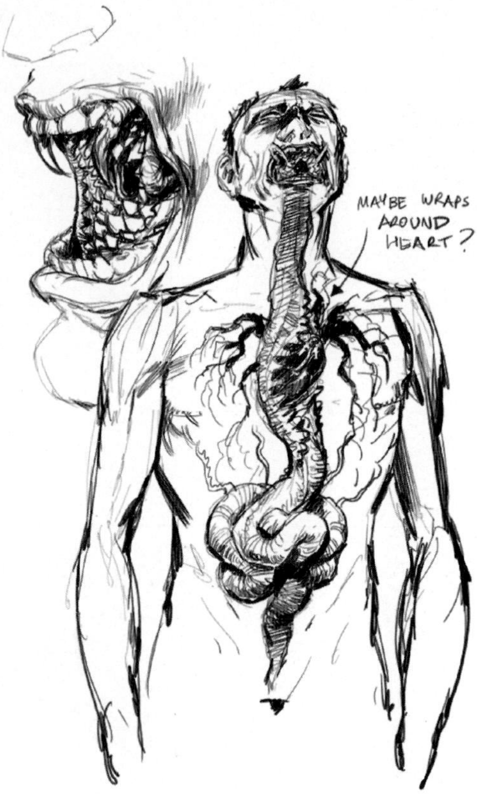
MAYBE WRAPS AROUND HEART?

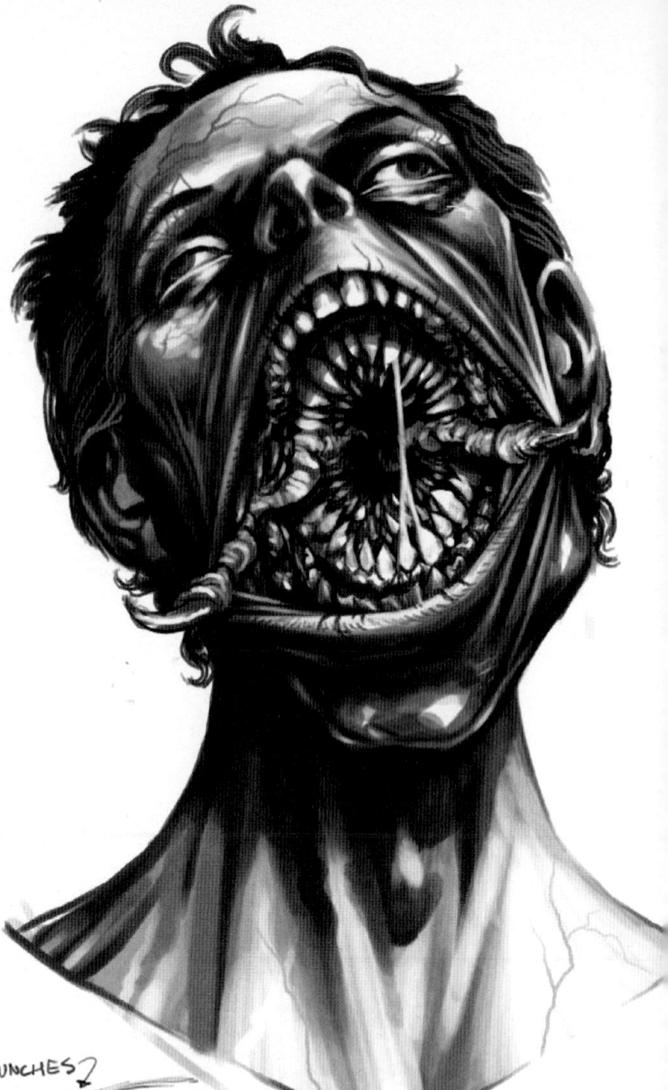

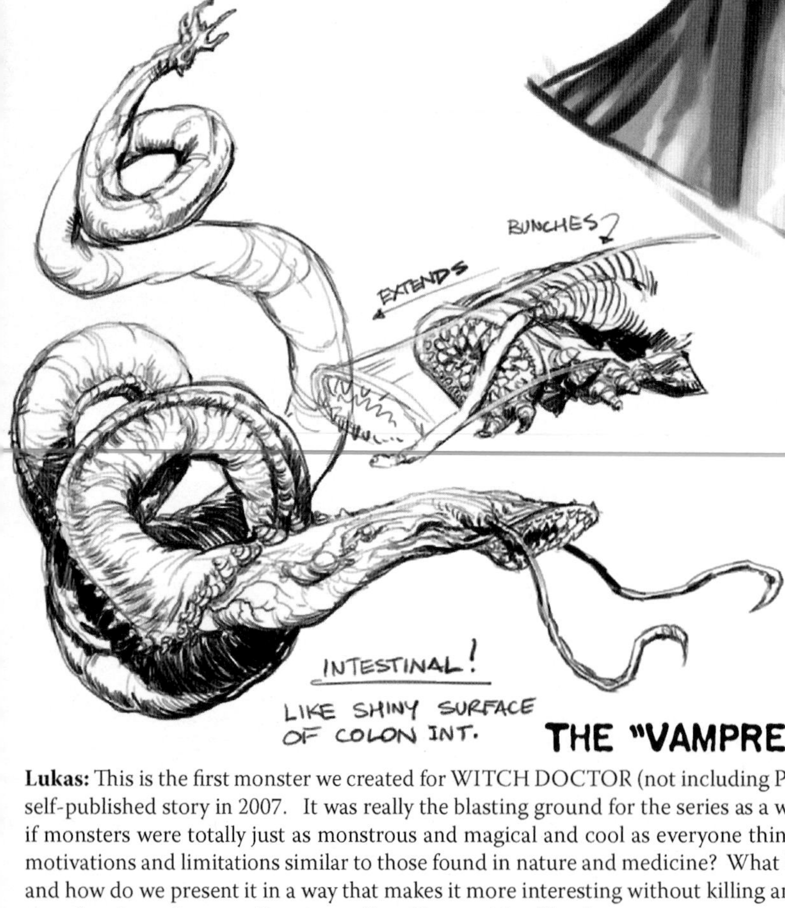
BUNCHES?
EXTENDS
INTESTINAL!
LIKE SHINY SURFACE OF COLON INT.

VAMPIRES
THE "VAMPREY" AND "VLAD DOE"

Lukas: This is the first monster we created for WITCH DOCTOR (not including Penny) back when we created our first self-published story in 2007. It was really the blasting ground for the series as a whole. The main question was, "what if monsters were totally just as monstrous and magical and cool as everyone thinks, but they had, like, real biological motivations and limitations similar to those found in nature and medicine? What kind of thing would we be looking at, and how do we present it in a way that makes it more interesting without killing any of its supernatural mystique?" I'm paraphrasing, of course. But we totally said something like that.

Brandon: The drawing of "Vlad Doe" on the top right is one of the first pieces Lukas did for this project. It's also still one of my favorite things I've ever seen him draw.

DR. MORROW

Brandon: Lukas' early sketches gave Morrow a very mad scientist, Dr. Horrible vibe. "Mad scientist" is definitely part of Morrow's DNA, but I never wanted people to view him as that kind of stock character — so I'm glad we've moved further and further from that over time. (A friend of ours once said, "I don't like Morrow's new outfit. It makes him look like a genteel Southern doctor, rather than a freaked-out maniac." And I was like, "Well, I don't want people to think he's a freaked-out maniac. So that works well!")

Lukas: When Brandon and I first began designing for WITCH DOCTOR, I had just discovered the wonders of '70s horror anthologies like *Creepy Magazine* and *House of Mystery*. The first time around Morrow was heavily influenced by Bernie Wrightson's Victor Frankenstein, so we see a meatier, more square-jawed character in the early drawings, and even the first self-published story (which may eventually be released as nothing more than an early curiosity). It wasn't until we made Morrow a little slimmer and sickly-chic that the character really began to stand on its own look. In the end, we wanted to create something a little more 'actual-size.' He's a flamboyant character, sure, but we wanted to create a world that sits on top of our own, not apart from it.

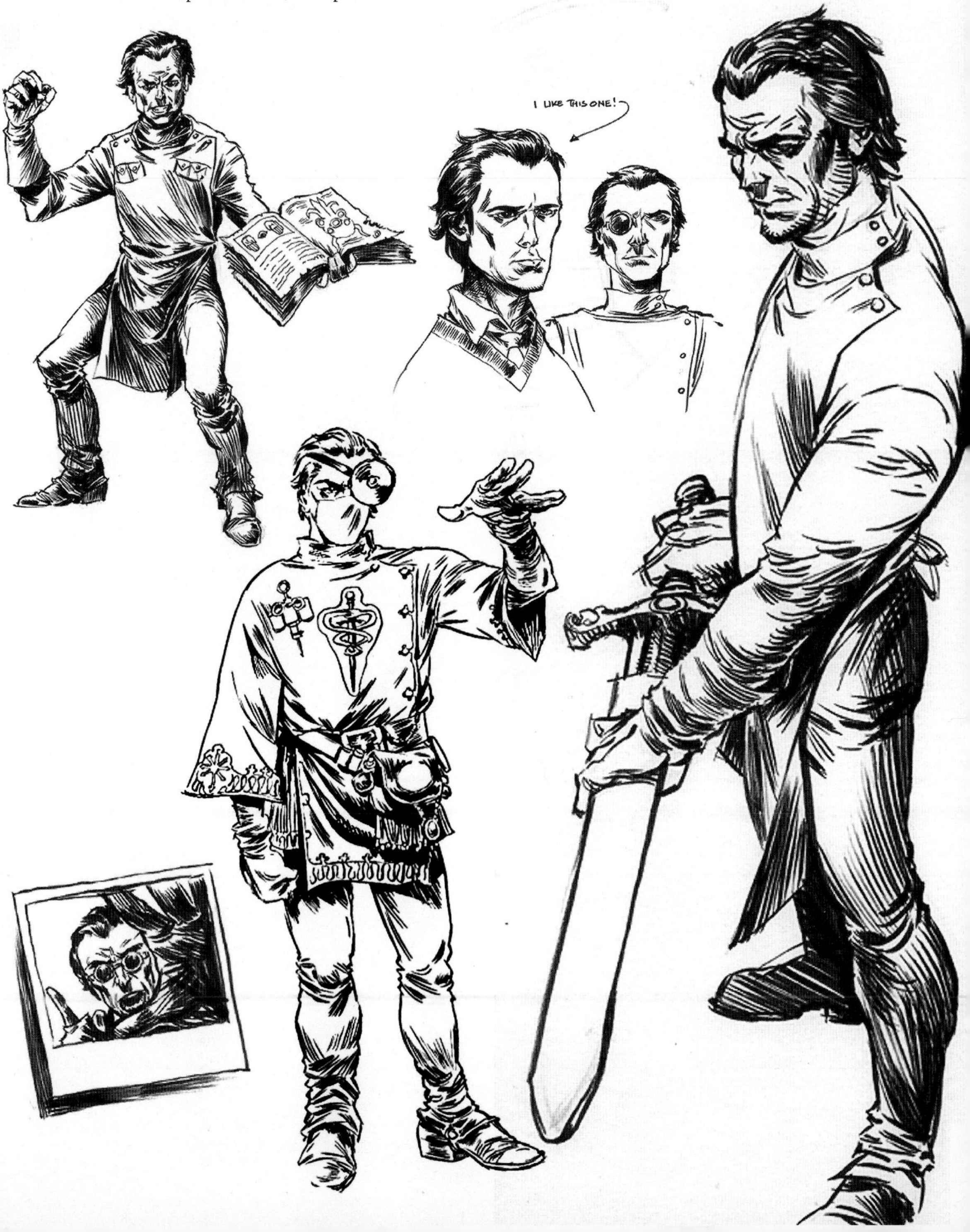
I LIKE THIS ONE!

PENNY DREADFUL

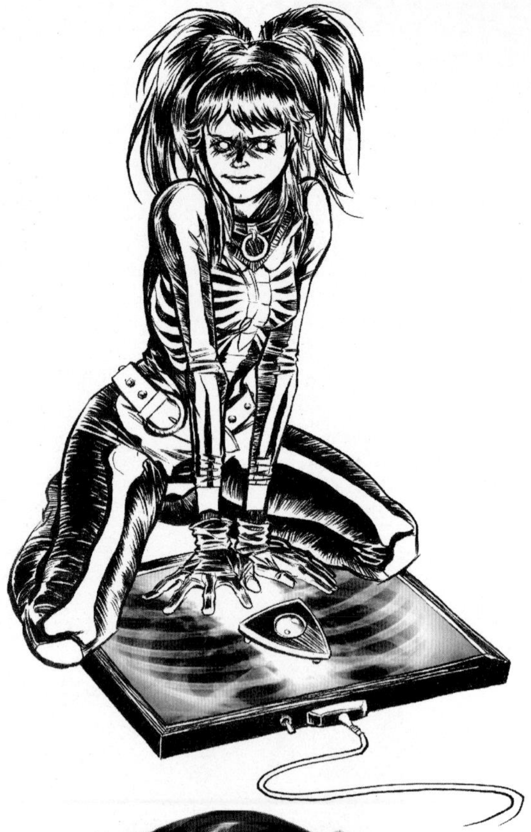

Brandon: Out of everything in the book, Penny's the thing that went through the most changes. Initially I was asking Lukas for sort of a goth fetish nurse, but he never really went for the fetish nurse stuff and she ended up looking like a goth cheerleader. We got a lot of criticism about her appearance and portrayal in the first WD story we self-published, and after that we sat down at a Portland bar called the Roadside Attraction and figured out a new direction to go for her, more patient than nurse. As you can see, her current look used to be even more J-Horror than it is now.

Lukas: We're not even showing every iteration that the character went through, we might even need a separate section for that. It was really her look that gave us the most trouble; her characterization has changed slightly, but her backstory has always been essentially the same. So how did her look change so much and why? It goes a bit alongside Morrow. The first version was really an attempt to make a cool-looking character. Trying to force cool out of something usually produces something cliché. It wasn't until we stopped trying to make her look good and started making her look like the character she actually was that we got something we wanted to see. The first version had too much obvious sex appeal for me. I enjoy drawing a character that might make the reader uncomfortable for finding her attractive.

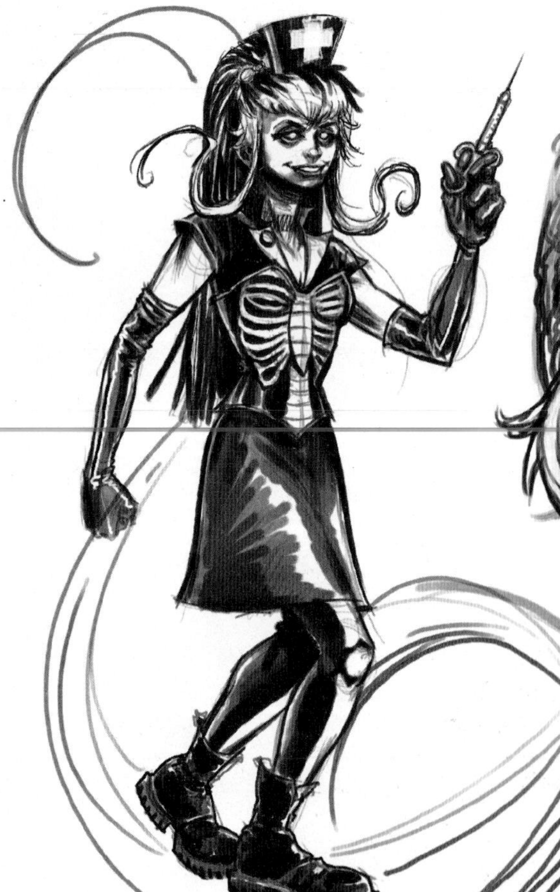

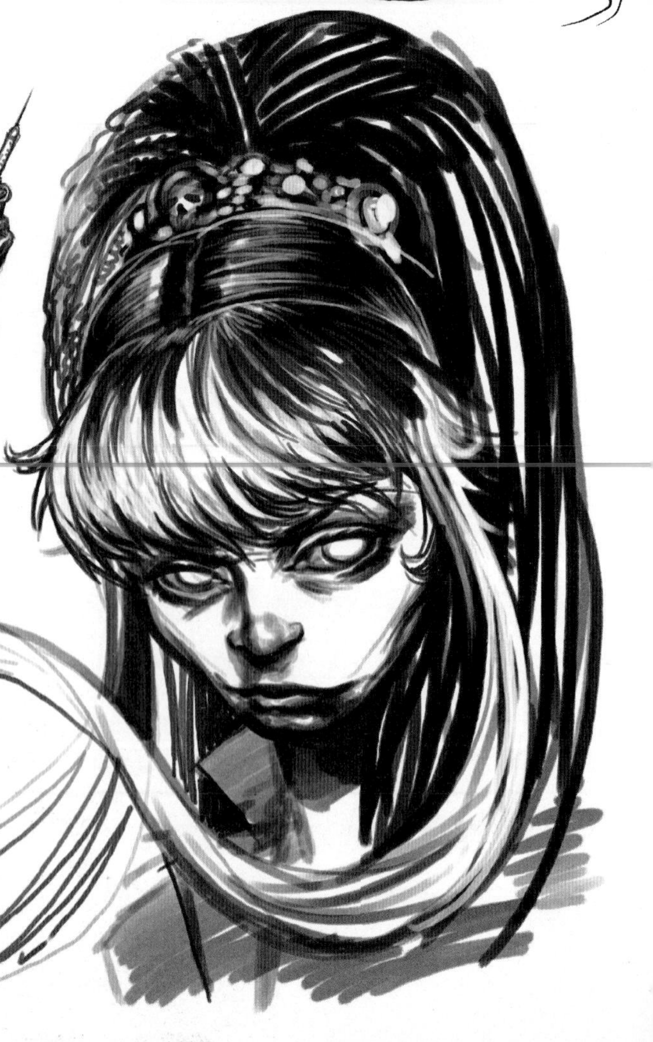

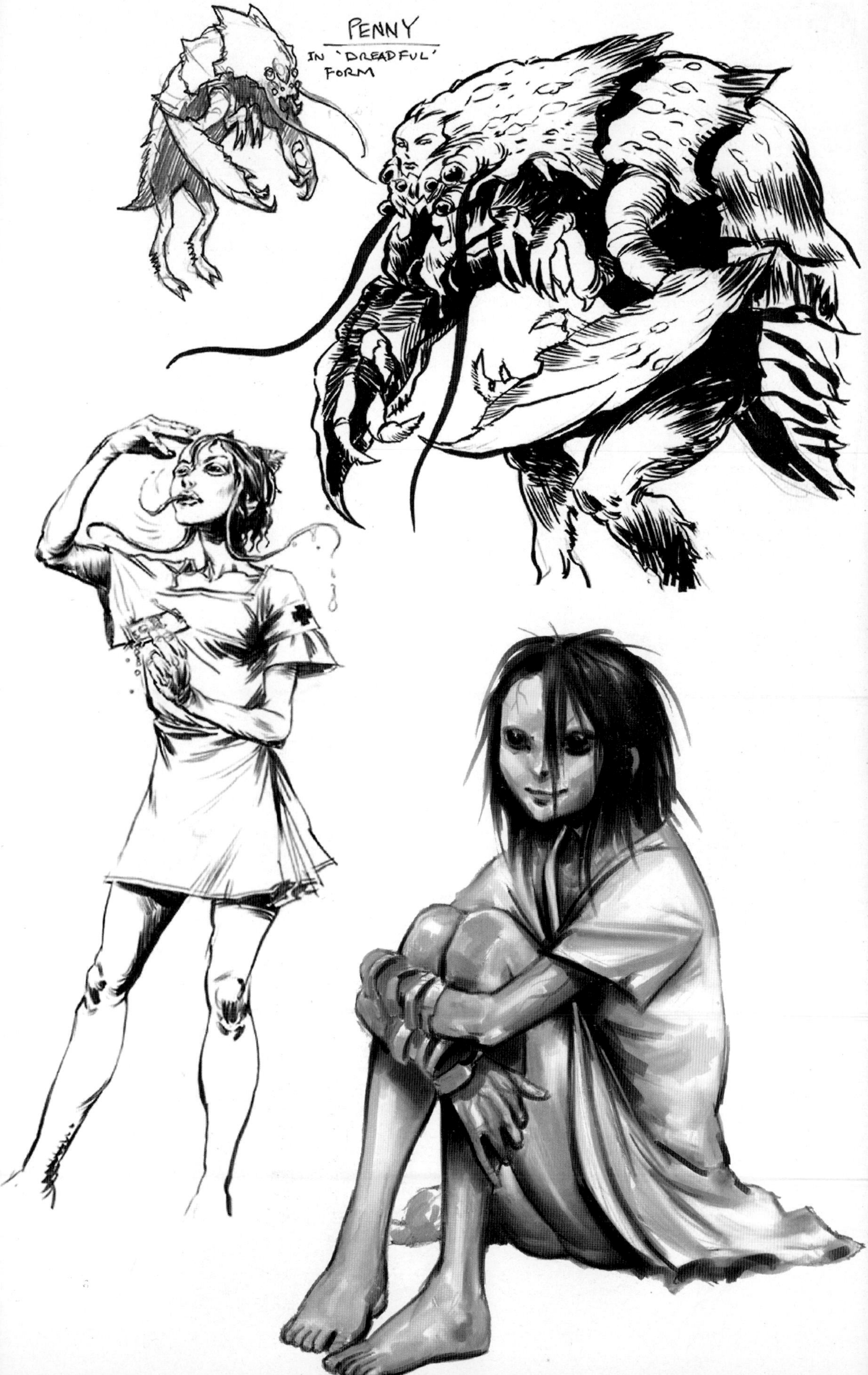
PENNY
IN 'DREADFUL' FORM

TOOLS

Lukas: The tools! Morrow has all of these magical artifacts. They're the sorts of things that any self-respecting magician would put on a pedestal and revere, but to Vincent Morrow, they really are just tools. He breaks them, bends them, and bastardizes them into a form that would be of use to a doctor or scientist. Early on, we went recognizably steampunk, but now I'm more interested in him building stuff out of discarded medical equipment from the '30s and '40s. The Killing Jar has pieces salvaged from an iron lung, he uses glass-bottle IVs, and some of the monitoring equipment is more modern. My favorite thing that I want to draw larger sometime? The magical CT scanner.

Brandon: I've said it before and I'm sure I'll say it again: One of the things I love about Lukas is how I can say something ridiculous like "stained-glass syringe!" to him, and his eyes will light up, and a few days later an amazing drawing like the one on the right will pop up in my inbox.

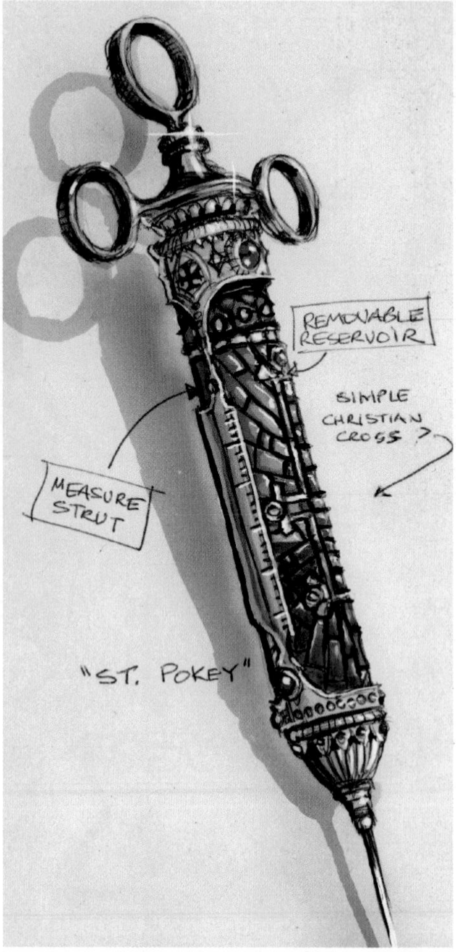

REMOVABLE RESERVOIR
SIMPLE CHRISTIAN CROSS ?
MEASURE STRUT
"ST. POKEY"

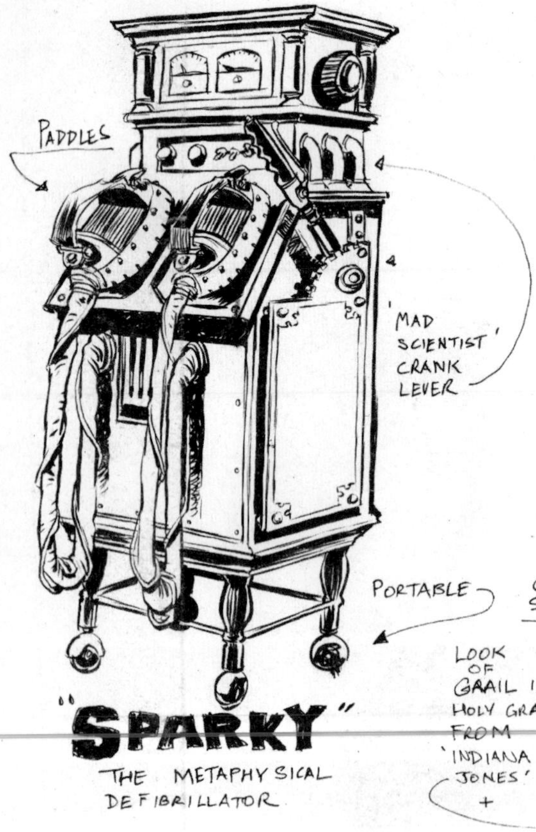

PADDLES
'MAD SCIENTIST' CRANK LEVER
PORTABLE
"SPARKY"
THE METAPHYSICAL DEFIBRILLATOR

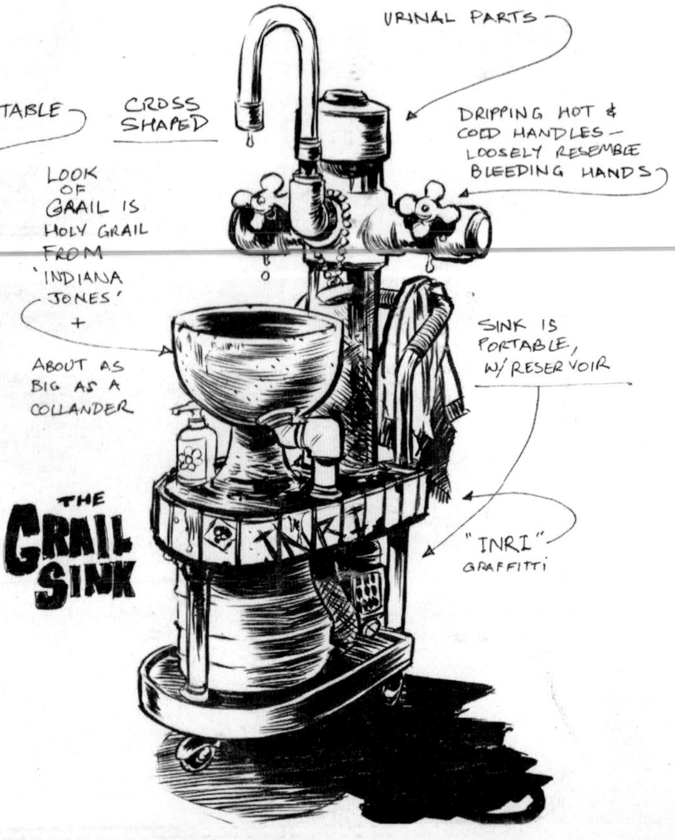

URINAL PARTS
CROSS SHAPED
DRIPPING HOT & COLD HANDLES — LOOSELY RESEMBLE BLEEDING HANDS
LOOK OF GRAIL IS HOLY GRAIL FROM 'INDIANA JONES' +
ABOUT AS BIG AS A COLLANDER
SINK IS PORTABLE, W/ RESERVOIR
"INRI" GRAFFITTI
THE GRAIL SINK